TUTOR DELIVERY PACK

ENGLISH LANGUAGE

— GCSE —

GRADES 3–5

Author: David Grant

AQA ENGLISH
Grades 3–5

Contents

Page		Learning Objectives
3	How to use this pack	
5	Information for parents and guardians	
7	Specification guidance	
8	Preparing for the exam	
11	Revise mapping guide	
13	Needs analysis	
15	Progress report	
16	End-of-lesson report	
17	Source texts	
23	1 Diagnostic: Reading	• To recap prior learning and identify areas for development

Reading

Page		Learning Objectives
29	2 Approaching an unseen text *3.1.1*	• To develop skills and confidence in deducing the meaning of unfamiliar words • To develop skills and confidence in tackling unseen texts • To develop skills in information retrieval
35	3 Explicit and implicit information *3.1.1*	• To understand the difference between explicit and implicit information • To be able to identify and infer implied meaning • To be able to identify precise evidence of implied meaning
41	4 Summarising using evidence *3.1.1*	• To be able to select relevant quotations • To be able to embed quotations • To be able to summarise a text using embedded quotations
47	5 Comparative summary *3.1.1*	• To be able to identify significant points of comparison in two texts • To be able to synthesise and summarise relevant evidence from two texts • To be able to structure an effective comparison
53	6 Analysing language 1 *3.1.1*	• To be able to identify significant choices of vocabulary and language features • To be able to recognise the writer's intention • To understand that language choice contributes to the writer's intention
59	7 Analysing language 2 *3.1.1*	• To develop language analysis skills • To understand connotation
65	8 Analysing language 3 *3.1.1*	• To develop language analysis skills • To craft effective critical writing
71	9 Analysing sentence forms 1 *3.1.1*	• To develop awareness of sentence forms and their effect • To be able to explore the impact of the writer's choice of sentence forms
77	10 Analysing sentence forms 2 *3.1.1*	• To be able to explore the impact of the writer's choice of sentence forms
83	11 Developing language analysis *3.1.1*	• To be able to comment on the writer's choice of words, phrases, language features and sentence forms • To be able to identify relevant evidence
89	12 Whole text structure *3.1.1*	• To be able to identify features and elements of structure • To understand the impact of structure
95	13 Narrative focus *3.1.1*	• To be able to identify features and elements of structure • To be able to explore the impact of whole text structure
101	14 Analysing whole text structure *3.1.1*	• To be able to identify features and elements of structure • To be able to explore the impact of whole text structure • To be able to write a critical response analysing text structure
107	15 Beginning an evaluation *3.1.1*	• To be able to identify relevant evidence to support a critical judgement • To be able to develop critical engagement with, and evaluation of, a text
113	16 Writing an evaluative response *3.1.1*	• To be able to develop critical engagement with, and evaluation of, a text • To be able to structure an effective evaluation
119	17 Developing critical evaluation *3.1.1*	• To be able to develop critical engagement with, and evaluation of, a text
125	18 Writing a comparison *3.1.1*	• To be able to identify the writers' attitudes in two texts • To be able to explore how the writers have conveyed their attitudes • To be able to structure an effective comparison

ENGLISH
Grades 3-5

CONTENTS

Page		Learning Objectives
131	19 Developing a comparison 3.1.1	• To be able to identify and compare the writers' attitudes in two texts • To be able to compare how the writers have conveyed their attitudes • To be able to structure an effective comparison
137	20 Consolidating comparisons 3.1.1	• To be able to structure an effective comparison • To be able to identify and compare the writers' attitudes in two texts • To be able to compare how the writers have conveyed their attitudes

Descriptive and narrative writing

Page		Learning Objectives
143	21 Gathering ideas 3.1.2	• To be able to gather ideas for a descriptive writing task • To be able to gather ideas for a narrative writing task
149	22 Structure and planning 3.1.2	• To be able to structure and sequence ideas for clarity and impact
155	23 Beginnings and endings 3.1.2	• To understand key elements of effective beginnings and endings • To be able to craft effective beginnings and endings
161	24 Using paragraphs for effect 3.1.2	• To be able to use paragraphs accurately • To be able to structure paragraphs for effect
167	25 Structuring sentences 3.1.2	• To develop understanding of clauses • To be able to structure sentences for clarity
173	26 Sentence structure for effect 3.1.2	• To be able to manipulate sentence structure • To be able to structure sentences for effect
179	27 Selecting vocabulary 3.1.2	• To be able to select vocabulary for concision and precision • To be able to consider connotation
185	28 Consolidation 3.1.2	• To be able to plan and write an effective piece of descriptive or narrative writing

Writing to present a viewpoint

Page		Learning Objectives
191	29 Gathering ideas 3.1.2	• To be able to identify the appropriate form, purpose and audience for a writing task • To be able to gather ideas to present a viewpoint
197	30 Structure and planning 3.1.2	• To understand how to structure an argument text • To be able to plan and shape an argument
203	31 Introductions and conclusions 3.1.2	• To be able to craft an effective introduction and conclusion
209	32 Building paragraphs 3.1.2	• To understand how to structure paragraphs in an argument text • To be able to link ideas using cohesive devices
215	33 Using structure for effect 3.1.2	• To understand that a writer's choices at text and sentence level can influence the reader's response • To be able to manipulate paragraph and sentence structure for effect
221	34 Selecting vocabulary 3.1.2	• To be able to select vocabulary for precision and impact
227	35 Writing a response 3.1.2	• To be able to plan and write an effective argument to present a viewpoint

SPaG

Page		Learning Objectives
233	36 Basic punctuation 3.1.2	• To be able to use full stops accurately • To be able to use commas accurately; to be able to use apostrophes accurately
239	37 Advanced punctuation 3.1.2	• To be able to use speech punctuation accurately • To be able to use colons and semi-colons accurately
245	38 Spelling and proofreading 3.1.2	• To develop awareness of homophones • To be able to proofread thoroughly
251	Mark scheme – writing	

ENGLISH
Grades 3–5

HOW TO USE THIS PACK

The *Tutors' Guild* English Language Tutor Delivery Pack gives you all of the tools you need to deliver effective GCSE 9–1 English Language lessons to students who are aiming for grades 3–5. Everything in this pack is available for you to download as an editable file. This means that every lesson can be edited to suit the needs of your student, and also that you can print off each resource as many times as you need.

LESSONS

There are 38 one-hour, six-page lessons in this Tutor Delivery Pack. Most tutors working for a full year will have around 38 lessons with a student. If you have less contact time, you can choose which lessons are most important to the student and build your own course, using the customisable digital version of this pack. Each lesson is standalone and can be taught independently from those preceding it.

If you have more than 38 lessons together, or your lessons are longer than one hour, you can incorporate assessment from the accompanying Tutor Assessment Pack (ISBN: 9781292195360). There is an *end-of-topic test* for every lesson in this pack, as well as *checkpoint challenges* and a *practice paper*. All of the papers can also be given as homework, used as diagnostic tests or incorporated into revision.

LESSON PLANS

The first page of each lesson is your *lesson plan*. It is designed specifically for tutors and is intended to guide you through a one-hour session in either a one-to-one or small group setting. It is not designed to be student-facing.

LEARNING OBJECTIVES AND SPECIFICATION LINKS

At the top of each lesson plan, you will find two lists. The first – *learning objectives* – is a list of your aims for the lesson. The learning objectives will be informed by the specification but may have been rephrased to make sure they are accessible to and useful for everyone. You can discuss these with the student or use them for your own reference when tracking progress. The second list – *specification links* – shows you where in the specification you can find the objectives relevant to the lesson. You can find out more about the specification on pages 7–10.

ACTIVITIES

The first five minutes of your lesson should be spent reviewing the previous week's homework. You should not mark the homework during contact time: instead, use the time to talk through what the student learned and enjoyed, and any difficulties they encountered.

The final five minutes should be used to set homework for the forthcoming week. There are three ways to do this: using the *end-of-lesson report* on page 16; orally with a parent or guardian; or simply using the *homework activity sheet* on the fifth page of each lesson.

In each lesson plan, you will find four types of activities.
- *Starter activities* are 5–10 minutes each and provide an introduction to the topic.
- *Main activities* are up to 40 minutes long and are more involved, focussing on the main objectives of the lesson.
- *Plenary activities* are 5–10 minutes each, require little to no writing and recap the main learning points or prepare for the homework.
- *Homework activities* can be up to an hour long and put learning into practice.

In the lesson plan, you will find a page reference (where the activity is paper-based), a suggested timeframe and teaching notes for each activity. The teaching notes will help to guide you in delivering the activity and will also advise you on any common misconceptions associated with the topic.

ENGLISH
Grades 3–5
AQA

How to use this pack

Support and extension ideas
This pack is aimed at students who are targeted grades 3–5, but every student is different: some will struggle with activities that others working at the same level find straightforward. In these sections, you will find ideas for providing some differentiation throughout the activities.

Progress and observations
This section is left blank for you to use as appropriate. You can then use the notes you make to inform assessment and future lessons, as well as to inform *progress reports* to parents or guardians.

Activities
There are four student-facing *activity sheets* for each lesson: one for the starter activities; two for the main activities and one for the homework activity. On each sheet, you'll find activity-specific lesson objectives, an equipment list and a suggested timeframe. All activities are phrased for one-to-one tutoring but are equally as appropriate for small group settings. If you have a small group and the task asks you to work in pairs or challenge each other, ask the students to pair up while you observe and offer advice as necessary. Where appropriate, answers can be found on the sixth page of the lesson.

Diagnostics
The first lesson in this pack is a diagnostic lesson, designed to help you find out more about your student: their likes and dislikes; strengths and weaknesses; and personality traits. As well as the diagnostic lesson, the *needs analysis* section (pages 13–14) allows you, the student and the student's parents or guardians to investigate together which areas of the subject will need greater focus. Together, these sections will help you deliver the most effective, best value tuition.

Progress report
This can be used to inform parents or guardians or for your own planning as frequently or infrequently as is useful for you. Spend some time discussing the statements on the report with the student. Be prepared, though – some students will tell you there isn't anything that they enjoy about the subject!

End-of-lesson report
Parent participation will vary greatly. The *end-of-lesson* report is useful for efficiently feeding back to parents or guardians who prefer an update after each lesson. There is space to review completed homework and achievements in the lesson, as well as space for the student to explain how confident they feel after the lesson. Finally, there is a section on what steps, including homework, the parent and student can take to consolidate learning or prepare for the following week. The *end-of-lesson* report may also be useful for communicating with some parents or guardians who speak English as a second language, as written information may be easier to follow.

Certificates
In the digital version of this pack, you will find two customisable certificates. These can be edited to celebrate achievements of any size.

AQA ENGLISH — Grades 3–5

INFORMATION FOR PARENTS AND GUARDIANS

INTRODUCTION
Your child's tutor will often make use of resources from the *Tutors' Guild* series. These resources have been written especially for the new 9–1 GCSEs and are tailored to the AQA English Language specification. The tutor will use their expert knowledge and judgement to assess the student's current needs. This will allow them to target areas for improvement, build confidence levels and develop skills as quickly as possible to ensure the best chance of success.

Just as a classroom teacher might do, the tutor will use lesson plans and activities designed to prepare the student for the 9–1 GCSEs. Each set of resources has been designed by experts in GCSE English Language and reviewed by tutors to ensure it offers great quality, effective and engaging teaching. All *Tutors' Guild* resources are flexible and fully adaptable, so you can be confident that the tuition the student receives is tailored to his or her needs.

GETTING STARTED
Before tuition can begin, the tutor will need to know more about your motives for employing them in order to set clear, achievable goals. They will also try to learn more about the student to ensure lessons are as useful and as engaging as possible.

To gather this information, the tutor will work through the *needs analysis* pages of this pack with you. It shouldn't take too long, but it will really maximise the value of the tuition time you pay for. You could also take this opportunity to discuss with the tutor any questions or concerns you may have.

LESSONS AND HOMEWORK
Each lesson will have the same structure: there will be a starter, which is a quick introduction to the topic; some main activities, which will look at the topic in greater detail; and a plenary activity, which will be used to round off the topic. Throughout the year, the student will become increasingly confident with the content of the specification, but will also improve his or her speaking, writing, reading, listening and co-ordination skills through a carefully balanced range of activities.

At the end of each lesson, the tutor will set some homework, which should take no longer than an hour to complete. If you don't want the tutor to set homework, please let them know. If you are happy for homework to be given, they will either discuss the homework task with you at the end of the lesson or give you an end-of-lesson report. All of the homework activities are designed to be completed independently, but if you would like to help with completion of homework, the tutor will be able to tell you what you can do.

FURTHER SUPPORT
Parents and guardians often ask a tutor what else they can do to support their child's learning or what resources they can buy to provide extra revision and practice. As a Pearson resource, *Tutors' Guild* has been designed to complement the popular *Revise* series. Useful titles you may wish to purchase include:
- *Revise* AQA GCSE (9–1) English Language Revision Guide 9781447988052
- *Revise* AQA GCSE (9–1) English Language Revision Workbook 9781447987833
- *Revise* AQA GCSE (9–1) English Language Revision Cards 9781292182056.

Using pages 11–12 of this pack, the tutor will be able to tell you which pages of the resources are appropriate for each lesson. If you purchase a set of Revision Cards, each card has a page reference in the top corner.

ENGLISH
Grades 3–5
AQA

INFORMATION FOR PARENTS AND GUARDIANS

WHAT'S IN THE TEST?

You may have heard a lot about the new 9–1 GCSEs from your child's school, from other parents or in the media. Here is a breakdown of the AQA GCSE (9–1) English Language exam.

Students will sit two tests that assess learning against the AQA GCSE (9–1) English Language specification.

Paper 1: *Explorations in creative reading and writing (50% of the total marks)*
Students are given 1 hour and 45 minutes to complete Paper 1. It comprises two sections: Section A, which assesses reading comprehension using one 'unseen' 20th- or 21st-century fiction text, and Section B, which assesses students' descriptive or narrative writing ability. 'Unseen' means that the text will not have been studied in class prior to the exam and 'descriptive or narrative writing' is what we often think of as creative writing.

Paper 2: *Writers' viewpoints and perspectives (50% of the total marks)*
Students are given 1 hour and 45 minutes to complete Paper 2. It, again, comprises two sections: Section A, which assesses reading comprehension using two 'unseen' non-fiction texts, and Section B, which assesses students' ability to write to present a viewpoint. Types of non-fiction texts include letters, journals, obituaries, reference books, speeches and reviews. One non-fiction text will be from the 20th century and one will be from the 21st century. Writing to present a viewpoint generally aims to inform, explain or review, although it can have other purposes too.

It is recommended that the 1 hour and 45 minutes' exam time for each paper is spent as follows:
- 15 minutes reading for Section A (read the questions, then skim read the text(s), and then read the text(s) again more thoroughly, annotating useful sections)
- 45 minutes answering Section A
- 10 minutes planning and checking for Section B
- 35 minutes writing for Section B.

SPELLING, PUNCTUATION AND GRAMMAR

The new GCSE (9–1) English Language exam awards 20% of the total marks available to accurate spelling, punctuation and grammar. These marks are awarded in Section B of each paper. Accurate spelling, punctuation and grammar in the writing tasks could, therefore, contribute 36 marks to the student's overall mark. If you think that this is an area for improvement, you may wish to support tuition with extra practice through the Revise GCSE Spelling, Punctuation and Grammar series (Revision Guide ISBN: 9781292211527, Revision Workbook ISBN: 9781292211497).

RESULTS AND GRADES

GCSE results day is typically the third or fourth Thursday in August. It is the same day across the country, so you can find out the exact date online. On results day, students will be given a slip of paper (or one per exam board, if the school hasn't collated them) with an overall grade for each GCSE. Grades for the 9–1 GCSE in English Language are given as numbers (9–1) instead of letters (A*–U). The diagram below shows roughly how the old-style grades translate to the new ones.

A*	A	B	C	D	E	F	G	U
9	8	7	6	5	4	3	2	1	U

As you can see, the new grade 9 is pitched higher than an A*. There is also a wider spread of grades available for students whose target would previously have been a B/C. English Language is not a tiered exam (there are no Foundation and Higher papers) so all of the above grades are available to your son or daughter.

ENGLISH
Grades 3–5

SPECIFICATION GUIDANCE

The new AQA GCSE (9–1) English Language qualification was introduced for first teaching in 2015 and first assessment in 2017.

Assessment of the specification is no longer tiered. This means that every student should cover the same subject content and will sit the same paper. There will be no Foundation or Higher papers. It also means that every student has the opportunity to attain any grade that can be awarded. This Tutor Delivery Pack is tailored for the needs of students aiming for grades 3 to 5, but its content is provided in an adaptable format to allow you to stretch or support your student as necessary. More information about the new grading structure can be found in the Tutors' Guild AQA GCSE (9–1) English Language Tutor Assessment Pack.

If you are new to tutoring GCSE (9–1) English Language, this page will give you a brief introduction to the qualification before you move on to pages 8–10. Further guidance on particular areas of the specification – including common misconceptions and barriers to learning – can be found in the lesson plans throughout this book. Full details of the specification can be found at http://www.aqa.org.uk/subjects/english/gcse/english-language-8700.

KEY FACTS

Scope of study

There are three main skills-based content areas in the new 9–1 GCSE.

- **Critical reading and comprehension**: The reading component is worth 50% of the total marks for the GCSE. Topics within this content area are critical reading and comprehension (for example, interpretation of themes, ideas and information); summary and synthesis (for example, summarising information from one text or bringing together analysis of themes in more than one text); evaluation of writer's choice of vocabulary, form, grammatical and structural features (for example, explanation of the contribution of linguistic features to the overall impact of a text, with accurate use of linguistic terms); and comparing texts (using all of the skills learnt to critically compare two or more texts).
- **Writing**: The writing component is also worth 50% of the total marks available. It is split into two main topics: producing clear and coherent text (for example, appropriately identifying and writing for a specific purpose and audience, and maintaining consistency and coherence throughout), and writing for impact (for example, effective selection and structuring of ideas delivered through creative use of language). Also within the writing component (and thus a part of its 50% weighting) are spelling, punctuation and grammar. The government has stated that spelling, punctuation and grammar must be worth 20% of the overall marks for the GCSE, which is a significant increase on past GCSEs. This reflects the government's commitment to improving literacy skills in general.
- **Spoken language**: Speaking and listening skills are no longer awarded a mark. Spoken language will be assessed by your student's teacher and graded as *pass*, *merit* or *distinction*. Although spoken language is not specifically dealt with in this pack, your student will have ample opportunity to practise oral responses. If you or your student's parents/guardians feel that more practice is needed, the guidelines in the specification are very clear.

Each lesson plan in this pack highlights which areas of the specification it covers. As the pack is not intended to replace classroom teaching, it will not cover all 9–1 GCSE content in full detail. It will instead focus on the most important areas and those students struggle with the most, in order to maximise your student's chances of success.

Exam papers
AQA GCSE (9–1) English Language is not a tiered exam, so all students will sit the same two papers:
- **Paper 1: Explorations in Creative Reading and Writing**
    - 1 hour 45 minutes; 80 marks; 50% of GCSE
    - Section A: Reading (one fiction text, four mandatory questions); Section B: Writing (one extended writing question from a choice of two)
- **Paper 2: Writers' Viewpoints and Perspectives**
    - 1 hour 45 minutes; 80 marks; 50% of GCSE
    - Section A: Reading (one non-fiction text and one literary non-fiction text, four mandatory questions); Section B: Writing (one mandatory extended writing question).

You can find further information about the exam itself in the accompanying Tutor Assessment Pack to this title (ISBN: 9781292195360).

ENGLISH
Grades 3-5

PREPARING FOR THE EXAM

The structure of the AQA GCSE (9–1) English Language exams is prescriptive. There are two papers, each with four reading questions and one writing question. Paper 1 provides a choice of two writing questions, one of which is accompanied by a prompt image, whereas there is no choice in Paper 2. The questions appear in a set order (from low to high demand), test specific assessment objectives and even have specific wording.

READING (SECTION A)

It's important that you understand which skills will be tested in which papers, and therefore on which text types. Note that there will be little variation in the question stems used in the exam, so you should base your own questions on those below.

PAPER 1

Paper 1 will be accompanied by one prose fiction extract from either the 20th or 21st century. It will be from the beginning, end or a transitional point within the story. Encourage your student to read as much post-1900 literature as possible.

Question 1: Identify explicit ideas and information within a specific section of the extract (AO1).
Example question stem: *List four things from this part of the text...*

Point out an explicit idea within a small section of the text (for example, what we learn about a setting) and challenge your student to find four pieces of information about it within that section. Question 1 won't ask your student to explain their response, simply to list the information they find – quoting or paraphrasing is acceptable.

Question 2: Explain and analyse the writer's use of language within a specific section of the extract (AO2).
Example question stem: *How does the writer use of language to…?*
You could include the writer's choice of:
- *words and phrases*
- *language features and techniques*
- *sentence forms.*

This questions explores how language is used to explain something about the idea identified in Question 1. For example, if your student noted information about a setting, they may now look at how language creates atmosphere in that setting.

Students will need to look at a range of aspects of language as suggested by the supporting bullet points in the question, remembering to use subject terminology accurately. However, it is not enough for your student to simply identify a word or phrase and name it appropriately. They must be able to analyse and explain the effect of its use.

For Question 2, students should not consider the text holistically. The question will ask them to look at a small section of the source (around 10 lines), so comments should be at word, phrase and sentence level, not paragraph or whole text level.

Question 3: Explain and analyse the writer's use of structure across the whole extract (AO2).
Example question stem: *This text is from…*
How has the writer structured the text to interest you as a reader?
You could write about:
- *what the writer focuses your attention on at the beginning*
- *how and why the writer changes this focus as the source develops*
- *any other structural features that interest you.*

This is a new approach to structural analysis, but it's actually very similar to the approach to language analysis in Question 2. Your student's discussion should include analysis of three levels of structure:
- whole text level – beginnings, ends, shifts in perspective (for example, from one character to another, from an inside setting to an outside one or from a character to the setting)
- paragraph level – cohesion and change of time period, topic or speaker
- sentence level – comment should only be made on sentences that affect the overall structure of the source. For example, it would be appropriate to discuss a sentence used to introduce a shift in perspective or further the reader's understanding of the whole text.

ENGLISH — Grades 3-5 —

Preparing for the exam

The phrase 'to interest you as a reader' reminds students that they must explain the effect of the structural devices, while allowing them the freedom to explain in what way the text is interesting. As with Question 2, it is important that your student remembers to use subject terminology and pick relevant examples that enhance and support their points.

Question 4: Evaluate a specific section of the extract critically (AO4).
Example question stem: *A student, having read this section of the text said: "…"*
To what extent do you agree?
In your response, you could:
- *consider your own impression of…*
- *evaluate how the writer creates…*
- *support your opinions with references to the text.*

Critical evaluation assesses your student synoptically; it requires them to bring together a range of skills: inference, analysis and evaluation. Your student should focus their response on the statement made in the question: how and why is the text effective or ineffective at what is claimed? It is acceptable to agree or disagree entirely with the statement. However, a more perceptive response might partially agree, discussing how the text is both successful and potentially unsuccessful in achieving its aim. Remind your student that the question is asking for their own opinion and thoughts.

Bullet points are provided within the question to support students in formulating a response. If your student seems a little daunted at first, point out that this question draws together the kind of observations needed for Questions 1–3 and has bullet points to help them structure their response. If they note down their answers to each point, they should find it much easier to pull those notes together into a coherent and structured evaluation.

Paper 2

Paper 2 will be accompanied by two texts: one non-fiction and one literary non-fiction. Non-fiction text types that students may find in the exam include newspaper or magazine articles, reviews, letters and leaflets. A literary non-fiction text, such as a diary, a piece of travel writing, a biography or a retelling of a historical event, is still factual in content but uses literary devices you would find in fictional prose. To help students practise the skills required, ensure they have access to a range of the text types listed above. On Paper 2, there will be some synthesis and comparison of texts, skills that are not tested in Paper 1.

Question 1: Identify and interpret explicit and implicit ideas within a specific section of the extract (AO1).
Example question stem: *Choose four statements below which are TRUE.*
- *Shade the boxes of the ones that you think are true.*
- *Choose a maximum of four statements.*

The skills needed to answer this question are similar to those for Question 1 on Paper 1. The difference here, however, is that your student will need to be able to interpret implicit information to decide whether some of the statements are correct.

Students who are generally risk-averse often find multiple-choice questions difficult to answer because they spend time finding a reason why each statement is either true or false. If they have read and digested the text, their 'gut feeling' is likely to be correct. Set some practice questions for your student under timed conditions and, if it looks as though their reasoning is sound, encourage them to listen to their instincts and use the text to verify their answers rather than to work them out.

Question 2: Synthesise implicit and explicit ideas (AO1) from two extracts.
Example question stem: *You need to refer to Source A and Source B for this question.*
Use details from both Sources. Write a summary of the differences between …

The example above asks students to summarise the differences between two texts, but could equally ask about the similarities. This question requires the most extended response of those assessing AO1, and for many students will be the most inaccessible. The key differences between this question and the other AO1 questions are that students need to bring together information from two texts throughout and refer to each text as a whole. To be successful, your student will need to work on and regularly practise the following skills:

- recognising what is to be summarised, for example, the similarities between two people
- locating appropriate evidence within each text and identifying what it tells them in relation to the question
- synthesising (bringing together) inferences and evidence to form a cohesive response.

Note that, although it asks for a comparison, Question 2 is only worth 8 marks and does not require in-depth analysis.

ENGLISH — Grades 3-5 — AQA

PREPARING FOR THE EXAM

Question 3: Explain and analyse the writer's use of language throughout half of the extract (AO2).
Example question stem: *How does Henry use language to...?*

The principles of this question are similar to those in Paper 1, Question 2: analysing the use of various linguistic features at word, phrase and sentence level. Although it will not provide suggestions of what the students' answers could include – the focus should be the same as in Paper 1. Furthermore, the student will need to look at language use in the whole extract, provide a broader range of examples and discuss these in more detail.

Having a clear idea of how to structure a response will help your student to approach the question in an organised manner. Give them an example question and ask them to identify the linguistic features they would like to discuss, and what they show. Then, ask them to categorise their ideas in a logical way: for example, grouping similar features or ideas and themes.

Question 4: Compare writers' ideas and perspectives and how they are conveyed throughout two extracts (AO3).
Example question stem: *Compare how the two writers convey their different attitudes to...*
> In your answer, you could:
> - compare their different attitudes
> - compare the methods they use to convey their attitudes
> - support your ideas with references to both texts.

This is the one reading question for which AQA suggests that students factor in planning time, as it is perhaps the most demanding of the reading questions. Fortunately, students will have practised many of the skills needed in Questions 1–3, such as writing about two texts together, discussing the methods used to convey an idea and providing evidence.

Students need to be able to identify the attitudes and viewpoints of both writers and support their ideas with evidence of the writers' methods, such as language and structure techniques. Identification of audience, purpose and form is essential, as these influence the writers' choices. Your student may need support and practice identifying tone and voice, skills which demand a sophisticated understanding of the holistic impact of the writers' craft.

Unlike Question 2, which asks for a comparison of the information in each text, this question asks the student to compare the ideas and perspectives of both writers. Students will then need to compare the texts in more depth than in Question 2 and will have the freedom to choose what to compare. This can be daunting. For example, one student may choose to compare how two writers use similes to portray an enthusiastic attitude, looking at the word choices in those figurative devices. Another may compare how writers create an enthusiastic tone in a different way – though energetic verb choices or through rhetorical questions, for example. The skill is being able to juggle both texts, while demonstrating a sophisticated understanding of the writer's craft.

Start preparing your student for this question with texts in which the writers use similar methods to convey clearly similar, or different, attitudes towards a topic. This practise with the core skills will increase their confidence. Then develop more perceptive comments by building up to texts in which the writers show broadly the same attitude, but for different reasons and in different ways. Remember, the student is asked to 'compare' so they should look for similarities *and* differences.

WRITING (SECTION B)

Paper 1: Question 5 offers students two creative writing tasks – with one written and one visual stimulus – closely linked to the theme of the source text in Section A. One task will require descriptive writing and the other will require narrative writing. While it will be useful to encourage your student to think critically about their own work and in which area their strengths lie, dissuade them from deciding definitively which question they are going to answer before reading the tasks.

Paper 2: Question 5 of Paper 2 does not offer a choice of writing tasks. The theme will be linked to that of the source texts in Section A, and the audience, purpose and form will be specified. Students will have to write to explain, instruct/advise, argue or persuade through a letter, article, leaflet, speech or essay, using characteristic linguistic, structural and presentational devices. Analysing good examples of each form together will increase your student's familiarity with its features.

AQA ENGLISH — Grades 3–5

REVISE MAPPING GUIDE

Parents may ask you if you know of any independent study resources that they can work through with their child, or you may wish to provide such resources yourself. Pearson's *Revise* series provides simple, clear support to students preparing for their GCSE (9–1) exams.

We have provided below a mapping guide for each lesson in this pack to a corresponding page in the *Revise* series, to make such recommendations easier for you. The Revision Guides and Revision Workbooks for each level correspond page-for-page, so the page references are the same for both. See page 5 for a list of recommended titles for students studying AQA GCSE (9–1) English Language.

REVISE AQA GCSE (9–1) ENGLISH LANGUAGE REVISION GUIDE

Lesson		Page
1	Diagnostic: Reading	
READING		
2	Approaching an unseen text	Covered throughout Revision Guide
3	Explicit and implicit information	Explicit information and ideas **13**; Implicit information and ideas **14**
4	Summarising using evidence	Skimming for the main idea **7**; Annotating the sources **8**; Point-Evidence-Explain **16**; Writing about two texts **39**; Selecting evidence for synthesis **40**
5	Comparative summary	Writing about two texts **39**; Selecting evidence for synthesis **40**; Answering a synthesis question **41**; Looking closely at language **42**; Planning to compare language **43**; Comparing language **44**; Comparing structure **45**; Comparing ideas **46**; Comparing perspective **47**; Answering a comparison question **48**
6	Analysing language 1	Word classes **19**; Connotations **20**; Figurative language **21**; Creation of character **22**; Creating atmosphere **23**; Narrative voice **24**; Rhetorical devices 1 **27**; Rhetorical devices 2 **28**
7	Analysing language 2	Word classes **19**; Connotations **20**; Figurative language **21**; Creation of character **22**; Creating atmosphere **23**; Narrative voice **24**; Rhetorical devices 1 **27**; Rhetorical devices 2 **28**
8	Analysing language 3	Word classes **19**; Connotations **20**; Figurative language **21**; Creation of character **22**; Creating atmosphere **23**; Narrative voice **24**; Rhetorical devices 1 **27**; Rhetorical devices 2 **28**
9	Analysing sentence forms 1	Identifying sentence types **31**; Commenting on sentences **32**
10	Analysing sentence forms 2	Identifying sentence types **31**; Commenting on sentences **32**
11	Developing language analysis	Inference **15**; Point-Evidence-Explain **16**; **19**; Connotations **20**; Figurative language **21**; Creation of character **22**; Creating atmosphere **23**; Narrative voice **24**; Rhetorical devices 1 **27**; Rhetorical devices 2 **28**; Identifying sentence types **31**; Commenting on sentences **32**; Looking closely at language **42**; Planning to compare language **43**
12	Whole text structure	Whole text structure: fiction **29**; Whole text structure: non-fiction **30**
13	Narrative focus	The writer's viewpoint **11**; Narrative voice **24**; Whole text structure: fiction **29**
14	Analysing whole text structure	Whole text structure: fiction **29**; Whole text structure: non-fiction **30**
15	Beginning an evaluation	Evaluating a fiction text 1 **35**; Evaluating a fiction text 2 **36**; Using evidence to evaluate **37**
16	Writing an evaluative response	Evaluating a fiction text 1 **35**; Evaluating a fiction text 2 **36**; Using evidence to evaluate **37**
17	Developing critical evaluation	Evaluating a fiction text 1 **35**; Evaluating a fiction text 2 **36**; Using evidence to evaluate **37**

ENGLISH — Grades 3-5 — AQA

REVISE MAPPING GUIDE

REVISE AQA GCSE (9–1) ENGLISH LANGUAGE REVISION GUIDE

Lesson		Page
18	Writing a comparison	Writing about two texts **39**; Selecting evidence for synthesis **40**; Answering a synthesis question **41**; Looking closely at language **42**; Planning to compare language **43**
19	Developing a comparison	Writing about two texts **39**; Selecting evidence for synthesis **40**; Answering a synthesis question **41**; Looking closely at language **42**; Planning to compare language **43**; Comparing language **44**; Comparing structure **45**; Comparing ideas **46**; Comparing perspective **47**; Answering a comparison question **48**
20	Consolidating comparisons	Answering a comparison question **48**
	DESCRIPTIVE AND NARRATIVE WRITING	
21	Gathering ideas	Writing for a purpose: creative 1 **54**; Writing for a purpose: creative 2 **55**
22	Structure and planning	Writing for a purpose: creative 1 **54**; Writing for a purpose: creative 2 **55**; Writing for a purpose: viewpoint 1 **56**; Writing for a purpose: viewpoint 2 **57**; Writing for an audience **58**; Ideas and planning: creative **65**; Structure: creative **66**; Beginnings and endings: creative **67**
23	Beginnings and endings	Beginnings and endings: creative **67**
24	Using paragraphs for effect	Paragraphing **74**; Linking ideas **75**
25	Structuring sentences	Sentence variety 1 **87**; Sentence variety 2 **88**
26	Sentence structure for effect	Sentences for different effects **89**
27	Selecting vocabulary	Vocabulary for effect: synonyms **79**; Vocabulary for effect: creative **80**
28	Consolidation	Writing questions: an overview **50**; Writing questions: Paper 1 **51**; Writing questions: time management **53**; Language for different effects 1 **82**; Language for different effects 2 **83**; Language for different effects 3 **84**
	WRITING TO PRESENT A VIEWPOINT	
29	Gathering ideas	Writing for a purpose: viewpoint 1 **56**; Writing for a purpose: viewpoint 2 **57**
30	Structure and planning	Writing for a purpose: viewpoint 1 **56**; Writing for a purpose: viewpoint 2 **57**; Writing for an audience **58**; Form: articles **61**; Form: letters and reports **62**; Form: speeches **63**; Ideas and planning: viewpoint 1 **69**; Ideas and planning: viewpoint 2 **70**
31	Introductions and conclusions	Openings: viewpoint **71**; Conclusions: viewpoint **72**
32	Building paragraphs	Paragraphing **74**; Linking ideas **75**
33	Using structure for effect	Paragraphing **74**; Sentence variety 1 **87**; Sentence variety 2 **88**; Sentences for different effects **89**
34	Selecting vocabulary	Vocabulary for effect: viewpoint **81**; Language for different effects 1 **82**; Language for different effects 2 **83**; Language for different effects 3 **84**
35	Writing a response	Writing questions: an overview **50**; Writing questions: Paper 1 **51**; Writing questions: time management **53**; Formality and standard English 1 **77**; Formality and standard English 2 **78**; Language for different effects 3 **84**
	SPaG	
36	Basic punctuation	Ending a sentence **91**; Commas **92**; Apostrophes and speech punctuation **93**
37	Advanced punctuation	Colons, semi-colons, dashes, brackets and ellipses **94**
38	Spelling and proofreading	Common spelling errors 1 **96**; Common spelling errors 2 **97**; Common spelling errors 3 **98**; Proofreading **99**

AQA ENGLISH — Grades 3–5

Needs Analysis

For parents and guardians

We have a tutor because...
(Briefly explain why you have employed a tutor.)

Where we are currently...
(Briefly explain the student's current progress. Do you have access to reports and predicted grades?)

For students

Use this space to tell your tutor about yourself.

I am...
Tell your tutor what type of person you think you are. Are you quiet or outgoing? Are you confident about your abilities?

I like...
Explain to your tutor how you like to work. Do you like to work independently or with more guidance? Do you like to write your answers down or talk through them first? Do you like to be creative?

How I feel about English...
Do you like English? Try to explain why or why not. What are your favourite and least favourite parts?

ENGLISH
Grades 3-5

NEEDS ANALYSIS

OUR GOALS

Work together to set small, achievable goals for the year ahead. Make them as positive as you can and don't limit your goals to areas of English – think about personal development too. Together, look back at this list often to see how you are progressing.

TICK OFF EACH GOAL WHEN YOU'VE ACHIEVED IT

In four weeks' time, I will...

- [ ] ....
- [ ] ....
- [ ] ....
- [ ] ....
- [ ] ....
- [ ] ....

In three months' time, I will...

- [ ] ....
- [ ] ....
- [ ] ....
- [ ] ....
- [ ] ....
- [ ] ....

By the time I sit my exam, I will...

- [ ] ....
- [ ] ....
- [ ] ....
- [ ] ....
- [ ] ....
- [ ] ....

AQA ENGLISH — Grades 3-5

PROGRESS REPORT

Fill in the boxes below with help from your tutor.

My strengths are...
Which areas of English do you think you've done well in recently? List at least three.

My favourite English topic is...
Which English topic is your favourite? It doesn't have to be the one you're best at!

because...

The areas of English I need to work on are...
In which areas of English do you think you need more practice?

To improve these areas, we are going to...
This space is for your tutor to explain how he/she is going to help you become confident in these areas.

ENGLISH
Grades 3-5

END-OF-LESSON REPORT

We have looked at last week's homework and my tutor thinks...
This space is for your tutor to give feedback on last week's homework.

Today, we worked on...
This space is for you to list all of the topics and skills that you and your tutor have worked on today.

I feel...
This space is for you to explain how you feel about today's lesson. Did you enjoy it? Do you feel confident?

My tutor thinks...
This space is for your tutor to explain how the lesson went.

At home this week, we can...
This space is for your tutor to explain what your homework is and give you other ideas for extra revision and practice.

Source A: Non-fiction text

This extract is taken from a biography called *The Napoleon of Crime: The Life and Times of Adam Worth, the Real Moriarty*, by Ben Macintyre. It was written in the 21st century, and describes the life of a criminal who operated in the 19th century.

The Napoleon of Crime

On a misty May midnight in the year 1876, three men emerged from a fashionable address in Piccadilly with top hats on their heads, money in their pockets, and burglary, on a grand scale, on their minds. At a deliberate pace the trio headed along the thoroughfare, and at the point where Piccadilly intersects with Old Bond Street, they came to a stop. Famed for its art galleries and antiques shops, the street by day was choked with the carriages of the wealthy, the well-bred, and the culturally well-informed. Now it was quite deserted.

The three men exchanged a few words at the corner of the street before one slipped into a doorway, invisible beyond the dancing gaslight shadows, while the other two turned right into Old Bond Street. They made an incongruous pair as they walked on: one was slight and dapper, some thirty-five years in age, with long, clipped mustaches, and dressed in the height of modern elegance, complete with pearl buttons and gold watch chain. The other, ambling a few paces behind, was a towering fellow with grizzled mutton-chop whiskers, whose ill-fitting frock coat barely contained a barrel chest. Had anyone been there to observe the couple, they might have assumed them to be a rich man taking the night air with his unprepossessing valet after a substantial dinner at his club.

Outside the art gallery of Thomas Agnew & Sons, at number 39, Old Bond Street, the two men paused, and while the aristocrat extinguished his cheroot and admired his own faint but stylish reflection in the glass, his brutish companion glanced furtively up and down the street. Then, at a word from his master, the giant flattened himself against the wall and joined his hands in a stirrup, into which the smaller man placed a well-shod foot, for all the world as if he were climbing onto a thoroughbred. With a grunt the big man heaved the little fellow up the wall and in a moment he had scrambled nimbly onto the window ledge some fifteen feet above the pavement. Balancing precariously, he whipped out a small crow bar, wrenched open the casement window, and slipped inside, as his companion vanished from sight beneath the gallery portal.

The room was unfurnished and unlit, but by the faint glow from the pavement gaslight a large painting in a gilt frame could be discerned on the opposite wall. The little man removed his hat as he drew closer.

The woman in the portrait, already famed throughout London as the most exquisite beauty ever to grace a canvas, gazed down with an imperious and inquisitive eye. Curls cascaded from beneath a broad-brimmed hat set at a rakish angle to frame a painted glance at once beckoning and mocking, and a smile just one quiver short of a full pout.

The faint rumble of a night watchman's snores wafted up from the room below, as the little gentleman unclipped a thick velvet rope that held the inquisitive public back from the painting during daylight hours. Extracting a sharp blade from his pocket, with infinite care he cut the portrait from its frame and laid it on the gallery floor. From his coat he took a small pot of paste, and using the tasseled end of the velvet rope, he daubed the back of the canvas to make it supple and then rolled it up with the paint facing outward to avoid cracking the surface, before slipping it inside his frock coat.

A few seconds later he had scrambled back down his monstrous assistant to the street below. A low whistle summoned the lookout from his street corner, and with jaunty step the little dandy set off back down Piccadilly, the stolen portrait pressed to his breast and his two rascally companions trailing behind.

Source B: Non-fiction text

This extract is from the autobiography of Montagu Williams, called *Round London: Down East and Up West*, written in 1894. In this section, he describes a burglary committed by a man named William Caseley and his gang.

Burglarious Bill

Caseley was known to be one of the most expert burglars in the metropolis, and he had already undergone one sentence of penal servitude[1], which proves that he must have entered upon a criminal career at an early age. He had two nicknames, one being "Counsellor Kelly," and the other "Tom the Madman."

The establishment broken into was that of Mr. Walker, a large jeweller's on Cornhill.

It appeared that on Saturday, the fourth of February, the assistant, after placing the whole of the stock in one of Milner's iron safes, left the premises at half-past seven in the evening. As usual, the gas was left burning in the shop, which was open to inspection by the police and other passers-by through apertures in the shutters. The safe was so placed as to be distinctly seen by anyone looking through these apertures, and by an ingenious arrangement of mirrors a person standing in any part of the shop would also be visible from the outside.

When the assistant returned to the premises on Monday morning at half-past eight o'clock, he found that the shop had been entered through a hole in the floor, and that the safe had been opened and ransacked. It appeared that the thieves had forced an entry into the rooms of Mr. Mitchell, a tailor, in the lower part of the building, and had cut their way through the ceiling. The value of Mr. Walker's stock was about six thousand pounds, and nearly the whole of it had been stolen. The booty included four hundred and sixty-five watches and one hundred and sixty gold chains. It was manifest that some considerable time had been occupied in the operations of the culprits. In all probability they had remained on the premises during Saturday night and the greater part of Sunday. The safe had been forced very cleverly, there being no external marks of violence upon it. During the trial the police declared that the tools used must have been "beautiful instruments."

The assistant lost no time in communicating with the police, and Inspector Potter, of the S Division, Inspector Brennan, Thomas Foulger, and Sergeant Moss, of the City Police, who were among the cleverest officers in the London force, were told off to investigate the matter. It appeared that, very soon after the burglary, Caseley opened a meat-pie shop at 142, Whitechapel Road, and there, on Friday, the twenty-fourth of February, Potter, Moss, and Brennan arrested the Brewertons and some of the other culprits. On the premises were discovered several articles of jewellery that were stolen from Mr Walker's shop, together with one hundred pounds in cash, and two receipts for money recently lodged at the London and Westminster Bank, one being for a sum of two hundred and fifty pounds and the other for a sum of one hundred and fifty pounds. The officers next proceeded to the Caseleys' private dwelling, in Ely Terrace, Bow Road. One of them knocked at the door, whereupon Mrs. Caseley put her head out of a window and said:
"Who are you?"
"We are police officers," was the reply.

They waited for a minute or two, but as the door was not opened they forced the lock, entered, and rushed upstairs. The two Caseleys were at once taken into custody, after which the house was searched, with the result that the officers discovered a box containing a number of Mr. Walker's watches and chains, gold coin to the amount of one hundred and ninety-six pounds, and a fifty-pound note. The proceeds of other burglaries were also found, together with a life preserver[2], which had been placed in the bed under the pillow, a collection of skeleton keys, several screwdrivers, a revolver, and some caps and bullets.

1: *sentence of penal servitude* – a prison sentence
2: *life preserver* – a heavy club or truncheon

ENGLISH
Grades 3–5

SOURCE C: NON-FICTION TEXT

In his book *Earth in the Balance*, Al Gore describes the damage that human beings have done to the Earth and calls for all of us to take action.

Earth in the Balance

One doesn't have to travel around the world to witness humankind's assault on the earth. Images that signal the distress of our global environment are now commonly seen almost anywhere. [...]
On some nights, in high northern latitudes[1], [...] if the sky is clear after sunset – and if you are watching from a place where pollution hasn't blotted out the night sky altogether – you can sometimes see a strange
5 kind of cloud high in the sky. This "noctilucent cloud"[2] occasionally appears when the earth is first cloaked in the evening darkness; shimmering above us with a translucent[3] whiteness, these clouds seem quite unnatural. And they should: noctilucent clouds have begun to appear more often because of a huge buildup of methane gas in the atmosphere. (Also called natural gas, methane is released from landfills, from coal mines and rice paddies, from billions of termites that swarm through the freshly cut forestland,
10 from the burning of biomass[4] and from a variety of other human activities.) Even though noctilucent clouds were sometimes seen in the past, all this extra methane carries more water vapor into the upper atmosphere, where it condenses at much higher altitudes to form more clouds that the sun's rays still strike long after sunset has brought the beginning of night to the surface far beneath them.

What should we feel toward these ghosts in the sky? Simple wonder or the mix of emotions we feel at
15 the zoo? Perhaps we should feel awe for our own power: just as men tear tusks from elephants' heads in such quantity as to threaten the beast with extinction, we are ripping matter from its place in the earth in such volume as to upset the balance between daylight and darkness. In the process, we are once again adding to the threat of global warming, because methane has been one of the fastest-growing greenhouse gases, and is third only to carbon dioxide and water vapor in total volume, changing the chemistry of the
20 upper atmosphere. But, without even considering that threat, shouldn't it startle us that we have now put these clouds in the evening sky which glisten with a spectral light? Or have our eyes adjusted so completely to the bright lights of civilization that we can't see these clouds for what they are – a physical manifestation[5] of the violent collision between human civilization and the earth?

Even though it is sometimes hard to see their meaning, we have by now all witnessed surprising
25 experiences that signal the damage from our assault on the environment – whether it's the new frequency of days when the temperature exceeds 100 degrees, the new speed with which the sun burns our skin, or the new constancy of public debate over what to do with growing mountains of waste. But our response to these signals is puzzling. Why haven't we launched a massive effort to save our environment?

1: *northern latitudes* – the northern hemisphere of the Earth
2: *noctilucent cloud* – a cloud that shines or glows at night due to pollution
3: *translucent* – allowing light to pass through; semi-transparent
4: *biomass* – wood and other natural substances burnt to generate energy
5: *manifestation* – a sign or symptom

ENGLISH
Grades 3-5

SOURCE D: FICTION TEXT

This extract is the opening of the novel *The Secret History* by Donna Tartt, published in 1992. It is set in a college in New England, America.

The Secret History

The snow in the mountains was melting and Bunny had been dead for several weeks before we came to understand the gravity[1] of our situation. He'd been dead for ten days before they found him, you know. It was one of the biggest manhunts in Vermont history – state troopers, the FBI, even an army helicopter; the college closed, the dye factory in Hampden shut down, people coming from New Hampshire, upstate
5 New York, as far away as Boston.

It is difficult to believe that Henry's modest plan could have worked so well despite these unforeseen events. We hadn't intended to hide the body where it couldn't be found. In fact, we hadn't hidden it at all but had simply left it where it fell in hopes that some luckless passer-by would stumble over it before anyone even noticed he was missing. This was a tale that told itself simply and well: the loose rocks, the
10 body at the bottom of the ravine with a clean break in the neck, and the muddy skidmarks of dug-in heels pointing the way down; a hiking accident, no more, no less, and it might have been left at that, at quiet tears and a small funeral, had it not been for the snow that fell that night; it covered him without a trace, and ten days later, when the thaw finally came, the state troopers and the FBI and the searchers from the town all saw that they had been walking back and forth over his body until the snow above it was packed
15 down like ice.

It is difficult to believe that such an uproar took place over an act for which I was partially responsible, even more difficult to believe I could have walked through it – the cameras, the uniforms, the black crowds sprinkled over Mount Cataract like ants in a sugar bowl – without incurring a blink of suspicion. But walking through it all was one thing; walking away, unfortunately, has proved to be quite another, and though once
20 I thought I had left that ravine forever on an April afternoon long ago, now I am not so sure. Now the searchers have departed, and life has grown quiet around me, I have come to realize that while for years I might have imagined myself to be somewhere else, in reality I have been there all the time: up at the top by the muddy wheel-ruts in the new grass, where the sky is dark over the shivering apple blossoms and the first chill of the snow that will fall that night is already in the air.

25 What are you doing up here? said Bunny, surprised, when he found the four of us waiting for him.
Why, looking for new ferns, said Henry.

And after we stood whispering in the underbrush – one last look at the body and a last look round, no dropped keys, lost glasses, everybody got everything? – and then started single file through the woods, I took one glance back through the saplings that leapt to close the path behind me. Though I remember the
30 walk back and the first lonely flakes of snow that came drifting through the pines, remember piling gratefully into the car and starting down the road like a family on vacation, with Henry driving clench-jawed through the potholes and the rest of us leaning over the seats and talking like children, though I remember only too well the long terrible night that lay ahead and the long terrible days and nights that followed, I have only to glance over my shoulder for all those years to drop away and I see it behind me again, the
35 ravine, rising all green and black through the saplings, a picture that will never leave me.

1: *gravity* – seriousness

SOURCE E: FICTION TEXT

This is the opening of a novel by Sarah Perry called *The Essex Serpent*. It was written in 2016 and is set in Victorian Essex. The story begins on New Year's Eve.

The Essex Serpent

A young man walks down by the banks of the Blackwater under the full cold moon. He's been drinking the old year down to the dregs, until his eyes grew sore and his stomach turned, and he was tired of the bright lights and bustle. 'I'll just go down to the water,' he said, and kissed the nearest cheek: 'I'll be back before the chimes.' Now he looks east to the turning tide, out to the estuary slow and dark, and the white gulls
5   gleaming on the waves.

It's cold, and he ought to feel it, but he's full of beer and he's got on his good thick coat. The collar rasps at the nape of his neck: he feels fuddled and constricted and his tongue is dry. I'll go for a dip, he thinks, that'll shake me loose; and coming down from the path stands alone on the shore, where deep in the dark mud all the creeks wait for the tide.

10   'I'll take a cup of kindness yet,' he sings in his sweet chapel tenor, then laughs, and someone laughs back. He unbuttons his coat, he holds it open, but it's not enough: he wants to feel the wind's edge strop itself sharp on his skin. Nearer he goes to the water, and puts out his tongue to the briny air: Yes – I'll go for a dip, he thinks, dropping his coat on the marsh. He's done it before, after all, when a boy and in good company: the brave tomfoolery of a midnight dip as the old year dies in the New Year's arms. The tide's
15   low – the wind's dropped – the Blackwater holds no fear: give him a glass and he'll drink it down, salt and seashell, oyster and all.

But something alters in a turn of the tide or a change of the air: the estuary surface shifts – seems (he steps forward) to pulse and throb, then grow slick and still; then soon after to convulse, as if flinching at a touch. Nearer he goes, not yet afraid; the gulls lift off one by one, and the last gives a scream of dismay.

20   Winter comes like a blow to the back of his neck: he feels it penetrate his shirt and go into his bones. The good cheer of drink is gone, and he's comfortless there in the dark – he looks for his coat, but clouds hide the moon and he's blind. His breath is slow, the air is full of pins; the marsh at his feet all at once is wet, as if something out there has displaced the water. Nothing, it's nothing, he thinks, patting about for his courage, but there it is again: a curious still moment as if he were looking at a photograph, followed by
25   a frantic uneven motion that cannot be merely the tug of the moon on the tides. He thinks he sees – is certain he sees – the slow movement of something vast, hunched, grimly covered over with rough and lapping scales; then it is gone.

SOURCE F: NON-FICTION TEXT

In this extract from *Six Thousand Years of History* by Edgar Sanderson, the writer looks back from the end of the 19th century at the progress humankind made in a hundred years.

A Century of Achievement

In the one hundred years now drawing to a close the world has made a greater advance in science and the arts than in all the preceding ages. The human mind reels when it tries to grasp the stupendous achievements of the Nineteenth Century, in every branch of discovery and invention. Because of their love of pure knowledge, men of gigantic intellect have sought out the mighty secrets of the universe and have
5 raised to the sky a temple to science on ground upon which stood, a century ago, only scattered and isolated stones. Close behind the worshipers of knowledge have followed the magicians of to-day; chemists, engineers and electricians. At their command the spirits of air, water, earth and fire have been made to do man's every bidding. They propel his steamships, railway cars and mighty engines; they make his garments; they build his houses; they illuminate his cities; they harvest his crops. For him they make ice
10 in the tropics or grow oranges amid snow. For him they fan a heated atmosphere into cooling breezes or banish icy winds. They flash his news around the globe; they carry the sound of his voice for thousands of miles, or preserve it after he is dead.

During the Nineteenth Century, man has made a messenger boy of the lightning, and harnessed vapor to his chariot wheels, and all this he regards as a matter of course. Men and women alive to-day can
15 remember the introduction of the first steamboat and the first locomotive. They can recall their delight at the first daguerreotype[1]. Yet their grandchildren from their cradles have been used to electric street cars[2], ocean greyhounds[3] and kodaks[4].

We are benefited by thousands of practical applications of the discoveries of wise and patient men, but do not pause to consider the wonder of it all, and how new a power science is in the world.

20 It is well-nigh impossible to realize the state of science one hundred years ago. All was inchoate[5]. Great truths, germs of much that has been developed since, had been discovered and were startling the world by their novelty and their simplicity. But they stood apart, nor did man dream of science as a single rounded and connected whole. When we regard the astonishing structure that has been built since then, the materials for which have been hewn in so many forests and quarried from so many mines, it seems
25 incredible that a single century can have witnessed so many brilliant achievements.

1: *daguerreotype* – an early form of photograph
2: *electric street cars* – public transport trams
3: *ocean greyhounds* – an ocean liner
4: *kodaks* – cameras
5: *inchoate* – confused, incoherent

ENGLISH
Grades 3-5

1 Diagnostic: Reading

LEARNING OBJECTIVES	SPECIFICATION LINKS
• To recap prior learning and identify areas for development	• A range of skills and assessment objectives

Starter activity

- **Reading skills self-assessment; 10 minutes; page 24**
  Ask the student to spend five minutes completing the self-assessment sheet, identifying those skills they are familiar with and their confidence in using them. You may need to clarify the definition of some skills, for example by showing the type of exam question in which those skills would be needed. Spend a further five minutes discussing those skills that the student finds difficult. You should identify the barrier that has inhibited them in each case, such as a misunderstanding of the concept, difficulty applying it to a text, difficulty expressing it in writing, etc.

Main activities

- **Responding to reading; 15 minutes; page 25**
  Give the student 3–5 minutes to read Source A: *The Napoleon of Crime* (page 17), a 21st century non-fiction extract. Explain that they will then complete a short activity to help you assess their reading skills and develop them in future sessions. Ask the student to complete the activity orally, sharing their thinking with you as they do. Point out that some questions may have more than one correct answer.
- **Writing about reading; 20 minutes; page 26**
  Ask the student to complete the writing task independently. Note the pace at which the student responds and writes as an indicator of confidence and ability. After completion, discuss the process of critical writing: how does the student approach it? Note those elements of critical writing which present the greatest challenge as priorities for future learning.

Plenary activity

- **Target setting; 5 minutes**
  Ask the student to review the day's activities and negotiate three key targets to work on. Note their targets to guide future learning and self- and teacher-assessment.

Homework activity

- **Diagnostic – writing; 45 minutes; page 27**
  Explain that the key aims of the activity are to produce an effective piece of writing *and* to show awareness of how and why it is effective. Explain that you will use the student's planning, writing and self-assessment to identify future learning needs.

Support ideas

- **Responding to reading** Where the student falters or asks for help, guide them with prompts to appropriate answers, noting where in the process they lose confidence or understanding. If the student is still challenged by a question after being prompted, move on swiftly, noting that area as a priority for future learning.
- **Writing about reading** Use the self-assessment criteria from the Starter activity as prompts to support the student's critical writing. Which prompts do they feel confident they can incorporate in their writing? In what order might they include them in the paragraph?

Extension ideas

- **Responding to reading** If time allows, encourage the student to provide textual evidence and analytical comment to support their responses.
- **Writing about reading** Encourage the student to include a range of evidence and analysis in their critical writing.

Progress and observations

ENGLISH
Grades 3–5

AQA

| STARTER ACTIVITY: READING SKILLS SELF-ASSESSMENT | TIMING: 10 MINS |

LEARNING OBJECTIVES
- To self-assess reading skills in English

EQUIPMENT
- sample or past exam papers

How would you rate your reading skills?
Tick the box that best describes how you feel about each of these key skills.

1. Finding key information in a text

I'm not sure what this means. | I find this difficult. | I'm pretty good at this. | I'm really confident with this.

☐————☐————☐————☐

2. Choosing relevant evidence from a text

I'm not sure what this means. | I find this difficult. | I'm pretty good at this. | I'm really confident with this.

☐————☐————☐————☐

3. Commenting on the writer's use of words and phrases

I'm not sure what this means. | I find this difficult. | I'm pretty good at this. | I'm really confident with this.

☐————☐————☐————☐

4. Commenting on the writer's use of sentence forms

I'm not sure what this means. | I find this difficult. | I'm pretty good at this. | I'm really confident with this.

☐————☐————☐————☐

5. Commenting on the writer's use of whole text structure

I'm not sure what this means. | I find this difficult. | I'm pretty good at this. | I'm really confident with this.

☐————☐————☐————☐

6. Evaluating a text

I'm not sure what this means. | I find this difficult. | I'm pretty good at this. | I'm really confident with this.

☐————☐————☐————☐

AQA ENGLISH — Grades 3–5

MAIN ACTIVITY: RESPONDING TO READING	**TIMING: 15 MINS**

LEARNING OBJECTIVES
- To evaluate reading skills

EQUIPMENT
- Source A: *The Napoleon of Crime*

1. **Read Source A: *The Napoleon of Crime*. Summarise the text in one sentence.**

   ----

2. **Read the first two paragraphs again.**

   a) When did the events take place? Tick one.

   ☐ Roman times   ☐ Medieval times   ☐ 19th century   ☐ 20th century   ☐ 21st century

   b) How do you know this? Circle three clues in the text that support your answer.

3. **Why did the writer write this text? Tick all that apply.**

   ☐ to entertain   ☐ to inform   ☐ to persuade   ☐ to argue   ☐ to explain

4. **What is the writer's intention?**

   ☐ to engage the reader's interest
   ☐ to influence the reader's opinion and ideas
   ☐ to make the reader feel sympathy
   ☐ to make the reader laugh
   ☐ to vividly describe something that happened

5. **How would you describe the mood the writer creates in the extract? Tick two.**

   ☐ tense   ☐ dramatic   ☐ aggressive   ☐ emotional   ☐ disturbing

6. **What impressions does the writer create of the people and/or events described in the extract? Summarise your ideas in three or four words.**

   ----

7. **How does the writer use language to achieve your answer to question 4, 5 or 6? Choose one example. Write your answer on a separate piece of paper.**

8. **How does the writer use sentence forms to achieve your answer to question 4, 5 or 6? Choose one example. Write your answer on a separate piece of paper.**

9. **Is the text successful? Give reasons for your answer. Write your answer on a separate piece of paper.**

ENGLISH
Grades 3–5

| MAIN ACTIVITY: WRITING ABOUT READING | TIMING: 20 MINS |

LEARNING OBJECTIVES
- To evaluate critical writing skills

EQUIPMENT
- Source A: *The Napoleon of Crime*

1. How does the writer grab the reader's attention in the opening paragraph of Source A: *The Napoleon of Crime*? Write one paragraph in response to the question.

   ....

   ....

   ....

   ....

   ....

   ....

   ....

   ....

2. Read your answer to question 1 again.

   a) Tick all the criteria you feel you have achieved.

   ☐ I have made a clear point identifying one way in which the writer grabs the reader's attention.
   ☐ I have supported my point with evidence from the text.
   ☐ I have commented on how the writer's choice of words or phrases helps to grab the reader's attention.
   ☐ I have commented on how the writer's choice of sentence forms helps to grab the reader's attention.
   ☐ I have expressed my ideas clearly.

   b) Underline and label your writing to show where you have included each of the features in the checklist in part a).

ENGLISH
Grades 3–5

HOMEWORK ACTIVITY: DIAGNOSTIC – WRITING   **TIMING: 45 MINS**

LEARNING OBJECTIVES
- To evaluate writing skills

EQUIPMENT
- none

1. **Describe an occasion when you did something you regretted.**
   Use the space below to plan your response.

2. **Write the opening paragraph of your response on a separate piece of paper.**
   Make sure you:
   - grab the reader's attention from the very start of your writing
   - write approximately 100–125 words.

3. **How have you tried to grab the reader's attention with your writing? Write down three examples.**

ENGLISH
Grades 3-5

1 ANSWERS

STARTER ACTIVITY: READING SKILLS SELF-ASSESSMENT
Student's own answers

MAIN ACTIVITY: RESPONDING TO READING
1. Example: Three men steal a valuable work of art from a gallery.
2. a) 19th century; b) Examples: 1876, top tops, carriages, gaslight.
3. Entertain, inform and explain
4. Accept either: engage the reader's interest or vividly describe something that happened.
5. Tense and dramatic
6. Accept any valid response.
7. Accept any valid response justified with textual reference.
8. Accept any valid response justified with textual reference.
9. Accept any valid response justified with textual reference.

MAIN ACTIVITY: WRITING ABOUT READING
1. Student's own answer
2. a) Check the student has selected all items that they have included in their paragraph.
b) Check the student has underlined and labelled all items that they have included in their paragraph.

HOMEWORK ACTIVITY: DIAGNOSTIC – WRITING
Look for responses that identify three features of the text specifically crafted to grab the reader's attention.

GLOSSARY

Evidence
A quotation from a text or an observation of a particular event or point of view that is used to support an argument or perspective

Evaluation
Judging, as a reader, how successful a particular aspect of a text is, with an explanation

Compare
Identifying similarities and differences between two or more texts

AQA ENGLISH — Grades 3–5

2 READING: APPROACHING AN UNSEEN TEXT

LEARNING OBJECTIVES

- To develop skills and confidence in deducing the meaning of unfamiliar words
- To develop skills and confidence in tackling unseen texts
- To develop skills in information retrieval

SPECIFICATION LINKS

- 3.1.1 critical reading and comprehension

STARTER ACTIVITY

- **Deducing meaning; 5 minutes; page 30**
  Fold page 30 along the dotted line. Ask the student to complete question 1 and then unfold the sheet. What additional clues can be gained from the context in which each word is used in the text? Ask the student to write improved definitions below their original ones, and then summarise the strategies that can be used to deduce meaning, for example word families and context.

MAIN ACTIVITIES

- **Reading and checking understanding; 20 minutes; page 31**
  Ask the student to read Source B: *Burglarious Bill* (page 18). Ask them to identify any further examples of challenging vocabulary they have encountered in the text and suggest possible meanings and/or whether it is 'safe' to overlook them (i.e. they do not inhibit overall understanding of the text). Fold page 31 in half along the dotted line. Ask the student to complete question 1, then unfold the sheet and ask them to complete questions 2 and 3.

- **Information retrieval; 20 minutes; page 32**
  Ask the student to re-read the source text, completing question 1 as they read. Ask them to stop reading when they have completed the question. Point out that this is a Paper 2, Section A exam-style information retrieval question and that some information may be the writer's opinion. Ask the student to complete question 2. Highlight that this is an effective method of familiarising yourself with the text.

PLENARY ACTIVITY

- **The verdict; 5 minutes**
  Ask the student to deliver their verdict on Caseley and his gang: guilty or not guilty? Ask the student to underline all the relevant evidence from the text that supports their verdict and explain the deductions they have drawn from it.

HOMEWORK ACTIVITY

- **Write an exam-style question; 30 minutes; page 33**
  Ask the student to write an exam-style question, typical of Paper 2, question 1. They may find it helpful to see an example from the AQA Sample Assessment Materials. You may want the student to answer their own question to check the accuracy of their question-writing and understanding of the text.

SUPPORT IDEA

- **Deducing meaning** Point out that some of the words may suggest membership of a word family, e.g. *burglarious/burglar*. Beware the similarity of *counsellor* (advisor) and *councillor* (member of a council).

EXTENSION IDEA

- **Reading and checking understanding** Experiment with reducing the sentence summary. In how few words can the source be summarised?

PROGRESS AND OBSERVATIONS

ENGLISH
Grades 3-5

STARTER ACTIVITY: DEDUCING MEANING **TIMING: 5 MINS**

LEARNING OBJECTIVES
- To develop skills and confidence in deducing the meaning of unfamiliar words

EQUIPMENT
none

1. What do these words and phrases mean? Write a short definition of each one.

    a) burglarious

    ----

    b) penal servitude

    ----

    c) counsellor

    ----

    d) life preserver

    --fold--

2. Read these short extracts the 19th century non-fiction text *Burglarious Bill*, and then improve your definitions to the words.

    > **Burglarious Bill**
    >
    > Caseley was known to be one of the most expert burglars in the metropolis, and he had already undergone one sentence of penal servitude[1], which proves that he must have entered upon a criminal career at an early age. He had two nicknames, one being "Counsellor Kelly", and the other "Tom the Madman".

    > The proceeds of other burglaries were also found, together with a life preserver[2], which had been placed in the bed under the pillow, a collection of skeleton keys, several screwdrivers, a revolver, and some caps and bullets.

AQA ENGLISH — Grades 3-5

MAIN ACTIVITY: READING AND CHECKING UNDERSTANDING   TIMING: 20 MINS

LEARNING OBJECTIVES
- To develop skills and confidence in tackling unseen texts

EQUIPMENT
- Source B: *Burglarious Bill*

1. Write one sentence of 25 words or fewer summarising Source B: *Burglarious Bill*. Make sure you include as much relevant information as you can.

....

....

....

....

---fold---

2. Review your sentence. Which of the following key pieces of information have you included? Tick all that apply.
   - ☐ Caseley was a known criminal.
   - ☐ He and his gang burgled a jeweller's shop.
   - ☐ The gang consisted of Caseley, his wife and others.
   - ☐ Police arrested the gang.
   - ☐ Stolen goods were found in Caseley's shop and house.

3. How could you revise your sentence to include more of the key information listed above? Rewrite it below.

....

....

....

....

ENGLISH
— Grades 3-5 —

MAIN ACTIVITY: INFORMATION RETRIEVAL   **TIMING: 20 MINS**

LEARNING OBJECTIVES
- To develop skills in information retrieval

EQUIPMENT
- Source B: *Burglarious Bill*

1. **Re-read Source B: *Burglarious Bill*. List four pieces of information about William Caseley.**

   ....

   ....

   ....

   ....

2. **Number the paragraphs in the extract from 1 to 6.**

   a) Which paragraphs focus on information about William Caseley's life? Circle the correct numbers below.

         1   2   3   4   5   6

   b) Which paragraphs focus on information about the burglary at Mr Walker's jewellery shop? Circle the correct numbers below.

         1   2   3   4   5   6

   c) What do the remaining paragraphs focus on? Complete the sentences below.

   Paragraph .... focuses on ....

   ....

   Paragraph .... focuses on ....

   ....

AQA ENGLISH
Grades 3–5

HOMEWORK ACTIVITY: WRITE AN EXAM-STYLE QUESTION   **TIMING: 30 MINS**

LEARNING OBJECTIVES
- To develop skills in information retrieval

EQUIPMENT
- Source B: *Burglarious Bill*

In Paper 2, Section A of your exam, you will face a question set out like the one below.

1. **Complete the question by adding:**
   a) four pieces of information about William Caseley and the burglary at Mr Walker's jewellery shop that can be found in the extract and are true
   b) four pieces of information about William Caseley and the burglary at Mr Walker's jewellery shop that cannot be found in the extract and are false.

Choose **four** statements below which are TRUE.

- Tick the ones that you think are true.
- Choose a maximum of four statements.

A. _____ ☐

B. _____ ☐

C. _____ ☐

D. _____ ☐

E. _____ ☐

F. _____ ☐

G. _____ ☐

H. _____ ☐

[4 marks]

ENGLISH
Grades 3–5

2 ANSWERS

STARTER ACTIVITY: DEDUCING MEANING
1 and 2. burglarious: of or relating to burglary; penal servitude: time spent in prison, a prison sentence; counsellor: an advisor; life preserver: a heavy club or truncheon

MAIN ACTIVITY: READING AND CHECKING UNDERSTANDING
1. Examples: William Caseley, a known criminal, and his gang were arrested for burgling a jeweller's shop when stolen jewellery was found in his home and shop.
2. Student's own answer
3. Student's own answer

MAIN ACTIVITY: INFORMATION RETRIEVAL
1. Examples: Caseley was known to be an expert burglar; he had already served a prison sentence;
he had probably started his criminal career at an early age; he had two nicknames: 'Counsellor Kelly' and 'Tom the Madman'.
2. a) 1; b) 2, 3, 4; c) Paragraph 5 focuses on the arrest of Caseley's gang; Paragraphs 6 focuses on the arrest of Caseley and his wife.

HOMEWORK ACTIVITY: WRITE AN EXAM-STYLE QUESTION
1. Examples:
William Caseley was an expert burglar.
Caseley had been to prison.
Caseley broke into a hat shop.
Caseley and his gang broke into the shop through the floor of the shop above.
Caseley subsequently opened a pub.
The police arrested his wife, but Caseley escaped.
Caseley was also known as 'Tom the Madman'.
The shop was owned by Mr Walker.

GLOSSARY

Deduce
Coming to a conclusion through reasoning and careful consideration of facts

Retrieval
To find something within a text

AQA ENGLISH — Grades 3-5

3 READING: EXPLICIT AND IMPLICIT INFORMATION

LEARNING OBJECTIVES

- To understand the difference between explicit and implicit information
- To be able to identify and infer implied meaning
- To be able to identify precise evidence of implied meaning

SPECIFICATION LINKS

- 3.1.1 critical reading and comprehension

STARTER ACTIVITY

- **Explicit or implicit?; 5 minutes; page 36**
  Ask the student to complete the questions, taking feedback after each to ensure understanding. Note the relationship between the word *implicit* and the verb *to imply*. Point out that the student will not be tested on the terms themselves, only their ability to explore ideas and information that are explicitly and implicitly expressed in a text.

MAIN ACTIVITIES

- **Exploring implied ideas; 20 minutes; page 37**
  Ask the student to read Source C: *Earth in the Balance* by Al Gore (page 19). This is a challenging text, so the student may need additional support. Ask them to summarise and explain the ideas expressed as succinctly as possible.
- **Identifying explicit and implicit ideas; 20 minutes; page 38**
  Work with the student to complete the questions, prompting where necessary.

PLENARY ACTIVITY

- **Checking understanding; 5 minutes**
  Ask the student to identify any words and phrases in the source text that focus on damage to the environment, and then identify any words and phrases in the source text that suggest humankind is responsible for that damage.

HOMEWORK ACTIVITY

- **Implied meaning; 30 minutes; page 39**
  You may want to encourage the student to select their evidence and briefly summarise their ideas during the lesson to ensure understanding.

SUPPORT IDEAS

- **Exploring implied ideas** Model how to annotate, focusing on brevity and the relevance of notes.
- **Identifying explicit and implicit ideas** Provide specific examples for the student to comment on, e.g. what is implied by the words 'distress' and 'ripping'?

EXTENSION IDEA

- **Throughout** Encourage the student to explore layers of meaning; for example, the word 'assault' implies violence and criminality, and represents the Earth as a victim.

PROGRESS AND OBSERVATIONS

ENGLISH
Grades 3-5

STARTER ACTIVITY: EXPLICIT OR IMPLICIT?

TIMING: 5 MINS

LEARNING OBJECTIVES
- To understand the difference between explicit and implicit information

EQUIPMENT
none

1. Look at the terms and definitions below. Draw lines linking each term to the correct definition.

| explicit information | Information or ideas that are clearly and directly stated. |

| implicit information | Information or ideas that are suggested but not clearly stated. |

2. Look at the introduction and title of Source C: *Earth in the Balance,* then read the information and ideas below.

> One doesn't have to travel around the world to witness humankind's assault on the earth. Images that signal the distress of our global environment are now commonly seen almost anywhere.

Which information in the text is explicit and which is implicit?
- Circle 'Explicit' for those points that are explicitly stated in the title or introduction of the text.
- Circle 'Implicit' for those points that are implicitly suggested by the title or introduction of the text.
- Circle 'Not in text' for those points that are neither explicitly stated nor implied in the title or introduction of the text.

Humankind is damaging the Earth.	Explicit	Implicit	Not in text
Evidence of this damage can be seen in many different places.	Explicit	Implicit	Not in text
Humankind needs to stop damaging the Earth.	Explicit	Implicit	Not in text
The Earth is a fragile planet and is easily damaged.	Explicit	Implicit	Not in text

AQA ENGLISH — Grades 3–5

MAIN ACTIVITY: EXPLORING IMPLIED IDEAS   **TIMING: 20 MINS**

LEARNING OBJECTIVES
- To be able to identify and infer implied meaning

EQUIPMENT
- Source C: *Earth in the Balance*

Look closely at this sentence from Source C: *Earth in the Balance*.

> Perhaps we should feel awe for our own power: just as men tear tusks from elephants' heads in such quantity as to threaten the beast with extinction, we are ripping matter from its place in the earth in such volume as to upset the balance between daylight and darkness.

1. What impression does this sentence give you of humankind? Write a sentence explaining your ideas.

   ----

2. Which words and phrases in the sentence from the source focus on humankind's activities?
   a) Underline them.
   b) Annotate the words and phrases you have underlined, noting what they imply about humankind's activities.

3. Which words and phrases in the sentence from the source focus on humankind's attitudes to their activities?
   a) Circle them.
   b) Annotate the words and phrases you have circled, noting what they imply about humankind's attitudes.

4. Look at this list of key words and phrases in the sentence from the source. Tick those that you identified and commented on in questions 1–3.
   ☐ awe for our own power
   ☐ tear
   ☐ threaten
   ☐ ripping
   ☐ upset the balance

5. Look at the words and phrases in the checklist above that you have not ticked. What does each one imply about the writer's opinion of humankind, and of their activities and attitudes? Annotate them.

ENGLISH
— Grades 3-5 —

MAIN ACTIVITY: IDENTIFYING EXPLICIT AND IMPLICIT IDEAS   **TIMING: 20 MINS**

LEARNING OBJECTIVES
- To be able to identify precise evidence of implied meaning

EQUIPMENT
- Source C: *Earth in the Balance*

Look again at the final paragraph of Source C: *Earth in the Balance*.

> Even though it is sometimes hard to see their meaning, we have by now all witnessed surprising experiences that signal the damage from our assault on the environment – whether it's the new frequency of days when the temperature exceeds 100 degrees, the new speed with which the sun burns our skin, or the new constancy of public debate over what to do with growing mountains of waste. But our response to these signals is puzzling. Why haven't we launched a massive effort to save our environment?

1. **Find one idea that is explicitly stated in the extract about the Earth or the people who live there.**
   a) Write it down.

   ....

   ....

   ....

   b) Where in the text is this idea explicitly stated? Underline the evidence in the text and label it 'explicit'.

2. **Find one idea that is implied in the extract about the Earth or the people who live there.**
   a) Write it down.

   ....

   ....

   ....

   b) Where in the text is this idea implied? Underline the evidence in the text and label it 'implicit'.
   c) Write two sentences explicitly stating what the writer has implied in your chosen example.

   ....

   ....

   ....

3. **What other explicit or implicit ideas can you identify in the extract above?**
   a) Underline each example and label it 'implicit' or 'explicit'.
   b) Annotate all the words and phrases you have labelled 'implicit', noting what the writer is suggesting about the Earth or the people who live there.

AQA ENGLISH — Grades 3-5

Homework activity: Implied meaning

Timing: 30 mins

Learning objectives
- To be able to identify precise evidence of implied meaning

Equipment
- Source C: *Earth in the Balance*

1. Choose two words, phrases or sentences from the source text in which the writer most strongly implies his ideas about the Earth and/or humankind. Choose from the ideas below, or pick your own.

> On some nights, in high northern latitudes[1], [...] if the sky is clear after sunset – and if you are watching from a place where pollution hasn't blotted out the night sky altogether – you can sometimes see a strange kind of cloud high in the sky.

> methane is released from landfills, from coal mines and rice paddies, from billions of termites that swarm through the freshly cut forestland, from the burning of biomass[4] and from a variety of other human activities

> we are once again adding to the threat of global warming

> shouldn't it startle us that we have now put these clouds in the evening sky which glisten with a spectral light?

> the violent collision between human civilization and the earth

2. Write a paragraph about each of the two words, phrases or sentences you have chosen, commenting on how the writer implies and/or explicitly expresses his ideas.

ENGLISH
Grades 3–5

3 ANSWERS

STARTER ACTIVITY: EXPLICIT OR IMPLICIT?

1. Explicit information: information or ideas that are clearly and directly stated.
Implicit information: information or ideas that are suggested but not clearly stated.
2. Implicit: Humankind is damaging the Earth.
Explicit: Evidence of this damage can be seen in many different places.
Implicit: Humankind needs to stop damaging the Earth.
Not in text: The Earth is a fragile planet and is easily damaged.

MAIN ACTIVITY: EXPLORING IMPLIED IDEAS

1. Example: Humankind is destroying the Earth.
2. a) and b) Examples:
'Tear tusks' and 'threaten the beast with extinction' imply humankind's violent and ruthless treatment of animals.
'Ripping matter from its place' suggests that we are destroying the environment.
3. a) and b) Example: 'Feel awe for our own power' suggests humankind may, but should not, see its actions as impressive achievements.
4. Student's own answer
5. Student's own answer

MAIN ACTIVITY: IDENTIFYING EXPLICIT AND IMPLICIT IDEAS

1. a) and b) Responses are likely to focus on the environmental damage and its consequences. Examples:
Our actions are harming the Earth ('the damage from our assault on the environment').
We are more likely to experience sunburn ('the new speed with which the sun burns our skin').
2. a), b) and c) Responses are likely to focus on the significance of environmental damage and our response to it. Examples:
Our environment is changing ('the new speed with which the sun burns our skin').
We must do more to prevent this damage ('Why haven't we launched a massive effort to save our environment?').
3. a) and b) as above

HOMEWORK ACTIVITY: IMPLIED MEANING

Responses should include relevant evidence and comment on meaning implied through clearly identified elements of that evidence.

GLOSSARY

Explicit
Stated clearly and in detail, leaving no room for confusion or doubt

Implicit
Suggested but not directly expressed

Infer
To read between the lines

ENGLISH
— Grades 3–5 —

4 READING: SUMMARISING USING EVIDENCE

LEARNING OBJECTIVES
- To be able to select relevant quotations
- To be able to embed quotations
- To be able to summarise a text using embedded quotations

SPECIFICATION LINKS
- 3.1.1 critical reading and comprehension

STARTER ACTIVITY
- **Selecting evidence; 5 minutes; page 42**
  As the student completes the activity, emphasise the importance of selecting relevant words/phrases/clauses only. Ask them to explain how and why they select their evidence to support the points.

MAIN ACTIVITIES
- **Embedding quotations; 20 minutes; page 43**
  Ask the student to read Source A: *The Napoleon of Crime* (page 17). Ask the student to complete question 1 then discuss the advantages of using short, relevant embedded quotations to make a point succinctly and demonstrate the ability to identify key ideas.
- **Summarising using quotations; 15 minutes; page 44**
  Check the student's understanding of the term *summary*. Monitor carefully to ensure key ideas and short relevant quotations are selected and effectively expressed in the summary.

PLENARY ACTIVITY
- **Review; 10 minutes**
  Ask the student to review their response to the summary activity. Are all essential key points included? Are all the quotations embedded? Ask the student how they would explain to another student how to select and embed quotations and write a summary.

HOMEWORK ACTIVITY
- **Write a summary; 30 minutes; page 45**
  Check understanding of the activity. Emphasise that the summary should focus only on implied and explicit information in the text. There is no need to comment on their impressions of the criminals or how the writer has created them.

SUPPORT IDEA
- **Selecting evidence** Encourage the student to think aloud during this activity and when selecting evidence throughout the lesson. This will allow them to clarify their thought process and you to monitor it.

EXTENSION IDEA
- **Summarising using quotations** Encourage the student to be ruthless in cutting extraneous detail and/or exposition from their summaries, while also focusing on including a broad range of ideas and information.

PROGRESS AND OBSERVATIONS

ENGLISH
Grades 3-5

| STARTER ACTIVITY: SELECTING EVIDENCE | TIMING: 5 MINS |

LEARNING OBJECTIVES
- To be able to select relevant quotations

EQUIPMENT
- Source A: *The Napoleon of Crime*

1. Read the opening paragraph of Source A: *The Napoleon of Crime*. Around the opening paragraph below, three key pieces of information have been noted. Choose three short quotations from the paragraph as evidence to support each of these points. Underline your chosen evidence and draw a line linking it to either A, B or C.

A. The criminals appear to be wealthy.

B. The criminals are intending to commit a significant crime.

On a misty May midnight in the year 1876, three men emerged from a fashionable address in Piccadilly with top hats on their heads, money in their pockets, and burglary, on a grand scale, on their minds. At a deliberate pace the trio headed along the thoroughfare, and at the point where Piccadilly intersects with Old Bond Street, they came to a stop. Famed for its art galleries and antiques shops, the street by day was choked with the carriages of the wealthy, the well-bred, and the culturally well-informed. Now it was quite deserted.

C. Bond Street is an area of London which caters for the wealthy.

AQA ENGLISH — Grades 3-5

Main activity: Embedding quotations

Timing: 20 mins

Learning objectives
- To be able to embed quotations

Equipment
- Source A: *The Napoleon of Crime*

1. Compare these two comments about the criminals described in Source A: *The Napoleon of Crime*. Which one is more effective? Why?

   Comment 1

   > The two criminals described in the source are very different: 'one was slight and dapper, some thirty-five years in age, with long, clipped mustaches, and dressed in the height of modern elegance, complete with pearl buttons and gold watch chain. The other, ambling a few paces behind, was a towering fellow with grizzled mutton-chop whiskers, whose ill-fitting frock coat barely contained a barrel chest'.

   Comment 2

   > The two criminals described in the source are very different. One is described as 'slight and dapper' and is 'dressed in the height of modern elegance' whereas the other is 'a towering fellow with grizzled mutton-chop whiskers' and an 'ill-fitting frock coat'.

   ----

2. Read the comment below and underline all the key words and phrases in the quotation that show the criminal's expertise in dealing with valuable works of art.

   > The criminal seems very expert in dealing with valuable works of art: 'From his coat he took a small pot of paste, and using the tasseled end of the velvet rope, he daubed the back of the canvas to make it supple and then rolled it up with the paint facing outward to avoid cracking the surface, before slipping it inside his frock coat...'

3. Rewrite the comment in question 2, embedding some or all of the evidence you have underlined.

ENGLISH
— Grades 3-5 —

Main activity: Summarising using quotations   Timing: 15 mins

Learning objectives	Equipment
• To be able to summarise a text using embedded quotations	• Source A: *The Napoleon of Crime*

You are going to write a short summary of Source A: *The Napoleon of Crime* using embedded quotations.

1. **Complete the table below to plan your summary.**
   a) Write down the most important idea or piece of information in each paragraph of the text.

   b) Select a short, relevant quotation that most effectively conveys each of the ideas or pieces of information you have noted.

	Key idea/information	Quotation
A		
B		
C		
D		
E		
F		
G		

2. **Look again at the table above.**
   a) Which key ideas and information *are not* essential to an effective summary of the text? Cross them out.

   b) Which key ideas and information *are* essential to an effective summary of the text? Tick them.

3. **Write your summary of the text on a separate piece of paper.**
   Make sure you:
   - include all the key ideas you have selected
   - embed all the quotations you have selected.

ENGLISH
Grades 3–5

HOMEWORK ACTIVITY: WRITE A SUMMARY	TIMING: 30 MINS

LEARNING OBJECTIVES
- To be able to summarise a text using embedded quotations

EQUIPMENT
- Source A: *The Napoleon of Crime*

In this source, the writer describes two criminals. You are going to write a summary of all the information you are given about the criminals, using embedded evidence.

In your summary, you should include information about:
- the criminals' appearance
- their actions
- their skills
- anything else you think is important or relevant.

1. Use the table below to plan your summary.

	Key idea/information	Quotation
Appearance		
Actions		
Skills		
Anything else		

2. On a separate piece of paper, use the ideas you have gathered to write your summary of the two criminals described in the source.
   Make sure you:
   - include all the key ideas you have selected
   - embed all the quotations you have selected.

ENGLISH
— Grades 3-5 —

4 ANSWERS

STARTER ACTIVITY: SELECTING EVIDENCE
1. A: 'money in their pockets'; B: 'burglary, on a grand scale, on their minds'; C: 'choked with the carriages of the wealthy'.

MAIN ACTIVITY: EMBEDDING QUOTATIONS
1. Comment 2 is far more succinct and precise as it uses a selection of embedded quotations.
2. 'expert'; 'he took a small pot of paste'; 'using the tasselled end of the velvet rope'; 'he daubed the back of the canvas to make it supple'; 'rolled it up with the paint facing outward to avoid cracking the surface'
3. Example: The criminal seems very expert in dealing with valuable works of art. He has brought 'a small pot of paste' to the burglary, which he uses to make the canvas 'supple' so he can 'avoid cracking the surface' when he rolls it up.

MAIN ACTIVITY: SUMMARISING USING QUOTATIONS
1. a) and b) Examples:
A: Three men are planning a burglary: 'burglary... on their minds'
B: The two men who will burgle the art gallery are very different: 'an incongruous pair'
C: The larger man helps the confident vain man to enter the gallery: 'as if he were climbing onto a thoroughbred'
D: The burglar is intending to steal a painting: 'a large painting in a gilt frame... he drew closer'
E: The painting is of a beautiful woman: 'the most exquisite beauty'
F: The burglar is an expert art thief: 'rolled it up with the paint facing outward to avoid cracking'
G: The burglars make off: 'set off back down Piccadilly'
2. a) and b) All of the above can be effectively incorporated into a summary.
3. The summary should include details of: the two very different criminals; the method they use to break into the gallery; the painting they steal.

HOMEWORK ACTIVITY: WRITE A SUMMARY
The summary should include details of the criminals' appearance, actions and skills. It may also include comments on their precision, efficiency and calmness under pressure.

GLOSSARY

Summary
A concise and clear description presenting the main facts or ideas in a text

5 Reading: Comparative summary

Learning objectives
- To be able to identify significant points of comparison in two texts
- To be able to synthesise and summarise relevant evidence from two texts
- To be able to structure an effective comparison

Specification links
- 3.1.1 critical reading and comprehension/summary and synthesis

Starter activity
- **Spot the difference; 5 minutes; page 48**
  Ask the student to spot and note any differences in the criminals described. Prompt the student to consider the criminals' appearance, social status, past, etc. In question 2, note that *but* and *whereas* are conjunctions and can be used to signal contrast mid-sentence; *however* is a conjunct and therefore signals contrast mid-sentence or in a second separate sentence.

Main activities
- **Identifying points of comparison; 20 minutes; page 49**
  The student may have seen these texts in lessons 2 and 4. Give them time to read both texts. Introduce the Paper 2, Section A exam-style question that will be set for homework, explaining that this is what you are working towards in the lesson. Ask the student to complete the questions, monitoring them carefully to ensure understanding and progression.
- **Planning a response; 20 minutes; page 50**
  Refer to the work completed in the previous activity.

Plenary activity
- **Review; 5 minutes**
  Ask the student to review their planning. Do they feel they have identified significant differences and relevant quotations? Are they confident in their ability to structure their response and use conjunctions/conjuncts to signal comparisons?

Homework activity
- **Write a response; 30 minutes; page 51**
  Ensure the student is aware of the time limits on this kind of question in the exam. Explain that their speed in planning and writing responses to this type of question will increase with practice.

Support ideas
- **Identifying points of comparison** You may need to offer focused prompt questions to enable the student to identify significant differences.
- **Planning a response** Reduce the number of points of comparison required. Encourage the student to focus on quality – the relevance of their points of comparison and supporting evidence – rather than quantity.

Extension idea
- **Planning a response** Encourage more confident students to synthesise evidence from different parts of the text, e.g. two quotes showing that one is a wealthy, sophisticated criminal; two quotes showing that the other is a violent, habitual criminal.

Progress and observations

ENGLISH
Grades 3-5

STARTER ACTIVITY: SPOT THE DIFFERENCE

TIMING: 5 MINS

LEARNING OBJECTIVES
- To be able to identify significant points of comparison in two texts

EQUIPMENT
none

You are going to compare the criminals described in the first few sentences of Source A and Source B.

Source A:
On a misty May midnight in the year 1876, three men emerged from a fashionable address in Piccadilly with top hats on their heads, money in their pockets, and burglary, on a grand scale, on their minds. At a deliberate pace the trio headed along the thoroughfare, and at the point where Piccadilly intersects with Old Bond Street, they came to a stop.

Source B:
Caseley was known to be one of the most expert burglars in the metropolis, and he had already undergone one sentence of penal servitude[1], which proves that he must have entered upon a criminal career at an early age. He had two nicknames, one being "Counsellor Kelly", and the other "Tom the Madman".

1. What differences can you identify in the criminals described in the two texts? Write your ideas in the box below.

2. Choose one or two of your ideas. For each one, write one or two sentences explaining how the criminals in each text are different. Make sure you use one of the words below to signal that you are contrasting two different ideas.

   but   whereas   however

AQA ENGLISH — Grades 3-5

| MAIN ACTIVITY: IDENTIFYING POINTS OF COMPARISON | TIMING: 20 MINS |

LEARNING OBJECTIVES
- To be able to identify significant points of comparison in two texts

EQUIPMENT
- Source A: *The Napoleon of Crime*
- Source B: *Burglarious Bill*

One way to compare the information and ideas in two texts is to summarise one and compare it with the other.

1. Look at these extracts from one student's summary of the information and ideas given about the criminals in Source A: *The Napoleon of Crime*. Compare each point with the information and ideas in Source B: *Burglarious Bill* by answering the questions below, circling 'yes' or 'no'.

a) wealthy and respectable	Are the criminals in *Burglarious Bill* wealthy and respectable?	yes	no
b) Two very different partners in crime: one is 'brutish', the other 'stylish'.	Are the criminal gang in *Burglarious Bill* very different to each other?	yes	no
c) daring and ingenious burglars	Are the burglars in *Burglarious Bill* daring and ingenious?	yes	no
d) steal a very valuable painting	Do the burglars in *Burglarious Bill* steal one very valuable painting?	yes	no
e) expert in art theft	Are the burglars in *Burglarious Bill* expert thieves?	yes	no
f) cool and calm under pressure	Are the burglars in *Burglarious Bill* cool and calm under pressure?	yes	no

2. Look at Source B: *Burglarious Bill* again. What further significant details about the criminals make them very different to those described in Source A: *The Napoleon of Crime*? Give examples to support your answer.

....

....

....

....

....

ENGLISH
— Grades 3-5 —

Main activity: Planning a response

Timing: 20 mins

Learning objectives
- To be able to synthesise and summarise relevant evidence from two texts

Equipment
- Source A: *The Napoleon of Crime*
- Source B: *Burglarious Bill*

You are going to plan your response to this Paper 2, Section A exam-style question:

> You need to refer to Source A: *The Napoleon of Crime* and Source B: *Burglarious Bill* for this question.
>
> The criminal gangs described in the two sources are different.
> Use details from **both** sources to write a summary of the differences.
>
> [8 marks]

1. Look again at your answers to the previous activity. Choose the three most significant differences between the criminals described in the two sources. Write them in the first column of the table below.

Differences between Source A and Source B	Evidence from Source A: *The Napoleon of Crime*	Evidence from Source B: *Burglarious Bill*
1.	1. 2.	1. 2.
2.	1. 2.	1. 2.
3.	1. 2.	1. 2.

2. Now select one or two relevant quotations from each source to support each of the differences you have noted. Write them in the second and third columns of the table above. When you have finished you should have selected at least six quotations altogether.

3. What would be the best order in which to write about these three differences in your response to the exam-style question? Number them to show how you will sequence them.

50

AQA ENGLISH
Grades 3-5

HOMEWORK ACTIVITY: WRITE A RESPONSE	TIMING: **30 MINS**

LEARNING OBJECTIVES
- To be able to structure an effective comparison

EQUIPMENT
- Source A: *The Napoleon of Crime*
- Source B: *Burglarious Bill*

1. Using your planning from the previous activities, write a response to the Paper 2, Section A exam-style question below on a separate piece of paper. Use the checklist at the bottom of the page to remind yourself of all the things you should achieve in your response.

> You need to refer to Source A: *The Napoleon of Crime* and Source B: *Burglarious Bill* for this question.
>
> The criminal gangs described in the two sources are different.
> Use details from **both** sources to write a summary of the differences.
>
> [8 marks]

2. When you have written your response, check you have achieved all of the success criteria below.

   a) Tick all the criteria you feel you have achieved.

   - ☐ I have identified at least three significant differences.
   - ☐ I have used relevant evidence from each text to support each point.
   - ☐ I have clearly signalled comparisons using conjuncts and conjunctions, e.g. *but, whereas, however*.
   - ☐ I have written in paragraphs.
   - ☐ I have carefully checked for accurate spelling and punctuation, and clear written expression.

   b) Look at any of the criteria you feel you have not achieved. Add to and improve your response so that you can tick all of them.

5 Answers

Starter activity: Spot the difference

1. Student's own answer
2. Examples:
In Source B, the writer gives details of the criminal's name, whereas the criminals in Source A are not named and seem much more mysterious.
In Source B, it is suggested that Caseley is a ruthless criminal as he has been to prison and is known as 'Tom the Madman'. However, the criminals described in Source A appear wealthy and respectable as they are wearing top hats and have money in their pockets.

Main activity: Identifying points of comparison

1. a) No, Caseley has a criminal record and owns a meat-pie shop.
b) No, there is no evidence to suggest this.
c) Yes, they break in through the shop below and spend more than a day in the jeweller's shop.
d) No, they steal a large quantity of less valuable jewellery.
e) Yes, they use 'beautiful instruments' and are successful – until they are arrested.
f) Yes, they spend more than a day in the jeweller's shop.
2. Examples:
They are ultimately unsuccessful and are arrested.
They are career criminals with implements that suggest violence.

Main activity: Planning a response

1. and 2. Examples: social class: 'dressed in the height of modern elegance', 'one sentence of penal servitude'; the quantity and value of the items they steal: 'a large painting in a gilt frame', 'four hundred and sixty-five watches and one hundred and sixty gold chains'; the implied use of violence in Source B: 'a life preserver… a revolver'.
3. Ensure the student's planned response follows a logical sequence.

Homework activity: Write a response

1.

Marks	Criteria
7–8 marks	• Insightful inferences from both texts • A carefully selected range of relevant, focused evidence from both texts • A range of insightful differences
5–6 marks	• Clear inferences from both texts • A range of relevant, focused textual evidence from both texts • Clear differences between texts
3–4 marks	• Some inference from one or both texts • Relevant and focused textual evidence from one or both texts • Significant differences between texts
1–2 marks	• Largely literal, rather than inferential, understanding • Largely relevant textual evidence from one or both texts • Simple differences between texts
No marks	• No creditable response

2. Ensure the student has achieved all, or the majority of, the success criteria.

Glossary

Synthesise
To combine a number of things into a coherent whole

AQA ENGLISH — Grades 3-5

6 READING: ANALYSING LANGUAGE 1

LEARNING OBJECTIVES
- To be able to identify significant choices of vocabulary and language features
- To be able to recognise the writer's intention
- To understand that language choice contributes to the writer's intention

SPECIFICATION LINKS
- 3.1.1 critical reading and comprehension

STARTER ACTIVITY
- **Revising figurative language; 10 minutes; page 54**
  Before starting, explain to the student that just naming a figurative language feature is ineffective. Their analysis should identify significant vocabulary choices and describe their effect.

MAIN ACTIVITIES
- **Thinking about intention; 20 minutes; page 55**
  Start by confirming the student's understanding of the term *intention*. Ask them to read Source D: *The Secret History* (page 20) and then summarise the events to confirm their understanding. Explain that every writer has an intention: the impact or influence that they want their writing to have on the reader. Pause after each question to check understanding.
- **Identifying rich vocabulary choices; 15 minutes; page 56**
  Explain to the student that writers choose some language to convey meaning and information, e.g. *the*, *and*, *we* and *have*. Other language choices are made for impact, to help the writer achieve their intention. The student may find it helpful to refer to the list of possible intentions from the previous activity.

PLENARY ACTIVITY
- **Review; 5 minutes**
  Discuss with the student how confident they feel about completing the Homework activity. Ask them to review the language choices they have circled in the text and decide which they feel may be particularly rich and significant. Discuss the reasons for their choices and their thoughts on how these language choices contribute to the writer's intention.

HOMEWORK ACTIVITY
- **Write a response; 30 minutes; page 57**
  Explain to the student that subsequent lessons will focus on language analysis and that this is only the start of their work on this challenging skill.

SUPPORT IDEA
- **Identifying rich vocabulary choices** Suggest that the student crosses out those words in the first two sentences that definitely do not contribute to the writer's intention – e.g. 'it', 'is', 'to', 'that' – before focusing on those that might contribute, then those that definitely do contribute.

EXTENSION IDEA
- **Identifying rich vocabulary choices** Encourage the student to explore the impact of language beyond its immediate effect on the reader, e.g. how does language choice reflect the narrator's thoughts and feelings about the murder?

PROGRESS AND OBSERVATIONS

ENGLISH
Grades 3-5
AQA

STARTER ACTIVITY: REVISING FIGURATIVE LANGUAGE   **TIMING: 10 MINS**

LEARNING OBJECTIVES
- To be able to identify significant choices of vocabulary and language features

EQUIPMENT
none

1. Draw lines linking these figurative language devices to the correct definition.

simile	A kind of metaphor in which a non-human creature or object is described as if it is human.
metaphor	A comparison made using 'like' or 'as', intended to create an image in the reader's mind.
personification	A direct comparison, made without using 'like' or 'as', intended to create an image in the reader's mind.

2. Which of the three figurative language devices in question 1 have the writers used in the three short extracts below? Underline any you can find and label them as 'simile', 'metaphor' or 'personification'.

> It is difficult to believe that such an uproar took place over an act for which I was partially responsible, even more difficult to believe I could have walked through it – the cameras, the uniforms, the black crowds sprinkled over Mount Cataract like ants in a sugar bowl – without incurring a blink of suspicion.
>
> *The Secret History*

> But, without even considering that threat, shouldn't it startle us that we have now put these clouds in the evening sky which glisten with a spectral light? Or have our eyes adjusted so completely to the bright lights of civilization that we can't see these clouds for what they are – a physical manifestation[5] of the violent collision between human civilization and the earth?
>
> *Earth in the Balance*

> The three men exchanged a few words at the corner of the street before one slipped into a doorway, invisible beyond the dancing gaslight shadows, while the other two turned right into Old Bond Street.
>
> *The Napoleon of Crime*

ENGLISH
Grades 3–5

MAIN ACTIVITY: THINKING ABOUT INTENTION **TIMING: 20 MINS**

LEARNING OBJECTIVES
- To be able to recognise the writer's intention
- To understand that language choice contributes to the writer's intention

EQUIPMENT
- Source D: *The Secret History*

Read the opening paragraph of Source D: *The Secret History*.

1. Which of the following might be the writer's intention in this opening paragraph? Tick all that you agree with.

    ☐ to shock the reader
    ☐ to grab the reader's attention
    ☐ to intrigue the reader
    ☐ to encourage the reader's sympathy
    ☐ to explain recent events in the narrator's life
    ☐ to describe the setting of the story
    ☐ to introduce one or more of the characters in the story

2. Which do you think is the most significant of these intentions in the opening paragraph? Underline it.

3. Which one word or phrase in the opening paragraph makes the biggest contribution to the writer achieving this intention? Explain your choice.

ENGLISH
— Grades 3-5 —

AQA

MAIN ACTIVITY: IDENTIFYING RICH VOCABULARY CHOICES   TIMING: 15 MINS

LEARNING OBJECTIVES
- To be able to identify significant choices of vocabulary and language features
- To understand that language choice contributes to the writer's intention

EQUIPMENT
none

Read the second paragraph of Source D: *The Secret History*.

> It is difficult to believe that Henry's modest plan could have worked so well despite these unforeseen events. We hadn't intended to hide the body where it couldn't be found. In fact, we hadn't hidden it at all but had simply left it where it fell in hopes that some luckless passer-by would stumble over it before anyone even noticed he was missing. This was a tale that told itself simply and well: the loose rocks, the body at the bottom of the ravine with a clean break in the neck, and the muddy skidmarks of dug-in heels pointing the way down; a hiking accident, no more, no less, and it might have been left at that, at quiet tears and a small funeral, had it not been for the snow that fell that night; it covered him without a trace, and ten days later, when the thaw finally came, the state troopers and the FBI and the searchers from the town all saw that they had been walking back and forth over his body until the snow above it was packed down like ice.

1. What is the writer's intention in this paragraph? What impact do they want this description of the murder to have on the reader? Summarise it in five words or fewer.

2. Focus on the first two sentences of the paragraph above. Which one word or phrase makes the greatest contribution to the intention you summarised in question 1? Circle it.

3. Look at the rest of the paragraph and circle any other words or phrases that you feel make a significant contribution to the writer's intention.

4. Choose one of the words or phrases you have circled in the paragraph. Explain how this language choice contributes to the writer's intention.
   Think about:
   - the meaning of the word or phrase and what it suggests
   - the impact that this choice of word or phrase might have on the reader.

AQA ENGLISH — Grades 3-5

HOMEWORK ACTIVITY: WRITE A RESPONSE   **TIMING: 30 MINS**

LEARNING OBJECTIVES
- To be able to identify significant choices of vocabulary and language features

EQUIPMENT
none

1. **On a separate piece of paper, answer the Paper 1, Section A exam-style question below.**
   Make sure you:
   - select at least two significant words or phrases
   - comment on how they contribute to the writer's intention.

Look in detail at this extract from **lines 1 to 15** of Source D: *The Secret History*.

> The snow in the mountains was melting and Bunny had been dead for several weeks before we came to understand the gravity of our situation. He'd been dead for ten days before they found him, you know. It was one of the biggest manhunts in Vermont history – state troopers, the FBI, even an army helicopter; the college closed, the dye factory in Hampden shut down, people coming from New Hampshire, upstate New York, as far away as Boston.
>
> It is difficult to believe that Henry's modest plan could have worked so well despite these unforeseen events. We hadn't intended to hide the body where it couldn't be found. In fact, we hadn't hidden it at all but had simply left it where it fell in hopes that some luckless passer-by would stumble over it before anyone even noticed he was missing. This was a tale that told itself simply and well: the loose rocks, the body at the bottom of the ravine with a clean break in the neck, and the muddy skidmarks of dug-in heels pointing the way down; a hiking accident, no more, no less, and it might have been left at that, at quiet tears and a small funeral, had it not been for the snow that fell that night; it covered him without a trace, and ten days later, when the thaw finally came, the state troopers and the FBI and the searchers from the town all saw that they had been walking back and forth over his body until the snow above it was packed down like ice.

How does the writer use language here to describe the murder he and his friends have committed?

[8 marks]

---

2. **When you have written your response, check you have achieved all of the success criteria below.**

   a) Tick all the criteria you feel you have achieved.

   ☐ I have identified the writer's intention(s) in the source.
   ☐ I have focused on at least two of the writer's language choices.
   ☐ I have commented on how these language choices contribute to the writer's intention.
   ☐ I have written in paragraphs.
   ☐ I have carefully checked for accurate spelling and punctuation, and clear written expression.

   b) Look at any of the criteria you feel you have not achieved. Add to and improve your response so that you can tick all of them.

6 ANSWERS

STARTER ACTIVITY: REVISING FIGURATIVE LANGUAGE

1. Simile: a comparison made using 'like' or 'as', intended to create an image in the reader's mind
Metaphor: a direct comparison, made without using 'like' or 'as', intended to create an image in the reader's mind
Personification: a kind of metaphor in which a non-human creature or object is described as if it is human
2. Simile: 'the black crowds sprinkled over Mount Cataract <u>like ants in a sugar bowl</u>' (*The Secret History*)
Metaphor: '<u>have our eyes adjusted so completely to the bright lights of civilisation</u>' (*Earth in the Balance*)
Personification: '<u>dancing</u> gaslight shadows' (*The Napoleon of Crime*)

MAIN ACTIVITY: THINKING ABOUT INTENTION

1. Student's own answer
2. One of: to shock the reader; to grab the reader's attention; to intrigue the reader
3. Words such as 'dead', 'gravity' or 'manhunt' are the most likely choices, suggesting the murder and its impact.

MAIN ACTIVITY: IDENTIFYING RICH VOCABULARY CHOICES

1. To shock, intrigue or engage
2. Example: 'body'
3. Examples: 'where it fell', 'clean break', 'quiet tears', 'back and forth'
4. Examples: The phrase 'clean break' conjures shocking images of the sudden and extreme violence of the murder. The phrase 'where it fell' suggests a disregard for the life they have taken, implying the ruthlessness of the murder.

HOMEWORK ACTIVITY: WRITE A RESPONSE

1.

Marks	Criteria
7–8 marks	• Clear and detailed analysis of the effect of the writer's language choices • A carefully selected range of relevant, focused textual evidence • A range of subject terminology to achieve clarity and precision
5–6 marks	• Clear comments on the effect of the writer's language choices • A range of relevant, focused textual evidence • A range of subject terminology to achieve clarity
3–4 marks	• Some comments on the effect of the writer's language choices • Relevant and focused textual evidence • Largely accurate use of subject terminology
1–2 marks	• Straightforward comments on the effect of the writer's language choices • Largely relevant textual evidence • Some use of subject terminology, with inconsistent accuracy
No marks	• No creditable response

2. Ensure the student has achieved all, or the majority of, the success criteria.

GLOSSARY

Writer's intention
The impact or influence that the writer wants their text to have on the reader

AQA ENGLISH — Grades 3–5

7 READING: ANALYSING LANGUAGE 2

LEARNING OBJECTIVES
- To develop language analysis skills
- To understand connotation

SPECIFICATION LINKS
- 3.1.1 critical reading and comprehension

STARTER ACTIVITY
- **Forensics; 10 minutes; page 60**
Explain that textual analysis is similar to forensic analysis at a crime scene: gathering clues, looking closely at every small detail and trying to piece the clues together to uncover what has been done – and how.

MAIN ACTIVITIES
- **Connotations; 20 minutes; page 61**
Explore the student's understanding of *connotation* and clarify if needed. Ask the student to read Source E: *The Essex Serpent* (page 21) and complete the questions.
- **Effect and impact; 15 minutes; page 62**
Ensure the student understands the difference between *effect* (what the language choice suggests about the object, character etc. that it refers to) and *impact* (how this might influence the reader's response to that object, character etc.).

PLENARY ACTIVITY
- **Review; 5 minutes**
Ask the student to look again at the *Effect and impact* worksheet and respond to similar questioning on another word of their own choice from the short extract, e.g. the word 'scream' to describe the cry of a gull.

HOMEWORK ACTIVITY
- **Write a response; 30 minutes; page 63**
Suggest that the student refer to their work on the *Effect and impact* worksheet to clarify the kinds of comments they can make on connotation, effect and impact. Explain that in the GCSE (9–1) English Language exam this style of question will also ask for comment on sentence forms (which will be the focus of lessons 9 and 10). In this activity, they need to focus on words and phrases only.

SUPPORT IDEA
- **Connotations** Encourage the student to create spider diagrams, noting the connotations of e.g. 'beast' and 'puppy'. Begin by simply noting whether each has positive or negative connotations before refining their ideas.

EXTENSION IDEA
- **Connotations** Encourage the student to consider the impact of the contrast in the connotations of 'bright lights', 'bustle', and 'full cold moon'. How does this contrast contribute to the mood of the opening paragraph?

PROGRESS AND OBSERVATIONS

ENGLISH
— Grades 3-5 —

STARTER ACTIVITY: FORENSICS **TIMING: 10 MINS**

LEARNING OBJECTIVES
- To develop language analysis skills

EQUIPMENT
none

Look at some of the writer's vocabulary choices from the source you are going to read, which is the opening of a novel.

Blackwater	convulse	comfortless
the full cold moon	flinching	courage
dark	afraid	frantic
pulse	scream	vast

1. What kind of story do you think this will be?

   ....

   ....

2. What kind of mood do you think the writer is trying to create?

   ....

   ....

3. How did the writer's vocabulary choices help you to answer questions 1 and 2?

   ....

   ....

ENGLISH
— Grades 3-5 —

MAIN ACTIVITY: CONNOTATIONS   **TIMING: 20 MINS**

LEARNING OBJECTIVES
- To understand connotation

EQUIPMENT
- Source E: *The Essex Serpent*

All of the words below could be used to fill the gap in this sentence:

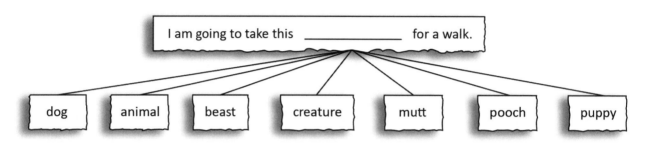

1. How do the tone and the speaker's attitude change depending on which word is used?

   ....

   ....

2. Choose two of the words. What are the connotations of each of your choices? Annotate them with two or three of the ideas or feelings they create as you read them.

3. Look carefully at the opening paragraph of Source E: *The Essex Serpent*. This section of the novel is entitled 'New Year's Eve'.

   > A young man walks down by the banks of the Blackwater under the full cold moon. He's been drinking the old year down to the dregs, until his eyes grew sore and his stomach turned, and he was tired of the bright lights and bustle. 'I'll just go down to the water,' he said, and kissed the nearest cheek: 'I'll be back before the chimes.' Now he looks east to the turning tide, out to the estuary slow and dark, and the white gulls gleaming on the waves.

   a) Which words describe the New Year's Eve celebrations that this young man has just left? Circle them.

   b) What are the connotations of these vocabulary choices? Annotate the words you have circled, noting the ideas and feelings they create as you read them.

4. Now look at this phrase from the extract. What are the connotations of these vocabulary choices? Annotate the phrase and/or the individual words, noting the ideas and feelings they create as you read them.

   > full cold moon

ENGLISH
— Grades 3-5 —

Main activity: Effect and impact

Timing: 15 mins

Learning objectives
- To develop language analysis skills

Equipment
none

When you analyse a writer's choice of words, phrases and language features, you need to comment on:
- their connotations
- their effect
- their impact.

Look at these sentences from Source E: *The Essex Serpent*.

> But something alters in a turn of the tide or a change of the air: the estuary surface shifts – seems (he steps forward) to pulse and throb, then grow slick and still; then soon after to convulse, as if flinching at a touch. Nearer he goes, not yet afraid; the gulls lift off one by one, and the last gives a scream of dismay.

Focus on the verb 'convulse' that the writer uses to describe the movement of the water.
In your answers to the questions below, you could use some of these phrases:

| this suggests | it implies | creates an image of | creates the impression that | making the reader |

1. What kind of movement is a convulsion? When do people experience convulsions?

   ....

   ....

   ....

2. What does the writer's choice of word suggest about the movement of the water?

   ....

   ....

   ....

3. How might the reader respond to the ideas and effect created by this language choice? Would they be shocked? Engaged by this dramatic description? Intrigued? Or something else?

   ....

   ....

   ....

ENGLISH
— Grades 3–5 —

HOMEWORK ACTIVITY: WRITE A RESPONSE   **TIMING: 30 MINS**

LEARNING OBJECTIVES
- To develop language analysis skills

EQUIPMENT
- Source E: *The Essex Serpent*

1. Write a response to the Paper 1, Section A exam-style question below.

Make sure you:
- select at least *two* significant words or phrases
- write a paragraph about each significant word or phrase
- in each paragraph, comment on the word or phrase's connotations, effect and impact on the reader.

> Look in detail at this extract from **lines 20 to 27** of Source E: *The Essex Serpent*:
>
> Winter comes like a blow to the back of his neck: he feels it penetrate his shirt and go into his bones. The good cheer of drink is gone, and he's comfortless there in the dark – he looks for his coat, but clouds hide the moon and he's blind. His breath is slow, the air is full of pins; the marsh at his feet all at once is wet, as if something out there has displaced the water. *Nothing, it's nothing*, he thinks, patting about for his courage, but there it is again: a curious still moment as if he were looking at a photograph, followed by a frantic uneven motion that cannot be merely the tug of the moon on the tides. He thinks he sees – is *certain* he sees – the slow movement of something vast, hunched, grimly covered over with rough and lapping scales; then it is gone.
>
> How does the writer use language here to describe the thoughts and feelings of the young man?
> You could include the writer's choice of:
>
> - words and phrases
> - language features and techniques.
>
> **[8 marks]**

2. When you have written your response, check you have achieved all of the success criteria below.

   a) Tick all the criteria you feel you have achieved.

   - ☐ I have focused on two of the writer's language choices.
   - ☐ I have commented on the connotations of each language choice.
   - ☐ I have commented on the effect of each language choice.
   - ☐ I have commented on the impact of each language choice.
   - ☐ I have written in paragraphs.
   - ☐ I have carefully checked for accurate spelling and punctuation, and clear written expression.

   b) Look at any of the criteria you feel you have not achieved. Add to and improve your response so that you can tick all of them.

7 ANSWERS

STARTER ACTIVITY: FORENSICS

1. Examples: gothic horror, thriller.
2. Examples: tense, dramatic, exciting.
3. Vocabulary choices suggest elements typical of these genres. For example: setting ('the full cold moon', 'dark', 'vast'); emotion ('afraid', 'pulse', 'courage', 'frantic') and action ('flinching', 'scream').

MAIN ACTIVITY: CONNOTATIONS

1. The connotations and mood suggested range from affection, to neutral, to revulsion.
2. Student's own answer
3. a) 'the bright lights and bustle'
b) This phrase would suggest a crowded and perhaps extravagant or glamorous party.
4. 'Full moon' suggests the supernatural; 'cold' creates a tone of unemotional aggression.

MAIN ACTIVITY: EFFECT AND IMPACT

1. Feverish and uncontrolled shaking suggesting serious illness
2. An extreme, irregular and perhaps unnatural movement
3. Intrigued and disturbed

HOMEWORK ACTIVITY: WRITE A RESPONSE

1.

Marks	Criteria
7–8 marks	• Clear and detailed analysis of the effect of the writer's language choices • A carefully selected range of relevant, focused textual evidence • A range of subject terminology to achieve clarity and precision
5–6 marks	• Clear comments on the effect of the writer's language choices • A range of relevant, focused textual evidence • A range of subject terminology to achieve clarity
3–4 marks	• Some comments on the effect of the writer's language choices • Relevant and focused textual evidence • Largely accurate use of subject terminology
1–2 marks	• Straightforward comments on the effect of the writer's language choices • Largely relevant textual evidence • Some use of subject terminology, with inconsistent accuracy
No marks	• No creditable response

2. Ensure the student has achieved all, or the majority of, the success criteria.

GLOSSARY

Connotation
The idea or feeling that a vocabulary choice can suggest to the reader

AQA ENGLISH — Grades 3-5

8 READING: ANALYSING LANGUAGE 3

LEARNING OBJECTIVES
- To develop language analysis skills
- To craft effective critical writing

SPECIFICATION LINKS
- 3.1.1 critical reading and comprehension

STARTER ACTIVITY
- **Refresher; 5 minutes; page 66**
  Remind the student that in a successful text, the intention and impact may well be similar, e.g. the reader responds as the writer intended.

MAIN ACTIVITIES
- **Annotating the text; 20 minutes; page 67**
  Explain to the student that they need to focus on the most relevant intentions and the most significant language choices.
- **Structuring your response; 15 minutes; page 68**
  Read through the questions with the student. Encourage them to give verbal reasoning for their answers before they write them down.

PLENARY ACTIVITY
- **Review; 5 minutes**
  Ask the student to review, evaluate and summarise what they have learned about analysing the writer's choices of words, phrases and language features. How confident do they feel about completing the Homework activity?

HOMEWORK ACTIVITY
- **Write a response; 30 minutes; page 69**
  Note that this activity will be revisited in lesson 10, which focuses on the writer's choice of sentence forms.

SUPPORT IDEA
- **Review** If time allows, ask the student to identify three further language choices in the extract and discuss their effect/impact, in preparation for the Homework activity.

EXTENSION IDEA
- **Structuring your response** Encourage the student to experiment with different sequences/structures, and not simply to follow the P-Q-C or P-E-E model. Make sure you conclude that there are a number of possible structures that can be used successfully.

PROGRESS AND OBSERVATIONS

ENGLISH
— Grades 3-5 —

AQA

STARTER ACTIVITY: REFRESHER   **TIMING: 5 MINS**

LEARNING OBJECTIVES   **EQUIPMENT**
- To develop language analysis skills   none

In this lesson, you are going to apply your language analysis skills.

1. Draw lines linking the terms on the left with the correct definition and example.

Terms	Definition	Example
intention	What the writer's language choice suggests about the place, object, idea etc. that it refers to.	This word creates an impression of confusion and chaos.
connotation	How the reader might respond to the writer's choices.	The writer is aiming to show the impact that science has had on our lives.
effect	The ideas or feelings that a word creates in the reader's mind.	It emphasises to the reader the scale of the achievements made in the nineteenth century.
impact	The response the writer wants to create in the reader.	The word suggests that the human mind is overwhelmed and unable to comprehend how much science has achieved.

AQA ENGLISH — Grades 3-5

MAIN ACTIVITY: ANNOTATING THE TEXT **TIMING: 20 MINS**

LEARNING OBJECTIVES
- To develop language analysis skills

EQUIPMENT
none

Look at the first paragraph of Source F: *A Century of Achievement*.

> In the one hundred years now drawing to a close the world has made a greater advance in science and the arts than in all the preceding ages. The human mind reels when it tries to grasp the stupendous achievements of the Nineteenth Century, in every branch of discovery and invention. Because of their love of pure knowledge, men of gigantic intellect have sought out the mighty secrets of the universe and have raised to the sky a temple to science on ground upon which stood, a century ago, only scattered and isolated stones. Close behind the worshipers of knowledge have followed the magicians of to-day; chemists, engineers and electricians. At their command the spirits of air, water, earth and fire have been made to do man's every bidding. They propel his steamships, railway cars and mighty engines; they make his garments; they build his houses; they illuminate his cities; they harvest his crops. For him they make ice in the tropics or grow oranges amid snow. For him they fan a heated atmosphere into cooling breezes or banish icy winds. They flash his news around the globe; they carry the sound of his voice for thousands of miles, or preserve it after he is dead.

1. What is the writer's main intention in this paragraph? Tick two of the following.

    ☐ to highlight the number of achievements made in the nineteenth century
    ☐ to highlight the impact that these achievements have had on people's lives
    ☐ to praise the scientists responsible for those achievements
    ☐ to compare life at the beginning and end of the nineteenth century
    ☐ to compare scientists to magicians
    ☐ to describe what scientists have done in the last one hundred years

2. Think about the writer's language choices in the paragraph above.

    a) Circle any of the words or phrases that make a significant contribution to the intentions you have identified.

    b) Annotate the words or phrases you have circled, noting:
    - their effect (what the word or phrase, and its connotations, suggests)
    - their impact (how the reader might respond to the writer's choice of word or phrase).

ENGLISH
— Grades 3-5 —

Main activity: Structuring your response

Timing: 15 mins

Learning objectives
- To craft effective critical writing

Equipment
- Source F: *A Century of Achievement*

1. Look at these sentences from a student's response to this Paper 2, Section A exam-style question.

> You now need to think about the whole of Source F: *A Century of Achievement*.
> How does the writer use language to try to convince the reader of his opinion?
> **[12 marks]**

A. The writer describes 'chemists, engineers and electricians' as 'the magicians of to-day.'

B. The writer tries to show how impressive the scientists and their achievements are.

C. This shows how impressive they are.

D. The word 'magicians' suggests that these scientists can perform amazing tricks that seem unbelievable and astonishing.

E. It gives the impression that they have achieved things that normal people like the reader cannot understand and might not think were possible.

   a) Add a label 'P' to the response in which the student has clearly identified the writer's intention.
   b) Add a label 'Q' to the response in which they have used a quotation as evidence to support their ideas.
   c) Add a label 'WP' to the response in which they have identified a significant choice of word or phrase.
   d) Add a label 'E' to the response in which they have commented on the effect of that word or phrase.
   e) Add a label 'I' to the response in which they have commented on the impact of that word or phrase.

2. How could you use these sentences to construct a response?
   a) Which of the student's sentences would you include in a paragraph responding to the exam-style question? Tick them.
   b) In what order would you sequence the sentences you have ticked? Number them.

3. Which sentences would you not include in a paragraph responding to the exam-style question above? Explain why.

AQA ENGLISH — Grades 3-5

HOMEWORK ACTIVITY: WRITE A RESPONSE

TIMING: 30 MINS

LEARNING OBJECTIVES
- To develop language analysis skills
- To craft effective critical writing

EQUIPMENT
- Source F: *A Century of Achievement*

Look at this Paper 2, Section A exam-style question.

> You now need to think about the whole of Source F: *A Century of Achievement*. How does the writer use language to try to convince the reader of his opinion?
> **[12 marks]**

1. Write two paragraphs in response to this question, focusing on the writer's choice of words, phrases and language features.

   _____
   _____
   _____
   _____
   _____
   _____
   _____
   _____
   _____

2. When you have written your response, check you have achieved all of the success criteria below.

   a) Tick all the criteria you feel you have achieved.

      ☐ I have focused on two of the writer's language choices.
      ☐ I have commented on the connotations of each language choice.
      ☐ I have commented on the effect of each language choice.
      ☐ I have commented on the impact of each language choice.
      ☐ I have written in paragraphs.
      ☐ I have carefully checked for accurate spelling and punctuation, and clear written expression.

   b) Look at any of the criteria you feel you have not achieved. Add to and improve your response so that you can tick all of them.

8 Answers

Starter activity: Refresher

1. Intention: the response the writer wants to create in the reader. Example: the writer is aiming to show the impact that science has had on our lives.
Connotation: the ideas or feelings that a word creates in the reader's mind. Example: this word creates an impression of confusion and chaos.
Effect: what the writer's language choice suggests about the place, object, idea, etc. that it refers to. Example: the word suggests that the human mind is overwhelmed and unable to comprehend how much science has achieved.
Impact: how the reader might respond to the writer's choices. Example: it emphasises to the reader the scale of the achievements made in the nineteenth century.

Main activity: Annotating the text

1. Two of: to highlight the number of achievements made in the nineteenth century; to highlight the impact that these achievements have had on people's lives; to praise the scientists responsible for those achievements
2. a) and b) Examples: 'gigantic': hyperbole suggests the scale of intellect and achievement; 'every branch' suggests the scale and range of achievements; 'mighty secrets' suggests the power of their discoveries; 'temple' suggests the god-like power of science and the forces that have been harnessed; 'command' suggests power and control.

Main activity: Structuring your response

1. A:Q; B:P; C:E; D:WP; E:I
2. a) Sentences A, B, D and E are all valid analytical comments
b) The most effective responses are likely to be: A, B, D, E; or B, A, D, E.
3. Sentence C simply repeats B.

Homework activity: Write a response

1.

Marks	Criteria
10–12 marks	• Clear and detailed analysis of the effect of the writer's language choices • A carefully selected range of relevant, focused textual evidence • A range of subject terminology to achieve clarity and precision
7–9 marks	• Clear comments on the effect of the writer's language choices • A range of relevant, focused textual evidence • A range of subject terminology to achieve clarity
4–6 marks	• Some comments on the effect of the writer's language choices • Relevant and focused textual evidence • Largely accurate subject terminology
1–3 marks	• Straightforward comments on the effect of the writer's language choices • Largely relevant textual evidence • Some use of subject terminology, with inconsistent accuracy
No marks	• No creditable response

2. Ensure the student has achieved all, or the majority of, the success criteria.

ENGLISH
Grades 3–5

9 Reading: Analysing sentence forms 1

Learning objectives
- To develop awareness of sentence forms and their effect
- To be able to explore the impact of the writer's choice of sentence forms

Specification links
- 3.1.1 critical reading and comprehension

Starter activity
- **Thinking about sentence forms; 5 minutes; page 72**
  Confirm understanding of the sentence forms, but avoid discussing in detail the impact of specific sentence types. Use this activity to assess awareness and subsequent activities to reinforce or develop analysis skills. Emphasise to the student that, as with analysis of language devices and vocabulary choices, terminology is far less important than discussing the effect/impact.

Main activities
- **Looking at sentence length; 20 minutes; page 73**
  Support the student as they complete the questions, monitoring their understanding and progress. Summarise some of the effects that sentence length can have, e.g. short sentences can add impact, emphasis or drama to an idea; longer sentences can be used to list events etc.
- **How sentences end; 20 minutes; page 74**
  Support the student as they complete the questions, monitoring their understanding and progress. Discuss possible ways in which the ideas could be sequenced in question 1, e.g. chronological order.

Plenary activity
- **Review; 5 minutes**
  Ask the student to summarise some ways in which sentences can be structured for impact, e.g. shorter sentences add impact and drama to key pieces of information; longer sentences listing information suggest range or variety; delaying significant information to the end of a longer sentence adds impact.

Homework activity
- **Writing sentences; 30 minutes; page 75**
  Check understanding evaluated in the Plenary activity against the demands of the Homework activity. Ensure the student is confident that they know what is required and how to achieve it.

Support idea
- **Looking at sentence length; How sentences end** Read the various versions of sentences aloud to the student to emphasise how shorter or longer, or differently sequenced sentences, alter the impact of the text.

Extension idea
- **How sentences end** Ask the student to identify other shorter or longer sentences in the extract that have been structured to achieve similar effects.

Progress and observations

ENGLISH
— Grades 3-5 —

STARTER ACTIVITY: THINKING ABOUT SENTENCE FORMS   **TIMING: 5 MINS**

LEARNING OBJECTIVES
- To develop awareness of sentence forms and their effect

EQUIPMENT
none

1. Which of the following sentence forms could you identify in a text?

    ☐ a long sentence
    ☐ a short sentence

    ☐ a simple sentence
    ☐ a compound sentence
    ☐ a complex sentence

    ☐ a single clause sentence
    ☐ a multi-clause sentence

    ☐ a question
    ☐ a statement
    ☐ an exclamation
    ☐ a command

2. Which of the following effects and impacts can a writer's choice of sentence forms have on the reader?

    ☐ add emphasis to an idea
    ☐ create tension
    ☐ add dramatic impact
    ☐ suggest a faster or slower pace of events
    ☐ create a vivid image in the reader's mind
    ☐ link ideas clearly
    ☐ convey the writer's mood or tone
    ☐ convey a character's mood or tone
    ☐ influence the reader's opinions or actions
    ☐ engage the reader's interest or opinions

AQA ENGLISH — Grades 3–5

MAIN ACTIVITY: LOOKING AT SENTENCE LENGTH	**TIMING: 20 MINS**

LEARNING OBJECTIVES
- To be able to explore the impact of the writer's choice of sentence forms

EQUIPMENT
none

Look carefully at the sentence forms in the opening paragraph of Source D: *The Secret History*.

> The snow in the mountains was melting and Bunny had been dead for several weeks before we came to understand the gravity of our situation. He'd been dead for ten days before they found him, you know. It was one of the biggest manhunts in Vermont history – state troopers, the FBI, even an army helicopter; the college closed, the dye factory in Hampden shut down, people coming from New Hampshire, upstate New York, as far away as Boston.

1. Circle the shortest sentence in the paragraph.

2. Look at the sentence you have circled and the one before it. Rewrite the two sentences below, linking them using a conjunction (e.g. *and*, *because*, *although*) to create one long sentence.

   ----

3. Compare the longer sentence you have written with the sentence you circled. Why do you think the writer chose to isolate this piece of information in its own, short sentence? Explain your ideas.

   ----

4. Underline the longest sentence in the paragraph.

5. Long sentences are used to link ideas or information. What is the connection between the information in the sentence you have underlined? What does all this information suggest about the death of Bunny? Explain your ideas.

ENGLISH
Grades 3–5

| MAIN ACTIVITY: HOW SENTENCES END | TIMING: 20 MINS |

LEARNING OBJECTIVES
- To be able to explore the impact of the writer's choice of sentence forms

EQUIPMENT
none

Writers often place significant information or ideas at the end of longer sentences.
Look at this very long sentence from the end of Source D: *The Secret History*:

> Though I remember the walk back and the first lonely flakes of snow that came drifting through the pines, remember piling gratefully into the car and starting down the road like a family on vacation, with Henry driving clench-jawed through the potholes and the rest of us leaning over the seats and talking like children, though I remember only too well the long terrible night that lay ahead and the long terrible days and nights that followed, I have only to glance over my shoulder for all those years to drop away and I see it behind me again, the ravine, rising all green and black through the saplings, a picture that will never leave me.

Look at this list of all the information in the sentence.
a) The narrator remembers walking back after the murder.
b) He remembers driving away from the scene of the murder.
c) He remembers the days and nights that followed the murder.
d) He remembers the ravine where he murdered Bunny.
e) This picture will never leave him.

1. **How could the writer have structured these pieces of information in a different order? Experiment with sequencing the five ideas by adding the letters a–e in the boxes below.**

1st	2nd	3rd	4th	5th

2. **Compare the way you have sequenced the ideas in the sentence with the writer's choice in the text. Why do you think the writer chose to save the final piece of information for the very end of the sentence? Explain your ideas.**

AQA ENGLISH — Grades 3-5

HOMEWORK ACTIVITY: WRITING SENTENCES	TIMING: 30 MINS

LEARNING OBJECTIVES
- To be able to explore the impact of the writer's choice of sentence forms

EQUIPMENT
none

You are going to write an imaginative opening about a dramatic event you remember clearly.

1. **Write down some ideas in the table below.**

What was the dramatic event?	What was happening just before this dramatic event?	How did you feel after the dramatic event?

2. **Think about how you will structure the sentences in your opening.**

    a) Which of your ideas would work well in a dramatic shorter sentence? Label them 'short'.
    b) Which of your ideas could be linked together in a longer sentence? Label them 'long'.
    c) Which of the ideas in your longer sentence will you place at the very end? Label them 'end'.

3. **Write the first three sentences of the opening you have planned.**

----

4. **Annotate each of the sentences you have written for impact and effect, identifying:**
   - how you have structured it
   - the impact and effect you intended it to have.

ENGLISH
Grades 3-5
AQA

9 ANSWERS

STARTER ACTIVITY: THINKING ABOUT SENTENCE FORMS
1. Student's own answer. If not all are ticked, review sentence forms with the student.
2. All options are valid.

MAIN ACTIVITY: LOOKING AT SENTENCE LENGTH
1. 'He'd been dead for ten days before they found him, you know.'
2. Example: The snow in the mountains was melting and Bunny had been dead for several weeks before we came to understand the gravity of our situation, although he'd been dead for ten days before they found him, you know.
3. The short sentence adds impact to this shocking piece of information.
4. 'It was one of the biggest manhunts…as far away as Boston.'
5. The sentence lists all the consequences of the manhunt, emphasising their scale and variety.

MAIN ACTIVITY: HOW SENTENCES END
1. Examples: 1st: e, 2nd: d, 3rd: a, 4th: b, 5th: c
2. This is the most significant piece of information in the sentence. Delaying it to the end of the sentence gives it emphasis.

HOMEWORK ACTIVITY: WRITING SENTENCES
Student's own answers. Responses should be annotated, identifying longer and shorter sentences, and crafted for impact.

GLOSSARY

Single clause sentence
A sentence consisting of only one clause; also known as a simple sentence

Multi-clause sentence
A sentence consisting of two or more clauses; also known as a compound or complex sentence

Compound sentence
A sentence of two or more clauses of equal importance, linked by a co-ordinating conjunction, e.g. *and*, *but*

Complex sentence
A sentence of two or more clauses of differing importance (a main clause and at least one subordinate clause), linked by a subordinating conjunction, e.g. *because*, *although*, *if*, etc.

ENGLISH
— Grades 3-5 —

10 READING: ANALYSING SENTENCE FORMS 2

LEARNING OBJECTIVES
- To be able to explore the impact of the writer's choice of sentence forms

SPECIFICATION LINKS
- 3.1.1 critical reading and comprehension

STARTER ACTIVITY
- **Playing with sentences; 10 minutes; page 78**
  Ask the student to cut out each clause, word and punctuation mark, and then complete the question. Encourage them to experiment with restructuring the sentences and comment on how their impact is altered.

MAIN ACTIVITIES
- **Sentence forms and intention; 20 minutes; page 79**
  This activity builds on lesson 9. Ask the student to read Source F: *A Century of Achievement* (page 22). Point out that 19th century writers generally used longer sentences, and therefore sentence length is relative. Develop breadth of understanding by discussing which sentences have the most significant impact.
- **Repetitive sentence forms; 15 minutes; page 80**
  Highlight the persuasive effect of repetition in the source, which is used to emphasise the impact of 19th century achievement on people's lives.

PLENARY ACTIVITY
- **Review; 5 minutes**
  Ask the student to review, evaluate and summarise their learning on sentence forms and the impact they can have on a reader.

HOMEWORK ACTIVITY
- **Write a response; 30 minutes; page 81**
  This exam-style question was also set for homework in lesson 8, with a focus on the writer's choice of words, phrases and language features. Here, the focus is on sentence structure instead. The student may choose to re-use ideas from the lesson. This is valuable practice in expressing their understanding in the context of an exam-style response.

SUPPORT IDEA
- **Playing with sentences** Begin by linking just two clauses and build up from there. Experiment with using conjunctions, lists and short sentences to link clauses.

EXTENSION IDEAS
- **Sentences forms and intention** Ask the student to select two or three sentences from the source for comment.
- **Throughout** Encourage the student to use technical terminology to describe sentence forms.

PROGRESS AND OBSERVATIONS

ENGLISH
— Grades 3-5 —

STARTER ACTIVITY: PLAYING WITH SENTENCES   **TIMING: 10 MINS**

LEARNING OBJECTIVES
- To be able to explore the impact of the writer's choice of sentence forms

EQUIPMENT
- scissors

1. Cut out the words, clauses and examples of punctuation below. Re-arrange them to craft three sentences with impact. You can use as many of the clauses as you like.

| I do everything I am asked |
| I listen carefully |
| I try my hardest |
| I do not understand sometimes |
| I will succeed |

and	and	.
but	but	.
when	when	.
if	if	,
although	although	,
because	because	,

78

AQA ENGLISH
Grades 3–5

| MAIN ACTIVITY: SENTENCE FORMS AND INTENTION | TIMING: 20 MINS |

LEARNING OBJECTIVES
- To be able to explore the impact of the writer's choice of sentence forms

EQUIPMENT
- Source F: *A Century of Achievement*

1. What is the writer's intention in Source F: *A Century of Achievement?* Summarise your answer in one or two sentences.

   ....

   ....

   ....

2. Look carefully through the text and mark any sentence forms that add significant impact to the text.
   You could look for:
   - long sentences
   - short sentences
   - sentences that list events or ideas
   - sentences in which a significant idea is delayed until the end.

3. Look again at the sentences you have marked. Which one makes the most significant contribution to achieving the writer's intention? Tick it.

4. Tick the ways in which the form of the sentence you have chosen contributes to the writer's intention.

   ☐ adds emphasis to the point or idea expressed in the sentence
   ☐ creates a vivid image in the reader's mind
   ☐ links two or more ideas
   ☐ conveys the writer's mood or tone
   ☐ suggests the range and variety of events or ideas
   ☐ other effects

5. Write at least two sentences about the sentence form you have chosen, commenting on its impact and contribution to the writer's intention.

   ....

   ....

   ....

   ....

   ....

ENGLISH
Grades 3-5

AQA

| MAIN ACTIVITY: REPETITIVE SENTENCE FORMS | TIMING: 15 MINS |

LEARNING OBJECTIVES

- To be able to explore the impact of the writer's choice of sentence forms

EQUIPMENT

none

Look closely at these sentences from Source F: *A Century of Achievement.* In these sentences, the writer uses a number of very similar sentence forms.

> At their command the spirits of air, water, earth and fire have been made to do man's every bidding. They propel his steamships, railway cars and mighty engines; they make his garments; they build his houses; they illuminate his cities; they harvest his crops. For him they make ice in the tropics or grow oranges amid snow. For him they fan a heated atmosphere into cooling breezes or banish icy winds. They flash his news around the globe; they carry the sound of his voice for thousands of miles, or preserve it after he is dead.

1. Look at the circled words in the second sentence. What other repetitive sentence forms can you see? Circle them.

2. Tick the ways in which these repetitive sentence forms contribute to the writer's intention.

    ☐ add emphasis to the point or idea expressed in the sentence
    ☐ create a vivid image in the reader's mind
    ☐ link two or more ideas
    ☐ convey the writer's mood or tone
    ☐ suggest the range and variety of events or ideas
    ☐ other effects

3. Write one or two sentences about the repetitive sentence forms you have chosen, commenting on their impact and contribution to the writer's intention.

AQA ENGLISH
Grades 3–5

HOMEWORK ACTIVITY: WRITE A RESPONSE **TIMING: 30 MINS**

LEARNING OBJECTIVES
- To be able to explore the impact of the writer's choice of sentence forms

EQUIPMENT
- Source F: *A Century of Achievement*

Look at this Paper 2, Section A exam-style question:

> You now need to think about the whole of Source F: *A Century of Achievement*.
> How does the writer use language to try to convince the reader of his opinion?
> **[12 marks]**

1. Write two paragraphs in response to this question, focusing on the writer's choice of sentence forms.

_____

_____

_____

_____

_____

_____

_____

_____

_____

_____

2. When you have written your response, check you have achieved all of the success criteria below.

    a) Tick all the criteria you feel you have achieved.

     ☐ I have focused on two examples of sentence forms.
     ☐ I have commented on the effect of each sentence form.
     ☐ I have commented on the impact of each sentence form.
     ☐ I have written in paragraphs.
     ☐ I have carefully checked for accurate spelling and punctuation, and clear written expression.

    b) Look at any of the criteria you feel you have not achieved. Add to and improve your response so that you can tick all of them.

ENGLISH
Grades 3-5

10 ANSWERS

STARTER ACTIVITY: PLAYING WITH SENTENCES

1. Example: Although I do not understand sometimes, I do everything I am asked, I listen carefully, I try my hardest and I will succeed.

MAIN ACTIVITY: SENTENCE FORMS AND INTENTION

1. The writer's intention is to encourage the reader to appreciate the achievements of the 19th century.
2. Examples:
Short sentences: 'It is well-nigh impossible to realize the state of science one hundred years ago. All was inchoate.'
Long sentences that list events or ideas: 'They propel his steamships, railway cars and mighty engines; they make his garments; they build his houses; they illuminate his cities; they harvest his crops.'
Longer sentences in which a significant idea is delayed to the end: 'When we regard the astonishing structure that has been built since then, the materials for which have been hewn in so many forests and quarried from so many mines, it seems incredible that a single century can have witnessed so many brilliant achievements.'
3. Student's own answer
4. Student's own answer
5. Responses should focus on the impact of sentence form and its contribution to intention, e.g. how it underlines the catalogue of achievements described.

MAIN ACTIVITY: REPETITIVE SENTENCE FORMS

1. 'For him... For him... They flash... They carry'
2. Student's own answer
3. This rhetorical repetition of sentence forms emphasises the range of listed achievements, effectively conveying the writer's enthusiasm.

HOMEWORK ACTIVITY: WRITE A RESPONSE

1.

Marks	Criteria
10–12 marks	• Clear and detailed analysis of the effect of the writer's language choices • A carefully selected range of relevant, focused textual evidence • A range of subject terminology to achieve clarity and precision
7–9 marks	• Clear comments on the effect of the writer's language choices • A range of relevant, focused textual evidence • A range of subject terminology to achieve clarity
4–6 marks	• Some comments on the effect of the writer's language choices • Relevant and focused textual evidence • Largely accurate subject terminology
1–3 marks	• Straightforward comments on the effect of the writer's language choices • Largely relevant textual evidence • Some use of subject terminology, with inconsistent accuracy
No marks	• No comments on the writer's use of language • No rewardable response

2. Ensure the student has achieved all, or the majority of, the success criteria.

GLOSSARY

Rhetorical question
This is a question that does not require an answer, asked with the purpose of producing an effect or reaction

11 READING: DEVELOPING LANGUAGE ANALYSIS

LEARNING OBJECTIVES

- To be able to comment on the writer's choice of words, phrases, language features and sentence forms
- To be able to identify relevant evidence

SPECIFICATION LINKS

- 3.1.1 critical reading and comprehension

STARTER ACTIVITY

- **Assessing an example; 10 minutes; page 84**
  Give the student five minutes to re-read Source B: *Burglarious Bill* (page 18), focusing on the second half of the text. Ask the student to complete the activity, using the model paragraph to prompt discussion of key points to remember when responding to this type of exam question. Highlight where the student in the example has selected evidence that allows them to comment on the writer's use of both sentence forms and words, phrases and language features.

MAIN ACTIVITIES

- **Surveying the source; 20 minutes; page 85**
  Explain to the student that they are now going to collect evidence for the exam-style question they assessed in the Starter activity.
- **Structuring your response; 15 minutes; page 86**
  Remind the student of the exemplar paragraph they explored in the Starter activity.

PLENARY ACTIVITY

- **Review; 5 minutes**
  Ask the student to review, evaluate and summarise what they have learned about analysing words, phrases, language features and sentence forms.

HOMEWORK ACTIVITY

- **Write a response; 30 minutes; page 87**
  Ask the student to use one of the three pieces of evidence gathered in the *Surveying the source* activity to complete this task – but not the same evidence used in the *Structuring your response* activity.

SUPPORT IDEAS

- **Surveying the source** Encourage the student to consider the form of each sentence in turn. Prompt them with examples of sentence forms explored in lessons 9 and 10.
- **Write a response** Suggest to the student that they use the ideas gathered in the Structuring your response activity in their response to the exam-style question.

EXTENSION IDEA

- **Write a response** Ask the student to plan and write a new paragraph in response to the exam-style question.

PROGRESS AND OBSERVATIONS

ENGLISH
Grades 3-5

STARTER ACTIVITY: ASSESSING AN EXAMPLE

TIMING: 10 MINS

LEARNING OBJECTIVES

- To be able to comment on the writer's choices of words, phrases, language features and sentence forms

EQUIPMENT

- Source B: *Burglarious Bill*

Read Source B: *Burglarious Bill* and then look at this paragraph from a student's response to a Paper 2, Section A exam-style question.

> Look in detail at Source B: *Burglarious Bill* from **line 20 to the end.**
>
> How does the writer use language here to describe the police investigation and arrest of the burglars?
>
> [8 marks]

> The writer's choices of language and sentence forms makes the arrest of Caseley and his wife dramatic. For example, when the police arrive at Caseley's house, the writer uses dialogue to create an impression of the situation. Mrs Caseley leans out of her window and says:
>
> '"Who are you?"
> "We are police officers," was the reply.'
>
> The writer uses very short sentences and very simple language to suggest that this is a short and blunt conversation. It gives the reader the impression that Mrs Caseley does not bother being polite to people she does not know and that the police are being quite aggressive in confronting the criminals. It suggests that there is going to be a dramatic ending.

1. What has this student done well in their paragraph of analysis? Write your ideas below.

....

....

....

....

....

AQA ENGLISH — Grades 3-5

MAIN ACTIVITY: SURVEYING THE SOURCE	**TIMING: 20 MINS**

LEARNING OBJECTIVES
- To be able to identify relevant evidence

EQUIPMENT
- Source B: *Burglarious Bill*

In this activity, you are going to focus on this Paper 2, Section A exam-style question:

> Look in detail at Source B: *Burglarious Bill* from **line 20 to the end**.
>
> How does the writer use language here to describe the police investigation and arrest of the burglars?
>
> **[8 marks]**

When you are asked to analyse the writer's use of language, you need to think about the writer's choice of:
- words, phrases and language features
- sentence forms.

The most effective responses select quotations that allow comment on words and phrases *and* sentence forms.

1. **Look carefully at Source B: *Burglarious Bill* from line 22 to the end.**

   a) First, identify any sentences in this section of the source that are not relevant to the exam-style question you are focusing on: those sentences that do not describe or refer to the police's investigation and arrest of the burglars. Cross them out.

   b) Next, identify any sentence forms that you feel make a significant contribution to the writer's description of the police investigation and arrest of the burglars. Underline them.

   c) Finally, look at the sentences you have underlined. Identify any of the writer's choice of words or phrases that make a significant contribution to the writer's description of the police investigation and arrest of the burglars. Circle them.

   d) If you have underlined more than three sentences, choose three that you feel make the most significant contribution to the description of the police investigation and arrest of the burglars – or those which you feel you can analyse most thoroughly and effectively.

Look at the three sentences you have chosen, and the choice of words and phrases you have circled. These will be the evidence you use in your response to the exam-style question.

ENGLISH
— Grades 3–5 —

MAIN ACTIVITY: STRUCTURING YOUR RESPONSE

TIMING: 15 MINS

LEARNING OBJECTIVES
- To be able to comment on the writer's choice of words, phrases, language features and sentence forms

EQUIPMENT
- Source B: *Burglarious Bill*

1. **Choose one of the sentences you identified in the previous activity. Add it to the evidence row in the table.**

2. **Look carefully at the evidence you have chosen and complete the rest of table.**
   You should use:
   - everything you have learned about analysing words, phrases, language features and sentence forms
   - the example you have already seen.

	Your analysis	Example
Identify the writer's intention		The writer's choices of language and sentence forms makes the arrest of Caseley and his wife dramatic.
Evidence		'"Who are you?" "We are police officers," was the reply.'
Identify sentence forms		The writer uses very short sentences
Identify significant words and phrases		and very simple language
Comment on effect		to suggest that this is a short and blunt conversation.
Comment on impact		It gives the reader the impression that Mrs Caseley does not bother being polite to people she does not know and that the police are being quite aggressive in confronting the criminals. It suggests that there is going to be a dramatic ending.

ENGLISH
— Grades 3-5 —

HOMEWORK ACTIVITY: WRITE A RESPONSE **TIMING: 30 MINS**

LEARNING OBJECTIVES
- To be able to comment on the writer's choice of words, phrases, language features and sentence forms

EQUIPMENT
- Source B: *Burglarious Bill*

Look at this Paper 2, Section A exam-style question:

> Look in detail at Source B: *Burglarious Bill* from **line 20 to the end**.
>
> How does the writer use language here to describe the police investigation and arrest of the burglars?
>
> **[8 marks]**

1. Write one paragraph in response to this question, focusing on the writer's choice of words, phrases, language features and sentence forms.

....

....

....

....

....

....

2. When you have written your response, check you have achieved all of the success criteria below.

   a) Tick all the criteria you feel you have achieved.

      ☐ I have focused on two of the writer's language choices.
      ☐ I have commented on the connotations of each language choice.
      ☐ I have commented on the effect of each language choice.
      ☐ I have commented on the impact of each language choice.
      ☐ I have written in paragraphs.
      ☐ I have carefully checked for accurate spelling and punctuation, and clear written expression.

   b) Look at any of the criteria you feel you have not achieved. Add to and improve your response so that you can tick all of them.

11 Answers

STARTER ACTIVITY: ASSESSING AN EXAMPLE

1. Examples: the student writer's intention is identified; the use of evidence; the simultaneous comment on words/phrases and sentence forms; the comments on effect and impact.

MAIN ACTIVITY: SURVEYING THE SOURCE

1. a) All sentences are relevant.
b) Examples: sentences listing the goods stolen or the variety of weapons and tools discovered at the Caseleys' house; use of numerical detail; sequence of coordinate clauses suggesting pace of action
c) Examples: 'they forced the lock, entered, and rushed upstairs'; choice of verbs
d) Student's own answer

MAIN ACTIVITY: STRUCTURING YOUR RESPONSE

1. and 2. Check the validity of responses, ensuring in particular that impact and effect are clearly differentiated.

HOMEWORK ACTIVITY: WRITE A RESPONSE

1.

Marks	Criteria
7–8 marks	• Clear and detailed analysis of the effect of the writer's language choices • A carefully selected range of relevant, focused textual evidence • A range of subject terminology to achieve clarity and precision
5–6 marks	• Clear comments on the effect of the writer's language choices • A range of relevant, focused textual evidence • A range of subject terminology to achieve clarity
3–4 marks	• Some comments on the effect of the writer's language choices • Relevant and focused textual evidence • Largely accurate use of subject terminology
1–2 marks	• Straightforward comments on the effect of the writer's language choices • Largely relevant textual evidence • Some use of subject terminology, with inconsistent accuracy
No marks	• No creditable response

2. Ensure the student has achieved all, or the majority of, the success criteria.

AQA ENGLISH — Grades 3–5

12 READING: WHOLE TEXT STRUCTURE

LEARNING OBJECTIVES
- To be able to identify features and elements of structure
- To understand the impact of structure

SPECIFICATION LINKS
- 3.1.1 critical reading and comprehension

STARTER ACTIVITY
- **Effective openings; 5 minutes; page 90**
  Discuss the introduction to the activity and elicit the student's own ideas. Explain that the structure question in Paper 1 of the exam is likely to refer to the opening of a novel or short story. Ask the student to cut out each question and feature, and then complete the activity for question 2. You will use this worksheet again in lesson 23.

MAIN ACTIVITIES
- **Tracking structure; 20 minutes; page 91**
  Ask the student to read Source D: *The Secret History* (page 20). Discuss question 1, noting the possible intention behind the writer's use of non-chronological order, repetition and the slow release of information about the murder.
- **Beginnings; 15 minutes; page 92**
  Ask the student to complete the questions, directing their attention to the selection and sequence of events, and the thoughts and feelings described.

PLENARY ACTIVITY
- **Restructuring; 10 minutes**
  Ask the student to list everything they think might happen or be focused on in the remainder of this novel. How would the student have chosen to begin it? With the events that led up to the murder? With the murder? With the aftermath of the murder? Discuss their choices, the impact of those choices, and their reasons for making them.

HOMEWORK ACTIVITY
- **Write your own; 30 minutes; page 93**
  Point out to the student that, if they have completed the Homework activity in lesson 9, they may want to rework their ideas and use them on this worksheet. Emphasise that their story opening should be 150–200 words.

SUPPORT IDEA
- **Tracking structure** The list of events does not need to be entirely comprehensive. The student may only note more significant events. Prompt if key points are overlooked.

EXTENSION IDEAS
- **Effective openings** Ask the student to note their own ideas, without showing the prompts on the worksheet.
- **Beginnings** Encourage the student to consider how the three key focuses of the opening of the novel interact with each other, e.g. how the effect of the murder on the narrator's thoughts and feelings suggests its brutality.

PROGRESS AND OBSERVATIONS

ENGLISH
Grades 3-5

AQA

STARTER ACTIVITY: EFFECTIVE OPENINGS

TIMING: 5 MINS

LEARNING OBJECTIVES
- To be able to identify features and elements of structure
- To understand the impact of structure

EQUIPMENT
- scissors

1. What makes for an effective opening to a short story or a novel?

....

....

....

....

2. Cut out the boxes below and match them up to create questions. Think about how each feature is important to the structure of a short story or novel. You should ask yourself these questions when you are looking at a text.

| How many? |
| In what order? |
| How much? |
| What kind of...? |

plot	characters	settings	dialogue
action	questions	drama	tension
shocks and surprises	mystery	problems	description

90

ENGLISH
Grades 3-5

MAIN ACTIVITY: TRACKING STRUCTURE **TIMING: 20 MINS**

LEARNING OBJECTIVES
- To be able to identify features and elements of structure

EQUIPMENT
- Source D: *The Secret History*

1. **Read Source D: *The Secret History*. As you read, note down everything in the extract that:**
   - **happens**
   - **has already happened**
   - **is described.**

   ....
   ....
   ....
   ....
   ....
   ....
   ....
   ....
   ....
   ....

2. **Number the events you have noted in chronological order.**

3. **Write down three things that you notice about the structure of this opening.**

   ....
   ....
   ....

ENGLISH
Grades 3-5

AQA

| **MAIN ACTIVITY: BEGINNINGS** | **TIMING: 15 MINS** |

LEARNING OBJECTIVES
- To understand the impact of structure

EQUIPMENT
- Source D: *The Secret History*

Look again at Source D: *The Secret History*.

1. **Which of these do you think is the main focus of the novel's opening? Tick one.**

    ☐ the murder of Bunny
    ☐ the manhunt for Bunny
    ☐ the narrator's thoughts and feelings

2. **Why has the writer made this the main focus of the novel's opening? Explain your ideas.**

Writers often engage the reader by giving just enough ideas and information in the opening to hint at the story that will follow. This makes the reader ask questions and want to read on to find out the answers.

3. **What questions does this opening make you ask? Give at least two examples.**

ENGLISH
Grades 3-5

| HOMEWORK ACTIVITY: WRITE YOUR OWN | TIMING: 30 MINS |

LEARNING OBJECTIVES
- To understand the impact of structure

EQUIPMENT
none

You are going to plan the opening to an imaginative writing task about a dramatic event you remember clearly. Make sure you choose a different event to the one you chose in lesson 9.

1. **Write down some ideas below.**

What was the dramatic event?	What was happening just before this dramatic event?	How did you feel after the dramatic event?

2. **Consider how you can structure your story opening to make it as engaging and interesting as possible.**

   a) Tick which tense you will use to describe the events.
      ☐ the present tense, describing events as they happen
      ☐ the past tense, describing events as though they have just happened
      ☐ the past tense, describing the events as though they happened a long time ago

   b) Tick the order in which you will describe the events.
      ☐ chronological order
      ☐ non-chronological order

   c) When you have decided on an order, number the ideas in your plan to show how you will sequence them in your story opening.

   d) What will you focus on?
      ☐ the events you are describing
      ☐ the narrator's thoughts and feelings about these events

   e) What questions do you want your reader to ask as they read your story opening? Give at least two examples.

   ----

3. **Write your story opening on a separate piece of paper.**

ENGLISH
— Grades 3–5 —

12 ANSWERS

STARTER ACTIVITY: EFFECTIVE OPENINGS
1. Student's own answers
2. Student's own answers

MAIN ACTIVITY: TRACKING STRUCTURE
1. and 2. Examples:
Bunny is dead. 4
There was a huge manhunt for him. 9
The narrator and his friends murdered Bunny. 3
They tried to make it look like an accident. 5
The body was found when the snow melted. 11
The narrator witnessed the manhunt. 10
Even years later, the narrator cannot forget the murder. 12
Bunny was surprised to find his friends in the mountains. 1
Henry said they were looking for ferns. 2
After the murder, they checked the area to make sure they had everything. 6
They drove away from the murder scene. 7
The narrator had a long difficult night – and then more difficult days and nights. 8
The narrator cannot forget the murder. 13
3. Examples: non-chronological order; repetition; details of the murder emerging throughout the extract; the underdeveloped dialogue very much out of context. All suggest the narrator is confused and upset.

MAIN ACTIVITY: BEGINNINGS
1. The narrator constantly returns to his thoughts and feelings throughout the opening; the non-chronological, recursive structure reflects his emotional state.
2. Examples: it suggests that the impact of the murder on the narrator will be the focus of the novel; it allows the reader to sympathise with the narrator to an extent; it suggests the dramatic, shocking nature of the murder itself.
3. Examples: why did the narrator and his friends murder Bunny? What were the consequences of the murder, e.g. arrest and imprisonment, significant impact on the narrator and his relationship with his friends, etc.?

HOMEWORK ACTIVITY: WRITE YOUR OWN
1., 2. and 3. Student's own answers. Planning and story opening should show clear evidence of key decisions: tense/viewpoint, sequencing, focus, questions.

GLOSSARY

Chronological
The time order in which events happened

AQA ENGLISH — Grades 3-5

13 READING: NARRATIVE FOCUS

LEARNING OBJECTIVES
- To be able to identify features and elements of structure
- To be able to explore the impact of whole text structure

SPECIFICATION LINKS
- 3.1.1 critical reading and comprehension

STARTER ACTIVITY
- **Summarise; 5 minutes; page 96**
  Ask the student to complete the activity, ideally without referring to Source D: *The Secret History* (page 20). When completed, give the student time to review the source and refine their response if necessary.

MAIN ACTIVITIES
- **Narrative focus; 20 minutes; page 97**
  Explain to the student that you began to explore narrative focus in lesson 12 and you are now going to explore it more fully, again using Source D: *The Secret History*.
- **Changing focus; 20 minutes; page 98**
  Explain that the narrator's thoughts and feelings are more explicitly explained at some points than at others, e.g. before the murder. Point out that some careful reading will be needed.
  Encourage the student to think about the openings of stories and films they know well and to identify any that focus on a significant event or a change in someone's life.

PLENARY ACTIVITY
- **Review; 5 minutes**
  Encourage the student to review, evaluate and summarise what they have learned about whole text structure and the impact it can have.

HOMEWORK ACTIVITY
- **Planning a response; 30 minutes; page 99**
  Explain that in the next lesson you will focus on responding to exam-style questions about whole text structure.

SUPPORT IDEA
- **Changing focus** Limit the range of the activity, focusing on only the more explicitly related 'immediately after' and 'a long time after'.

EXTENSION IDEA
- **Changing focus** Encourage the student to explore what is implied by the narrator's changing thoughts and feelings, e.g. what it suggests about the narrator, his decision to commit murder etc.

PROGRESS AND OBSERVATIONS

ENGLISH
— Grades 3-5 —

STARTER ACTIVITY: SUMMARISE **TIMING: 5 MINS**

LEARNING OBJECTIVES
- To be able to identify features and elements of structure

EQUIPMENT
none

1. Without looking at the text, note down the key ideas, events and information you read about in Source D: *The Secret History*.

....

....

....

....

....

....

....

....

2. Write one sentence, summarising the key ideas, events and information in Source D.

....

....

....

....

AQA ENGLISH — Grades 3-5

Main activity: Narrative focus

Timing: 20 mins

Learning objectives
- To be able to identify features and elements of structure

Equipment
- Source D: *The Secret History*

In the opening of a novel, the narrative (or story) often focuses on one or more of these features:
- setting the scene or outlining the situation
- introducing characters and their relationships with each other
- describing a significant event or decision.

1. Read Source D: *The Secret History*. Which of the features above does the writer focus on? Tick them.

2. In the table below, write one thing you found out from the extract about each narrative focus that you ticked above.

The scene or situation	Characters and their relationships	A significant event or decision

3. Identify a short, relevant quotation from the source that supports each of your ideas in the table above. Add them to the table.

ENGLISH
— Grades 3-5 —

MAIN ACTIVITY: CHANGING FOCUS   **TIMING: 20 MINS**

LEARNING OBJECTIVES

- To be able to explore the impact of whole text structure

EQUIPMENT

- Source D: *The Secret History*

In the opening of a novel, a character or narrator will often respond to a significant event or change in their life. In the opening of *The Secret History*, the narrator focuses on a murder he has committed. Think about how the writer suggests this event has changed the narrator's life.

1. **Choose at least one short, relevant quotation that shows the narrator's thoughts and feelings:**

   a) before the murder

   ----

   b) during the murder

   ----

   c) immediately after the murder

   ----

   d) long after the murder

   ----

2. **How do the narrator's thoughts and feelings change? Explain your ideas.**

AQA ENGLISH — Grades 3–5

HOMEWORK ACTIVITY: PLANNING A RESPONSE

TIMING: 30 MINS

LEARNING OBJECTIVES
- To be able to explore the impact of whole text structure

EQUIPMENT
- Source D: *The Secret History*

You are going to plan your response to this Paper 1, Section A exam-style question.

> You now need to think about the **whole** of Source D: *The Secret History*.
>
> This text is from the opening of a novel.
>
> How has the writer structured the text to interest you as a reader?
>
> You could write about:
>
> - what the writer focuses your attention on at the beginning
> - how and why the writer changes this focus as the extract develops
> - any other structural features that interest you.
>
> **[8 marks]**

1. **Use the space below to write some ideas.**
   You could think about:
   - the writer's use of non-chronological structure
   - how the writer engages the reader's attention
   - questions that the reader is prompted to ask
   - the narrative focus in the extract
   - how the narrator's thoughts and feelings change over time.

   ----

2. On a separate piece of paper, write down quotations and comments to support each of your ideas.

ENGLISH
— Grades 3-5 —

13 ANSWERS

STARTER ACTIVITY: SUMMARISE

1. Student's own answer
2. Example: The opening describes a murder committed by the narrator, the manhunt that followed and the narrator's increasingly troubled thoughts and feelings.

MAIN ACTIVITY: NARRATIVE FOCUS

1. All options are featured.
2. The scene: a murder is committed in the mountains; the body is not found for some time because of heavy snowfall.
Characters: the narrator is clearly troubled by the murder he has committed.
A significant event: murder.
3. Examples: 'body at the bottom of the ravine… the snow above it was packed down like ice'; 'a picture that will never leave me'; 'a clean break in the neck'.

MAIN ACTIVITY: CHANGING FOCUS

1. Examples:
a) before the murder: The fact that the narrator was prepared to commit murder suggests he had not considered the impact it would have on him: 'It is difficult to believe that Henry's modest plan could have worked so well despite these unforeseen events.'
b) during the murder: The careful planning/staging suggests cold-blooded calmness: 'a clean break in the neck, and the muddy skidmarks of dug-in heels.'
c) immediately after the murder: The excited drive home suggests a failure to recognise what they have done: 'leaning over the seats and talking like children.'
d) long after the murder: 'walking through it all was one thing; walking away, unfortunately, has proved to be quite another … a picture that will never leave me.'
2. Example: As the narrator himself says, 'Bunny had been dead for several weeks before we came to understand the gravity of our situation.'

HOMEWORK ACTIVITY: PLANNING A RESPONSE

1. and 2.

Marks	Criteria
7–8 marks	• Clear and detailed analysis of the effect of the writer's use of structural features • A carefully selected range of relevant, focused examples • A range of subject terminology to achieve clarity and precision
5–6 marks	• Clear comments on the effect of the writer's use of structural features • A range of relevant, focused examples • A range of subject terminology to achieve clarity
3–4 marks	• Some comments on the effect of the writer's use of structural features • Relevant and focused examples • Largely accurate use of subject terminology
1–2 marks	• Straightforward comments on the effect of the writer's use of structural features • Largely relevant examples • Some use of subject terminology, with inconsistent accuracy
No marks	• No creditable response

AQA ENGLISH — Grades 3–5

14 READING: ANALYSING WHOLE TEXT STRUCTURE

LEARNING OBJECTIVES

- To be able to identify features and elements of structure
- To be able to explore the impact of whole text structure
- To be able to write a critical response analysing text structure

SPECIFICATION LINKS

- 3.1.1 critical reading and comprehension

STARTER ACTIVITY

- **First thoughts; 5 minutes; page 102**
  Read through Source E: *The Essex Serpent* (page 21) and discuss the questions with the student before they write their response to question 3.

MAIN ACTIVITIES

- **Gathering ideas; 20 minutes; page 103**
  Ask the student to read the remainder of Source E: *The Essex Serpent* (page 21) and complete the questions. Explain that this kind of analysis of whole text structure is likely to apply to most questions that they will have to answer in their exam.
  Emphasise that responses should focus on what the writer has done and its impact on the reader, and that there is no advantage in commenting on what the writer has not done.
- **Developing ideas; 20 minutes; page 104**
  Suggest to the student that they avoid the empty phrase *it makes the reader want to read on*, and focus on more specific observations instead, e.g. how the writer *prompts the reader to question the text…*, *engages the reader…*, *encourages the reader to think about the situation or characters…*, etc.

PLENARY ACTIVITY

- **Selecting and sequencing; 5 minutes**
  Ask the student to select three or four ideas from the previous activity to include in their homework. Discuss which ideas will allow them to comment most fully and effectively on the impact of the writer's choices on the reader.

HOMEWORK ACTIVITY

- **Write a response; 30 minutes; page 105**
  Explain to the student that there is less time in the exam for this kind of question, but that they will become quicker with practice.

SUPPORT IDEAS

- **Gathering ideas** The student may find it helpful to annotate the text, highlighting key features and noting their response to them.
- **Developing ideas** You may need to model the use of textual reference to avoid unnecessary use of long quotations.

EXTENSION IDEA

- **Developing ideas** Encourage the student to be as specific as possible when describing how the text's structural features may affect the reader, e.g. the rising tension and concern for 'the young man' as he repeatedly threatens to 'go for a dip'.

PROGRESS AND OBSERVATIONS

ENGLISH
— Grades 3-5 —

AQA

| STARTER ACTIVITY: FIRST THOUGHTS | TIMING: 5 MINS |

LEARNING OBJECTIVES
- To be able to identify features and elements of structure
- To be able to explore the impact of whole text structure

EQUIPMENT
- Source E: *The Essex Serpent*

Read the paragraph opener of Source E: *The Essex Serpent*, a novel by Sarah Perry.

> A young man walks down by the banks of the Blackwater under the full cold moon. He's been drinking the old year down to the dregs, until his eyes grew sore and his stomach turned, and he was tired of the bright lights and bustle. 'I'll just go down to the water,' he said, and kissed the nearest cheek: 'I'll be back before the chimes.' Now he looks east to the turning tide, out to the estuary slow and dark, and the white gulls gleaming on the waves.

Read the paragraph again, thinking about the features of whole text structure you have been exploring. You should consider the following points:

a) The ingredients the writer introduces at the start of the novel, such as:
   - the scene
   - the characters and their relationships
   - a significant event.

b) The narrative focus of this paragraph

c) The questions the reader is prompted to ask.

1. How does the writer engage the reader's interest in this opening paragraph? Write your ideas below.

AQA ENGLISH
— Grades 3-5 —

MAIN ACTIVITY: GATHERING IDEAS	TIMING: 20 MINS

LEARNING OBJECTIVES	EQUIPMENT
• To be able to identify features and elements of structure	• Source E: *The Essex Serpent*

Read Source E: *The Essex Serpent*, thinking about the structural features the writer has used.

1. **Are the events in the source recounted in chronological order? Use the table to note down what past events are mentioned, and what events happen in the extract.**

What has happened in the past	What happens in the extract

2. **Writers sometimes use contrast to shock and surprise the reader, or to emphasise the difference between two characters, settings or events. Does the writer use contrast in Source E: *The Essex Serpent*? If so, how? Explain your ideas.**

....

....

....

3. **Think about the ending of the extract and compare it to the beginning. How has the mood changed? Write your ideas below.**

....

....

....

ENGLISH
Grades 3-5

AQA

| MAIN ACTIVITY: DEVELOPING IDEAS | TIMING: 20 MINS |

LEARNING OBJECTIVES
- To be able to explore the impact of whole text structure

EQUIPMENT
- Source E: *The Essex Serpent*

You are going to use all the ideas you have gathered in the lesson so far about Source E: *The Essex Serpent* to plan a response to the Paper 1, Section A exam-style question below.

> You now need to think about the **whole** of Source E: *The Essex Serpent*.
>
> This text is from the opening of a novel.
>
> How has the writer structured the text to interest you as a reader?
>
> You could write about:
>
> - what the writer focuses your attention on at the beginning
> - how and why the writer changes this focus as the extract develops
> - any other structural features that interest you.
>
> **[8 marks]**

1. **Note all your ideas.**
   You should think about:
   - ingredients: setting the scene, introducing characters and their relationships, describing events
   - chronological or non-chronological structure
   - narrative focus
   - changes in focus
   - questions the reader might want to ask.

   ---

2. **For each idea you have noted, add some evidence from the text.**
   It could be:
   - a short, relevant quotation
   - a short summary of an event
   - a description of a structural feature.

3. **Think about the impact that these structural features have on the reader. For each idea you have noted, add your thoughts on how it may affect the reader.**

ENGLISH
— Grades 3-5 —

HOMEWORK ACTIVITY: WRITE A RESPONSE **TIMING: 30 MINS**

LEARNING OBJECTIVES
- To be able to write a critical response analysing text structure

EQUIPMENT
- Source E: *The Essex Serpent*

Look at this Paper 1, Section A exam-style question.

> You now need to think about the **whole** of Source E: *The Essex Serpent*.
>
> This text is from the opening of a novel.
>
> How has the writer structured the text to interest you as a reader?
>
> You could write about:
>
> - what the writer focuses your attention on at the beginning
> - how and why the writer changes this focus as the extract develops
> - any other structural features that interest you.
>
> [8 marks]

1. **Write a response to this question on a separate piece of paper. Make sure you write three to four paragraphs.**

2. **When you have written your response, check you have achieved all of the success criteria below.**

   a) Tick all the criteria you feel you have achieved.

   - ☐ I have focused on two structural features.
   - ☐ I have commented on the effect of each feature.
   - ☐ I have commented on the impact of each feature.
   - ☐ I have written in paragraphs.
   - ☐ I have carefully checked for accurate spelling and punctuation, and clear written expression.

   b) Look at any of the criteria you feel you have not achieved. Add to and improve your response so that you can tick all of them.

14 ANSWERS

STARTER ACTIVITY: FIRST THOUGHTS

1. Example: The opening paragraph focuses on the young man and the mysterious, dark water. What will he see, hear or experience?

MAIN ACTIVITY: GATHERING IDEAS

1. What has happened in the past: the narrator has been at a party; he has swum in the Blackwater.
What happens in the extract: he goes outside to the water; he notices something strange in the water and is afraid; he goes for a swim anyway.
2. Example: The writer contrasts the 'bright lights and bustle' of the party with the calm, quiet of the night, and then contrasts that calm with the disturbing hints of the creature in the water.
3. Example: The mood changes from the excitement of the party, to the calm outside, to a feeling of threat and danger.

MAIN ACTIVITY: DEVELOPING IDEAS

1. Examples: the narrative focus is on the young man and his experience at the water's edge; non-chronological references to the party are used to create contrast; the writer uses the description of the still Blackwater and the 'full cold moon' to establish a disarming mood that suddenly changes with the appearance of the creature in the water; the contrast of the calm night and the disturbing appearance of the creature prompts the reader to question what will happen next.
2. Student's own answer
3. Student's own answer

HOMEWORK ACTIVITY: WRITE A RESPONSE

1.

AO2
• Explain, comment on and analyse how writers use language and structure to achieve effects and influence readers, using relevant subject terminology to support their views

This question focuses on structure only.

Level	Skills descriptors
Level 4 7–8 marks	• Clear and detailed analysis of the effect of the writer's use of structural features • A carefully selected range of relevant, focused examples • A range of subject terminology to achieve clarity and precision
Level 3 5–6 marks	• Clear comments on the effect of the writer's use of structural features • A range of relevant, focused examples • A range of subject terminology to achieve clarity
Level 2 3–4 marks	• Some comments on the effect of the writer's use of structural features • Relevant and focused examples • Largely accurate use of subject terminology
Level 1 1–2 marks	• Straightforward comments on the effect of the writer's use of structural features • Largely relevant examples • Some use of subject terminology, with inconsistent accuracy
Level 0 No marks	• No comment on structural features

2. Ensure the student has achieved all, or the majority of, the success criteria.

ENGLISH
— Grades 3–5 —

15 READING: BEGINNING AN EVALUATION

LEARNING OBJECTIVES
- To be able to identify relevant evidence to support a critical judgement
- To be able to develop critical engagement with, and evaluation of, a text

SPECIFICATION LINKS
- 3.1.1 evaluation of a writer's choice of vocabulary, form, grammatical and structural features

STARTER ACTIVITY
- **Considering opinions; 5 minutes; page 108**
  Explain to the student that in their exam they will be presented with an opinion on the text and asked to respond to it. Give them time to remind themselves of Source D: *The Secret History* (page 20), then read and discuss the statements in question 1. All activity sheets should be available during the lesson.

MAIN ACTIVITIES
- **Exploring opinions 1; 20 minutes; page 109**
  Suggest that the student chooses the opinion that they most strongly agree with and/or the opinion that they are most able to justify with evidence from the text. Explain the process of evaluating a text: firstly identifying the parts of the text that are relevant to the opinion, and secondly identifying relevant evidence from those parts.
- **Exploring opinions 2; 20 minutes; page 110**
  Explain to the student that the aim of an evaluation question in the exam is to assess them synoptically: simultaneously assessing their skills of inference, analysis and evaluation. Ask the student to complete the questions, bearing in mind the opinion that they have chosen to explore.

PLENARY ACTIVITY
- **Review; 5 minutes**
  Ask the student to summarise and evaluate their understanding of how to begin evaluating a text.

HOMEWORK ACTIVITY
- **Exploring opinions 3; 30 minutes; page 111**
  Emphasise to the student that evaluating effectiveness requires more than a simple response of *yes, it's effective* or *no, it's not effective*. The judgement must be supported with an explanation of how and why.

SUPPORT IDEA
- **Exploring opinions 1** Explain that looking for evidence is a process of elimination and encourage the student to hone in on the source of an effect, e.g. in which paragraph did they get that impression? In which sentence in the paragraph did they get that impression?

EXTENSION IDEA
- **Considering opinions** Ask the student to suggest two similar statements of opinion in response to the extract.

PROGRESS AND OBSERVATIONS

ENGLISH
Grades 3–5

AQA

| STARTER ACTIVITY: CONSIDERING OPINIONS | TIMING: 5 MINS |

LEARNING OBJECTIVES
- To be able to develop critical engagement with, and evaluation of, a text

EQUIPMENT
- Source D: *The Secret History*

Read Source D: *The Secret History*.

1. **Circle a number on each scale to show how strongly you agree or disagree with each statement, based on the information in the source.**

I think the narrator and his friends had good reason to murder Bunny.

> 0   1   2   3   4   5   6   7   8   9   10
> Strongly disagree   Strongly agree

I get a very strong impression of the impact that Bunny's murder had on the narrator.

> 0   1   2   3   4   5   6   7   8   9   10
> Strongly disagree   Strongly agree

I feel that the narrator did not expect the consequences that Bunny's murder would have.

> 0   1   2   3   4   5   6   7   8   9   10
> Strongly disagree   Strongly agree

I feel sorry for the narrator.

> 0   1   2   3   4   5   6   7   8   9   10
> Strongly disagree   Strongly agree

AQA ENGLISH — Grades 3–5

Main activity: Exploring opinions 1

Timing: 20 mins

Learning objectives
- To be able to identify relevant evidence to support a critical judgement

Equipment
- Source D: *The Secret History*

1. Choose the statement from the Starter activity that you most strongly agree with and write it below.

2. Read through Source D: *The Secret History* and underline up to four parts of the text that led you to agree strongly with the statement you chose for question 1.

3. Choose three or four short, relevant quotations to support your agreement with the statement you have chosen. Write the quotations below and number them.

ENGLISH
Grades 3-5

AQA

MAIN ACTIVITY: EXPLORING OPINIONS 2　　　　　**TIMING: 20 MINS**

LEARNING OBJECTIVES
- To be able to develop critical engagement with, and evaluation of, a text

EQUIPMENT
- Source D: *The Secret History*

The evaluation task in your exam requires you to:
- explore what the writer implies about the characters, setting and/or events described in the source
- describe the impression this creates in the reader
- analyse how the writer has created that impression
- evaluate how effectively the writer has created that impression.

Choose the quotation from the previous activity that most strongly supports the opinion you agreed with.

1. **What is the writer implying in this quotation? Explain your ideas.**

   ....
   ....
   ....
   ....

2. **Think about the writer's choices in the quotation.**
   a) Circle any words or phrases that contribute to the opinion you are exploring.
   b) What do the words or phrases you have circled suggest? Write a sentence or two explaining your ideas.

   ....
   ....
   ....
   ....

3. **How effective are the writer's choices in this quotation? Do they strongly contribute to the opinion you are focusing on? Why? Explain your ideas.**

   ....
   ....
   ....
   ....

AQA ENGLISH — Grades 3-5

HOMEWORK ACTIVITY: EXPLORING OPINIONS 3

TIMING: 30 MINS

LEARNING OBJECTIVES
- To be able to develop critical engagement with, and evaluation of, a text

EQUIPMENT
- Source D: *The Secret History*

In this lesson, you identified up to four quotations that strongly supported an opinion that you agreed with. You then explored how, and how effectively, the writer had created that impression in one of the quotations you identified. You are now going to explore two more of the quotations you identified.

1. **Add your two chosen quotations to column 1 of the table below, and then fill in the other columns.**

Quotation	What does it imply?	What do the words and phrases suggest?	How effectively does it create an impression?

15 ANSWERS

STARTER ACTIVITY: CONSIDERING OPINIONS

1. Student's own answers. Note that there is no evidence to support the statement 'I think the narrator and his friends had good reason to murder Bunny'.

MAIN ACTIVITY: EXPLORING OPINIONS 1

1. and 2. Student's own answers

3. Ensure quotations are an appropriate length and relevant. Examples:

I get a very strong impression of the impact that Bunny's murder had on the narrator: 'even more difficult to believe I could have walked through it… walking away, unfortunately, has proved to be quite another… in reality I have been there all the time… I remember only too well the long terrible night that lay ahead and the long terrible days and nights that followed'.

I feel that the narrator did not expect the consequences that Bunny's murder would have: 'Bunny had been dead for several weeks before we came to understand the *gravity* of our situation… It is difficult to believe that Henry's modest plan could have worked so well… It is difficult to believe that such an uproar took place over an act for which I was partially responsible… leaning over the seats and talking like children'.

I feel sorry for the narrator: 'Walking away, unfortunately, has proved to be quite another… I remember only too well the long terrible night that lay ahead and the long terrible days and nights that followed… a picture that will never leave me'.

MAIN ACTIVITY: EXPLORING OPINIONS 2

1., 2. and 3. Student's own answers. Ensure responses are valid and as fully developed as possible.

HOMEWORK ACTIVITY: EXPLORING OPINIONS 3

1. Student's own answer. Ensure responses are valid and as fully developed as possible.

AQA ENGLISH — Grades 3–5

16 READING: WRITING AN EVALUATIVE RESPONSE

LEARNING OBJECTIVES
- To be able to develop critical engagement with, and evaluation of, a text
- To be able to structure an effective evaluation

SPECIFICATION LINKS
- 3.1.1 evaluation of a writer's choice of vocabulary, form, grammatical and structural features

STARTER ACTIVITY
- **Making a judgement; 5 minutes; page 114**
  Give the student time to recap Source D: *The Secret History* (page 20). Discuss the student's reasons for their response to question 1. Emphasise that all responses to the statement in the exam question are acceptable as long as they are justified and relevant.

MAIN ACTIVITIES
- **Gathering your ideas; 20 minutes; page 115**
  Focus on the rubric of the exam-style question: it asks the student to focus on the second half of the text only. Explain that the student will already have explored the whole text structure of the source in an earlier question in the exam – and although they will also have already explored the writer's use of language in an earlier question, this will have been focused on the first half of the text.
- **Crafting your response; 20 minutes; page 116**
  Discuss the contribution that each sentence in the model paragraph contributes (or otherwise) to the evaluation. If time allows, ask the student to write their own paragraph using the notes they compiled in 'Gathering your ideas'.

PLENARY ACTIVITY
- **Review; 5 minutes**
  Ask the student to summarise and evaluate their understanding of how to craft an evaluative response.

HOMEWORK ACTIVITY
- **Write a response; 30 minutes; page 117**
  Remind the student to refer to their work from the *Gathering your ideas* and *Crafting your response* activity sheets.

SUPPORT IDEA
- **Write a response** Ask the student to write just one paragraph and focus on carefully crafting it to ensure each of the criteria is achieved.

EXTENSION IDEA
- **Write a response** Encourage the student to consider any connections between, or the cumulative impact of, the ideas and evidence gathered.

PROGRESS AND OBSERVATIONS

ENGLISH
— Grades 3-5 —

STARTER ACTIVITY: MAKING A JUDGEMENT

TIMING: 5 MINS

LEARNING OBJECTIVES

- To be able to develop critical engagement with, and evaluation of, a text

EQUIPMENT

- Source D: *The Secret History*

You are going to develop your response to this Paper 1, Section A exam-style question.

> Focus this part of your answer on the second half of Source D: *The Secret History*, **from line 16 to the end.**
>
> A student, having read this section of the text, said: 'The writer clearly shows the narrator's thoughts and feelings about the murder of Bunny. It helps you understand how it has affected his whole life.'
>
> To what extent do you agree?
>
> - Write about your own impressions of the narrator's thoughts and feelings.
> - Evaluate how the writer has created these thoughts and feelings.
> - Support your opinions with quotations from the text.
>
> **[20 marks]**

1. Circle a number on the scale below to show how strongly you agree or disagree with this student's judgement.

```
0    1    2    3    4    5    6    7    8    9    10
Strongly                                          Strongly
disagree                                          agree
```

AQA ENGLISH — Grades 3-5

| **Main activity: Gathering your ideas** | **Timing: 20 mins** |

Learning objectives
- To be able to develop critical engagement with, and evaluation of, a text

Equipment
- Source D: *The Secret History*

When you have decided to what extent you agree or disagree with the student's statement in the exam question, you need to start gathering evidence from the source to support your judgement. Remember, you are only looking at the second half of the source.

1. **Which elements of the text's structure contribute to your judgement?**

   ....

   ....

   ....

2. **What other evidence is there to support your judgement?**

   a) Underline any words, phrases or sentences that you could quote or refer to in your response. You will need at least three quotations, ideally more. Label them A, B, C, etc.

   b) Look again at the quotations you have identified. Tick a few that:
      - support your judgement most strongly
      - will allow you to comment on the writer's use of words, phrases, language features and/or sentence forms and how these contribute to your judgement.

   c) Annotate your quotations, noting what the writer is implying about the narrator's thoughts and feelings.

   d) Look again at your chosen quotations. Circle any key words or phrases that make a significant contribution to your judgement.

   e) Add to your annotations, noting how the writer's choice of words, phrases, language features and/or sentence forms contribute to your judgement.

3. **Answer the questions below to review your chosen quotations and annotations.**

   a) Have you identified something that is implied in each quotation that makes a significant contribution to your response?

      ☐ yes ☐ no

   b) Have you identified a significant language feature in each quotation that you can analyse in your response?

      ☐ yes ☐ no

If you have ticked 'yes' for both questions, you are ready to start writing your evaluation. If you have ticked 'no' for either question, you need to review your chosen quotations and/or annotations.

ENGLISH
Grades 3-5

MAIN ACTIVITY: CRAFTING YOUR RESPONSE   **TIMING: 20 MINS**

LEARNING OBJECTIVES

- To be able to structure an effective evaluation

EQUIPMENT

- Source D: *The Secret History*

An effective response to an evaluation question needs to:
  a) evaluate the effect of the text on the reader
  b) show understanding of the writer's use of structure, sentence forms, words, phrases and language features
  c) support its argument with evidence from the text
  d) offer a clear and relevant response to the statement in the question.

> Focus this part of your answer on the second half of Source D: *The Secret History*, **from line 16 to the end.**
>
> A student, having read this section of the text, said: 'The writer clearly shows the narrator's thoughts and feelings about the murder of Bunny. It helps you understand how it has affected his whole life.'
>
> To what extent do you agree?
>
> - Write about your own impressions of the narrator's thoughts and feelings.
> - Evaluate how the writer has created these thoughts and feelings.
> - Support your opinions with quotations from the text.
>
> **[20 marks]**

1. **Label these sentences a), b), c) or d) to show which of the above criteria they achieve.**
2. **Tick the sentences you would include in a paragraph responding to the Paper 1, Section A exam-style question.**
3. **Number your chosen sentences in the order you would sequence them.**

A. The writer clearly shows the narrator's thoughts and feelings, but they are not all about how bad he feels about murdering his friend.

B. Some of the narrator's thoughts suggest he does not really understand what he did.

C. For example, 'It is difficult to believe that such an uproar took place over an act for which I was partially responsible'.

D. The word 'partially' implies that he does not fully accept responsibility for what he did.

E. This is the second time in the source that the writer has begun a paragraph with the phrase 'It is difficult to believe' which suggests that the narrator has still not come to terms with the murder and its consequences.

F. It shows that although he is still haunted by the memories of the murder and is obviously still deeply affected by it, he is not really sorry for what he did.

G. I don't really know whether I'm meant to feel sorry for him and forgive him or not.

AQA ENGLISH — Grades 3–5

HOMEWORK ACTIVITY: WRITE A RESPONSE | **TIMING: 30 MINS**

LEARNING OBJECTIVES
- To be able to structure an effective evaluation

EQUIPMENT
- Source D: *The Secret History*

Look again at the Paper 1, Section A exam-style question from the previous activity.

> Focus this part of your answer on the second half of Source D: *The Secret History*, **from line 16 to the end.**
>
> A student, having read this section of the text, said: 'The writer clearly shows the narrator's thoughts and feelings about the murder of Bunny. It helps you understand how it has affected his whole life.'
>
> To what extent do you agree?
>
> - Write about your own impressions of the narrator's thoughts and feelings.
> - Evaluate how the writer has created these thoughts and feelings.
> - Support your opinions with quotations from the text.
>
> [20 marks]

1. Write a response to this question on a separate piece of paper. Make sure you write three to four paragraphs.

2. When you have written your response, check you have achieved all of the success criteria below.

   a) Tick all the criteria you feel you have achieved.

      - ☐ I have evaluated the effect on the reader.
      - ☐ I have showed understanding of the writer's use of structure, sentence forms, words, phrases and language features.
      - ☐ I have supported evaluation with evidence from the text.
      - ☐ I have given a clear and relevant response to the statement in the question.
      - ☐ I have written in paragraphs.
      - ☐ I have carefully checked for accurate spelling and punctuation, and clear written expression.

   b) Look at any of the criteria you feel you have not achieved. Add to and improve your response so that you can tick all of them.

16 Answers

STARTER ACTIVITY: MAKING A JUDGEMENT
1. All responses are acceptable if they can be justified with evidence.

MAIN ACTIVITY: GATHERING YOUR IDEAS
1. Example: The recursive, non-chronological structure reflects the impact of the murder on the narrator, even after several years have passed.
2. Examples: 'partially responsible' – suggests denial/a failure to accept full responsibility; 'walking away, unfortunately, has proved to be quite another' – 'unfortunately' implies the desire to forget; 'one last look at the body' – 'the body' suggests a cold dehumanisation of the victim; 'leaning over the seats and talking like children' – implies that they did not face the reality of the murder at the time; 'a picture that will never leave me' – this text positioned at the end of the paragraph emphasises that the murder still haunts the narrator.
3. Student's own answers. If 'No', review the student's responses with them.

MAIN ACTIVITY: CRAFTING YOUR RESPONSE
1. A: d; B: a; C: c; D: b; E: b; F: a; G: this is not fully relevant to the task, or appropriate to an examination response.
2. Student's own answer
3. Student's own answer

HOMEWORK ACTIVITY: WRITE A RESPONSE
1.

Marks	Criteria
16–20 marks	• Clear and detailed analysis of the writer's choices • Clear and full evaluation of the effect on the reader • A carefully selected range of relevant, focused textual evidence • A developed and considered critical response to the statement
11–15 marks	• Clear comments on the writer's choices • Clear evaluation of the effect on the reader • A range of relevant, focused textual evidence • A relevant, focused response to the statement
6–10 marks	• Some comments on the writer's choices • Some evaluation of their effect on the reader • Relevant and focused textual evidence • A more developed response to the statement
1–5 marks	• Straightforward comments on the writer's choices • Straightforward evaluation of their effect on the reader • Largely relevant textual evidence • A straightforward response to the statement
No marks	• No creditable response

2. Ensure the student has achieved all, or the majority of, the success criteria.

ENGLISH
Grades 3-5

17 Reading: Developing critical evaluation

LEARNING OBJECTIVES	SPECIFICATION LINKS
• To be able to develop critical engagement with, and evaluation of, a text	• 3.1.1 evaluation of a writer's choice of vocabulary, form, grammatical and structural features

Starter activity

- **What is evaluation?; 5 minutes; page 120**
  Discuss which elements of the sentences analyse how, why and how effectively the writer has achieved their intention.

Main activities

- **Responding to the question; 20 minutes; page 121**
  Emphasise that the exam-style question asks the student to focus on the second half of the text only. Point out that statements in evaluation questions are often structured as two distinct sentences.
- **Evaluate your evaluation; 20 minutes; page 122**
  Complete the annotation activity with the student, negotiating and discussing to what extent their paragraph achieves the criteria.

Plenary activity

- **Review; 5 minutes**
  Ask the student to summarise and evaluate their understanding of how to craft an evaluative response.

Homework activity

- **Complete your response; 30 minutes; page 123**
  Remind the student to use their work from the lesson to help them craft the most effective evaluation. Remind them that, although the lesson has focused on evaluating the writer's use of language, their response can also include evaluation of the writer's structural choices.

Support ideas

- **What is evaluation?** Ask the student to rank the statements in order of effectiveness. Discuss why some are more effective than others before going on to explore the features of the more successful statements.
- **Evaluate your evaluation** Use annotated examples from the Starter activity to model effective analysis and evaluation.

Extension idea

- **Review** Ask the student to write their own version of the Starter activity, featuring statements that are ineffective, analyse but do not evaluate, and evaluate the source effectively.

Progress and observations

ENGLISH
— Grades 3–5 —

AQA

STARTER ACTIVITY: WHAT IS EVALUATION?

TIMING: 5 MINS

LEARNING OBJECTIVES

- To be able to develop critical engagement with, and evaluation of, a text

EQUIPMENT

none

Here is a definition of what 'evaluating' a text means.

> **Evaluating a text**: to explore and analyse how, why, and how successfully the writer has achieved their intention.

1. Which of the statements below would you say are effectively evaluating a text? Tick any that apply.

A. I think it's boring.

B. It's really good because I want to read on and find out what happens.

C. The writer emphasises how desperate the man is by repeating the word 'please' in a series of very short sentences. It immediately gives you a really strong impression of how he feels about the situation he is in.

D. The word 'crumbling' suggests an extremely old building that has been left to fall down, implying that the people who live there do not have any pride in their home.

E. The writer's use of verbs in the opening paragraph is particularly effective because it suggests how quickly the woman is running without revealing why, creating a sense of tension and mystery.

F. The old man is not a very appealing character because he talks to the child using negative language such as 'brat' and 'nuisance'.

AQA ENGLISH — Grades 3-5

Main activity: Responding to the question

Timing: 20 mins

Learning objectives
- To be able to develop critical engagement with, and evaluation of, a text

Equipment
- Source E: *The Essex Serpent*

In this lesson you are going to respond to a Paper 1, Section A exam-style question about the second half of Source E: *The Essex Serpent*, from line 16 to the end. The question features this statement:

> A student, having read this section of the text said: 'The writer gives only a limited but disturbing description of what the young man sees in the water. You know something dramatic is going to happen.'

1. **Identify and write down four relevant quotations from the source.**
   You should look for:
   - two quotations that you can use to support the first sentence of the statement (Evidence A)
   - two quotations that you can use to support the second sentence of the statement (Evidence B).

Evidence A	Evidence B

2. **Now think about the writer's use of language and sentence forms in your chosen quotations.**
   Annotate each quotation, noting:
   - what it implies
   - how the writer's choice of words, phrases, language features and/or sentence forms contribute to your judgement
   - why the writer has done this.

3. **How effectively will your four quotations support your response to the statement? Number them from 1 (the most effective) to 4 (the least effective).**

4. **Look again at the most and least effective quotations. Explain why you ranked these two quotations in that order.**

ENGLISH
Grades 3-5
AQA

MAIN ACTIVITY: EVALUATE YOUR EVALUATION

TIMING: 20 MINS

LEARNING OBJECTIVES
- To be able to develop critical engagement with, and evaluation of, a text

EQUIPMENT
- Source E: *The Essex Serpent*

Look at this Paper 1, Section A exam-style question.

> Focus this part of your answer on the second half of Source E: *The Essex Serpent*, **from line 17 to the end.**
>
> A student, having read this section of the text said: 'The writer gives only a limited but disturbing description of what the young man sees in the water. You know something dramatic is going to happen.'
>
> To what extent do you agree?
>
> In your response, you could:
> - write about your own impressions of what the young man sees in the water
> - evaluate how the writer has created these impressions
> - support your opinions with quotations from the text.
>
> **[20 marks]**

1. **On a separate piece of paper, write the first paragraph of your response to the exam-style question above. Use the reminders below to help you.**

   A. Write a clear and relevant response to the statement in the question.

   B. Support your answer with evidence from the text.

   C. Evaluate the effect on the reader.

   D. Include comments on what the writer is implying.

   E. Include comments on how the writer has used structure, sentence forms, words, phrases and/or language features.

   F. Explain why the writer has done this – the impact on the reader.

2. **Look at the reminders above. Have you achieved all of them in your response? Label your response to show where you have achieved each statement.**

ENGLISH
— Grades 3-5 —

| **HOMEWORK ACTIVITY: COMPLETE YOUR RESPONSE** | **TIMING: 30 MINS** |

LEARNING OBJECTIVES
- To be able to develop critical engagement with, and evaluation of, a text

EQUIPMENT
- Source E: *The Essex Serpent*

Look again at this Paper 1, Section A exam-style question.

> Focus this part of your answer on the second half of Source E: *The Essex Serpent*, **from line 17 to the end.**
>
> A student, having read this section of the text said: 'The writer gives only a limited but disturbing description of what the young man sees in the water. You know something dramatic is going to happen.'
>
> To what extent do you agree?
>
> In your response, you could:
> - write about your own impressions of what the young man sees in the water
> - evaluate how the writer has created these impressions
> - support your opinions with quotations from the text.
>
> [20 marks]

1. Write a further two or three paragraphs in response to the question on a separate piece of paper.

2. When you have written your response, check you have achieved all of the success criteria below.

   a) Tick all the criteria you feel you have achieved.

   - ☐ I have evaluated the effect on the reader.
   - ☐ I have shown clear understanding of the writer's use of structure, sentence forms, words, phrases and language features.
   - ☐ I have supported argument with evidence from the text.
   - ☐ I have made a clear and relevant response to the statement in the question.
   - ☐ I have written in paragraphs.

   b) Look at any of the criteria you feel you have not achieved. Add to and improve your response so that you can tick all of them.

17 ANSWERS

STARTER ACTIVITY: WHAT IS EVALUATION?

1. Statements A and B are evaluative in a very limited sense – and not at all analytical; statements C and E are good examples of effective evaluation; statements D and F are effective comments on the writer's language choices but do not evaluate or analyse their impact on the writer's intention.

MAIN ACTIVITY: RESPONDING TO THE QUESTION

1. Examples: Evidence A: 'something vast', 'hunched… grimly covered'; Evidence B: 'pulse… throb… convulse', 'a scream of dismay'.
2. Student's own answer
3. Student's own answer
4. Student's own answer

MAIN ACTIVITY: EVALUATE YOUR EVALUATION

1.

Marks	Criteria
16–20 marks	• Clear and detailed analysis of the writer's choices • Clear and full evaluation of the effect on the reader • A carefully selected range of relevant, focused textual evidence • A developed and considered critical response to the statement
11–15 marks	• Clear comments on the writer's choices • Clear evaluation of the effect on the reader • A range of relevant, focused textual evidence • A relevant, focused response to the statement
6–10 marks	• Some comments on the writer's choices • Some evaluation of their effect on the reader • Relevant and focused textual evidence • A more developed response to the statement
1–5 marks	• Straightforward comments on the writer's choices • Straightforward evaluation of their effect on the reader • Largely relevant textual evidence • A straightforward response to the statement
No marks	• No creditable response

2. Ensure that all, or the majority of, the annotations are present in the student's paragraph.

HOMEWORK ACTIVITY: COMPLETE YOUR RESPONSE

1. See mark scheme for *Evaluate your evaluation* question 1.
2. Ensure the student has achieved all, or the majority of, the success criteria.

AQA ENGLISH — Grades 3–5

18 READING: WRITING A COMPARISON

LEARNING OBJECTIVES
- To be able to identify the writers' attitudes in two texts
- To be able to explore how the writers have conveyed their attitudes
- To be able to structure an effective comparison

SPECIFICATION LINKS
- 3.1.1 comparing texts

STARTER ACTIVITY
- **Attitudes; 5 minutes; page 126**
  Point out that this type of exam question may ask for a comparison of attitudes, ideas, views, experiences, etc.

MAIN ACTIVITIES
- **Exploring comparison; 20 minutes; page 127**
  Encourage the student to focus simply on identifying points of similarity or difference. Structuring an effective comparison is covered in the next activity.
- **Writing a comparison; 20 minutes; page 128**
  Encourage the student to use appropriate language such as *analytical terms*, *conjunctions* and *adverbials* to describe similarities and differences.

PLENARY ACTIVITY
- **Check-up; 5 minutes**
  Ask the student to create a checklist of elements to include when writing a comparison. This might include: identifying attitudes; using relevant evidence; commenting on and comparing ideas, language choice, etc.; using conjunctions and adverbials.

HOMEWORK ACTIVITY
- **Identifying relevant evidence; 30 minutes; page 129**
  Explain that this activity will form the basis of the next lesson. Ensure the student understands that they must label their chosen evidence in the text.

SUPPORT IDEA
- **Writing a comparison** Encourage the student to re-read their paragraph from the beginning as they add to it, aiming to achieve fluency and to avoid repetition.

EXTENSION IDEA
- **Exploring comparison** Encourage the student to identify a range of significant choices in the extracts and any cumulative effect they might have.

PROGRESS AND OBSERVATIONS

ENGLISH
— Grades 3-5 —

Starter activity: Attitudes

Timing: 5 mins

Learning objectives
- To be able to identify the writers' attitudes in two texts

Equipment
none

Read this Paper 2, Section A exam-style question.

> For this question, you need to refer to Source A: *The Napoleon of Crime* together with Source B: *Burglarious Bill*.
>
> Compare how the two writers convey their different attitudes to crime.
>
> In your answer, you should:
> - compare their different attitudes
> - compare the methods they use to convey their attitudes
> - support your ideas with quotations from both texts.
>
> **[16 marks]**

Now read these two short extracts from the two sources.

Source A: *The Napoleon of Crime*

> Extracting a sharp blade from his pocket, with infinite care he cut the portrait from its frame and laid it on the gallery floor. From his coat he took a small pot of paste, and using the tasseled end of the velvet rope, he daubed the back of the canvas to make it supple and then rolled it up with the paint facing outward to avoid cracking the surface, before slipping it inside his frock coat.

Source B: *Burglarious Bill*

> The safe had been forced very cleverly, there being no external marks of violence upon it. During the trial the police declared that the tools used must have been "beautiful instruments".

1. How would you describe the writer's attitude to crime in each extract? Choose one or two of the ideas below – or add your own in the blank boxes – and label it as either 'Source A' or 'Source B'.

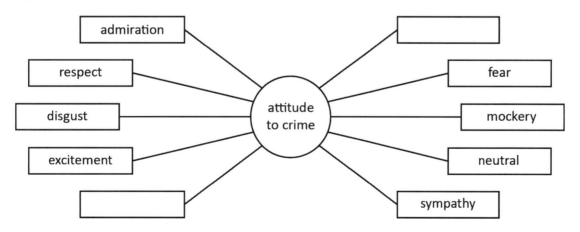

AQA ENGLISH — Grades 3–5

MAIN ACTIVITY: EXPLORING COMPARISON	**TIMING: 20 MINS**

LEARNING OBJECTIVES
- To be able to explore how the writers have conveyed their attitudes

EQUIPMENT
- *Attitudes* Starter activity sheet

Think about the writers' attitudes to crime in the two short extracts you have been looking at.

1. **Are the writers' attitudes similar in any way or very different? Explain your ideas.**

....

....

....

....

2. **Consider how the writers of the two sources have conveyed their attitudes in the two short extracts.**

   a) Circle any significant language choices that convey the writers' attitudes. Think about their choice of:
      - words, phrases or language features
      - sentence forms.

   b) Complete the sentences below to describe the effect of the language choices you circled.

In Source A:

....

....

In Source B:

....

....

3. **Look at your answers to question 2. Compare the writers' choices. Is there any similarity in the ways they have suggested their attitudes, or are they very different? Explain your ideas.**

....

....

....

....

ENGLISH
Grades 3-5

AQA

MAIN ACTIVITY: WRITING A COMPARISON

TIMING: 20 MINS

LEARNING OBJECTIVES
- To be able to structure an effective comparison

EQUIPMENT
- *Attitudes* Starter activity sheet

An effective comparison:
- identifies and compares the writers' attitudes and ideas
- supports this with evidence from both texts
- explores and compares how the writers' choices convey those ideas and attitudes.

1. Write two sentences on the lines below comparing the writers' attitudes and ideas. You can use the words and phrases below to help you.

2. Add evidence from both texts. You can use the words and phrases below to help you.

3. Add your analysis of the writers' choices in the evidence. Use the words and phrases below to help you.

in both texts	whereas	suggests	the choice of	both writers	however
on the other hand	refers to	describes	in Source...	whereas	similarly
for example	conveys	in the same way	however	expresses

128

ENGLISH
— Grades 3-5 —

HOMEWORK ACTIVITY: IDENTIFYING RELEVANT EVIDENCE   TIMING: 30 MINS

LEARNING OBJECTIVES
- To be able to identify the writers' attitudes in two texts

EQUIPMENT
- Source A: *The Napoleon of Crime*
- Source B: *Burglarious Bill*

Read Source A: *The Napoleon of Crime* and Source B: *Burglarious Bill.*

1. In both texts, underline any significant evidence that reveals the writers' attitude to crime. Label the evidence in each source A, B, C, etc.

2. What does each piece of evidence reveal about the writer's attitude to crime? Note your ideas in the table below.

	Source A: *The Napoleon of Crime*	Source B: *Burglarious Bill*
A		
B		
C		
D		
E		
F		
G		

18 Answers

STARTER ACTIVITY: ATTITUDES
1. Both sources suggest a respect for the criminals' skill.

MAIN ACTIVITY: EXPLORING COMPARISON
1. The writers' attitudes are similar.
2. Example: In Source A the writer describes the 'infinite care' taken by the thief as he cuts the painting from its frame and ensures it is not damaged, while the writer of Source B describes how the safe was opened 'cleverly' using 'beautiful instruments'.
3. Both writers describe the criminals' actions using positive language, praising their care and skill.

MAIN ACTIVITY: WRITING A COMPARISON
1. to 3. Student's own answers. Ensure the final paragraph is written fluently and avoids repetition of ideas or words/phrases.

HOMEWORK ACTIVITY: IDENTIFYING RELEVANT EVIDENCE
1. and 2. Examples for Source A: 'a fashionable address in Piccadilly with top hats on their heads'; 'one was slight and dapper… the other, ambling a few paces behind, was a towering fellow'; 'the faint rumble of a night watchman's snores wafted up from the room below'; 'with jaunty step the little dandy set off back down Piccadilly'. The quotes suggest that crime is lucrative, requiring intelligence, physical strength, bravery and boldness.

Examples for Source B: 'expert burglars'; 'Tom the Madman'; 'a number of Mr. Walker's watches and chains, gold coin to the amount of one hundred and ninety-six pounds, and a fifty-pound note'; 'a life preserver, which had been placed in the bed under the pillow, a collection of skeleton keys, several screwdrivers, a revolver, and some caps and bullets'. The quotes suggest that crime requires expertise and is a violent but lucrative profession.

AQA ENGLISH — Grades 3-5

19 READING: DEVELOPING A COMPARISON

LEARNING OBJECTIVES
- To be able to identify and compare the writers' attitudes in two texts
- To be able to compare how the writers have conveyed their attitudes
- To be able to structure an effective comparison

SPECIFICATION LINKS
- 3.1.1 comparing texts

STARTER ACTIVITY
- **Homework review; 5 minutes; page 132**
  Ask the student to talk you through their homework from the previous lesson (lesson 18), explaining their choice of quotations and what each implies about the writer's attitude to crime. As you talk, they should summarise the writers' attitudes on the activity sheet.

MAIN ACTIVITIES
- **Similarities and differences; 20 minutes; page 133**
  The student may find it helpful to label each point with the letter of the relevant quote from their homework.
- **Comparing choices; 20 minutes; page 134**
  Explain to the student that comparing the ways in which writers convey their attitudes is a high-level skill. Point out that more than one technique may be evident in each quotation.

PLENARY ACTIVITY
- **Review; 5 minutes**
  Ask the student to summarise and evaluate their understanding of how to compare the writers' ideas and attitudes in two texts.

HOMEWORK ACTIVITY
- **Write a response; 30 minutes; page 135**
  The student should write two new paragraphs comparing the texts, referring to their work from this and the previous lesson in order to craft the most effective comparison. Remind them that, although this lesson has focused on evaluating the writers' use of language and sentence forms, their response can also compare the writers' structural choices.

SUPPORT IDEA
- **Similarities and differences** Suggest that the student draws lines on the *Homework review* worksheet (Starter activity) linking similarities and pairing significant differences, before summarising their thinking.

EXTENSION IDEA
- **Write a response** Encourage the student to return to the sources and identify at least one previously unexplored similarity or difference in the two writers' attitudes to crime.

PROGRESS AND OBSERVATIONS

ENGLISH
— Grades 3-5 —

Starter activity: Homework review

Timing: 5 mins

Learning objectives
- To be able to identify and compare the writers' attitudes in two texts

Equipment
- Homework activity from lesson 18

1. What does the evidence you have gathered suggest about each writer's attitude to crime? Write your ideas below.

Source A	Source B

AQA ENGLISH — Grades 3–5

MAIN ACTIVITY: SIMILARITIES AND DIFFERENCES	TIMING: 20 MINS

LEARNING OBJECTIVES
- To be able to identify and compare the writers' attitudes in two texts

EQUIPMENT
- Homework activity from lesson 18
- *Homework review* Starter activity sheet
- Source A: *The Napoleon of Crime*
- Source B: *Burglarious Bill*

1. Review the evidence and ideas you have gathered, and summarise any similarities and differences you can identify in the two writers' attitudes to crime.

   Both writers…

   ....

   ....

   ....

   ....

   ....

The writer of Source A…	…whereas the writer of Source B…

ENGLISH
— Grades 3-5 —

MAIN ACTIVITY: COMPARING CHOICES   **TIMING: 20 MINS**

LEARNING OBJECTIVES
- To be able to compare how the writers have conveyed their attitudes

EQUIPMENT
none

In your comparison, you can also compare how writers convey their ideas and attitudes. For example, the writer's attitude may be revealed through:
- **implication**: the writer implies their attitude through the ideas or details they choose to include in their writing
- **language**: the writer explicitly states or implicitly suggests their attitude through their vocabulary choices
- **sentence forms**: the writer implies or emphasises their attitude through their choice of sentence forms.

Read the sources and think about how both writers suggest that crime can be a lucrative profession.

Source A: *The Napoleon of Crime*

> On a misty May midnight in the year 1876, three men emerged from a fashionable address in Piccadilly with top hats on their heads, money in their pockets, and burglary, on a grand scale, on their minds.

Source B: *Burglarious Bill*

> The two Caseleys were at once taken into custody, after which the house was searched, with the result that the officers discovered a box containing a number of Mr. Walker's watches and chains, gold coin to the amount of one hundred and ninety-six pounds, and a fifty-pound note.

1. **Complete the sentences below by crossing out the incorrect answers.**

   a) The writer of Source A conveys this attitude using   implication   language choice   sentence forms.

   b) The writer of Source B conveys this attitude using   implication   language choice   sentence forms.

2. **Write two sentences comparing how each writer uses their chosen method to suggest that crime can be a lucrative profession.**

134

ENGLISH
— Grades 3-5 —

HOMEWORK ACTIVITY: WRITE A RESPONSE

TIMING: 30 MINS

LEARNING OBJECTIVES
- To be able to structure an effective comparison

EQUIPMENT
- Source A: *The Napoleon of Crime*
- Source B: *Burglarious Bill*

Read this Paper 2, Section A exam-style question.

> For this question, you need to refer to Source A: *The Napoleon of Crime* together with Source B: *Burglarious Bill*.
>
> Compare how the two writers convey their different attitudes to crime.
>
> In your answer, you should:
> - compare their different attitudes
> - compare the methods they use to convey their attitudes
> - support your ideas with quotations from both texts.
>
> **[16 marks]**

1. Write two paragraphs in response to this question on a separate piece of paper.

2. When you have written your response, check you have achieved all of the success criteria below.

   a) Tick all the criteria you feel you have achieved.

   - ☐ I have identified and compared the writers' attitudes to crime.
   - ☐ I have supported my points with evidence from the text.
   - ☐ I have analysed and compared how the writers use structure, sentence forms, words, phrases and language features to convey their attitudes.
   - ☐ I have clearly signalled comparisons using conjunctions and adverbials such as *whereas* and *similarly*.
   - ☐ I have written in paragraphs.
   - ☐ I have carefully checked for accurate spelling and punctuation, and clear written expression.

   b) Look at any of the criteria you feel you have not achieved. Add to and improve your response so that you can tick all of them.

ENGLISH
Grades 3-5

19 ANSWERS

STARTER ACTIVITY: HOMEWORK REVIEW

1. Examples for Source A: 'a fashionable address in Piccadilly with top hats on their heads'; 'one was slight and dapper... the other, ambling a few paces behind, was a towering fellow'; 'the faint rumble of a night watchman's snores wafted up from the room below'; 'with jaunty step the little dandy set off back down Piccadilly'. The quotes suggest that crime is lucrative, requiring intelligence, physical strength, bravery and boldness.

Examples for Source B: 'expert burglars'; 'Tom the Madman'; 'a number of Mr. Walker's watches and chains, gold coin to the amount of one hundred and ninety-six pounds, and a fifty-pound note'; 'a life preserver, which had been placed in the bed under the pillow, a collection of skeleton keys, several screwdrivers, a revolver, and some caps and bullets'. The quotes suggest that crime requires expertise and is a violent but lucrative profession.

MAIN ACTIVITY: SIMILARITIES AND DIFFERENCES

1. Example similarities: both writers suggest that crime requires skill and boldness; both suggest that crime can be lucrative. Example differences: the arrest in Source B suggests that crime does not pay, whereas the narrative structure and mood of adventure in Source A suggest the excitement of a life of crime; Source B suggests the violence of crime, listing the weapons found in the Caseley's house, but there is no reference to physical violence in the Source A's more sophisticated crime.

MAIN ACTIVITY: COMPARING CHOICES

1. Incorrect answers: a) implication, language choice; b) implication, sentence forms
2. Example: The writer of Source A suggests that crime can be lucrative: the criminals wear 'top hats' and live at a 'fashionable address', both of which suggest wealth. The writer of Source B suggests a similar idea by emphasising the significant proceeds of the theft by listing them in a lengthy sentence.

HOMEWORK ACTIVITY: WRITE A RESPONSE

1.

Marks	Criteria
13–16 marks	• Clear and detailed analysis of the writers' choices • A carefully selected range of relevant, focused textual evidence from both texts • A developed and considered understanding of the different ideas and perspectives in both texts
9–12 marks	• Clear explanation on the writer's choices • A range of relevant, focused textual evidence from both texts • A clear understanding of the different ideas and perspectives in both texts
5–8 marks	• Some comments on the writer's choices • Relevant and focused textual evidence from one or both texts • Awareness of range of different ideas and perspectives
1–4 marks	• Straightforward comments on the writer's choices • Largely relevant textual evidence • Some awareness of ideas and or perspectives
No marks	• No creditable response

2. Ensure the student has achieved all, or the majority of, the success criteria.

GLOSSARY

Conjunction
A word used to connect clauses within sentences, e.g. *but, whereas*

Adverbial
A word or phrase that modifies a verb, adjective or another adverbial – adverbial conjuncts, such as *similarly, however* and *on the other hand*, are used both to link clauses within sentences and to make links between sentences

AQA ENGLISH — Grades 3-5

20 READING: CONSOLIDATING COMPARISONS

LEARNING OBJECTIVES

- To be able to structure an effective comparison
- To be able to identify and compare the writers' attitudes in two texts
- To be able to compare how the writers have conveyed their attitudes

SPECIFICATION LINKS

- 3.1.1 comparing texts

STARTER ACTIVITY

- **Refresh; 5 minutes; page 138**
  Discuss how each skill is applied when planning and writing a comparison.

MAIN ACTIVITIES

- **Planning a comparison; 25 minutes; page 139**
  Ask the student to read the two sources (Source C: *Earth in the Balance*, page 19, and Source F: *A Century of Achievement*, page 22) and the exam-style question, then complete the questions. Emphasise that this is guided exam practice, and so it is important to stick to the time limit.
- **A paragraph of comparison; 15 minutes; page 140**
  Ask the student to write one paragraph in response to the exam-style question.

PLENARY ACTIVITY

- **Review; 5 minutes**
  Ask the student to label the parts of their paragraph from the previous activity that show where they think they have achieved the success criteria identified in the Starter activity. Ask the student to evaluate their success in achieving all the criteria and to suggest how they could improve their paragraph.

HOMEWORK ACTIVITY

- **Complete your response; 30 minutes; page 141**
  Point out to the student that they should consider how they sequence their points of comparison. The paragraph they have already completed may not end up being the first paragraph of their final response.

SUPPORT IDEA

- **Planning a comparison** To allow more time for planning, move the student on as soon as one point of comparison is identified. They can then use that point as the focus for their paragraph of comparison in the next activity, and complete the remainder of their planning as part of their homework.

EXTENSION IDEA

- **Planning a comparison** Encourage the student to look for a range of evidence to support each attitude and explore how this evidence contributes to conveying each attitude.

PROGRESS AND OBSERVATIONS

ENGLISH
Grades 3-5

AQA

STARTER ACTIVITY: REFRESH   TIMING: 5 MINS

LEARNING OBJECTIVES
- To be able to structure an effective comparison

EQUIPMENT
none

1. Which of these skills do you need when comparing the writers' ideas and attitudes in two texts? Tick all that apply.

138

ENGLISH
— Grades 3-5 —

| MAIN ACTIVITY: PLANNING A COMPARISON | TIMING: 25 MINS |

LEARNING OBJECTIVES	EQUIPMENT
• To be able to identify and compare the writers' attitudes in two texts • To be able to compare how the writers have conveyed their attitudes	• Source C: *Earth in the Balance* • Source F: *A Century of Achievement* • Two different coloured pens

You are going to plan and write a response to the Paper 2, Section A exam-style question below.

> For this question, you need to refer to the whole of Source C: *Earth in the Balance* together with the whole of Source F: *A Century of Achievement*.
>
> Compare how the writers have conveyed their different attitudes to human beings.
>
> In your answer, you could:
> • compare their different attitudes
> • compare the methods they use to convey those attitudes
> • support your ideas with quotations from both texts.
>
> **[16 marks]**

1. Underline any significant evidence in the sources that suggests the writers' attitudes to human beings.
2. Look at the evidence you have underlined in each source. What does your chosen evidence reveal about the writer's attitude to human beings? Write down two or three different ideas for each source.

Source C: *Earth in the Balance*	Source F: *A Century of Achievement*

3. Compare the attitudes you have identified. Use a coloured pen to draw lines linking any that are similar, then use another colour to link any that are very different.
4. Look again at the evidence you have underlined in the two sources. Tick the quotations you will use in your response.
5. Annotate your chosen quotations, circling key words or phrases and noting ideas you can use in your analysis of the writers' choices.

ENGLISH
Grades 3-5

AQA

MAIN ACTIVITY: A PARAGRAPH OF COMPARISON

TIMING: 15 MINS

LEARNING OBJECTIVES
- To be able to structure an effective comparison

EQUIPMENT
- Source C: *Earth in the Balance*
- Source F: *A Century of Achievement*

1. Choose a point of comparison from your planning in the previous activity. Use it to write the first paragraph of your response to the Paper 2, Section A exam-style question below.

> For this question, you need to refer to the whole of Source C: *Earth in the Balance* together with the whole of Source F: *A Century of Achievement*.
>
> Compare how the writers have conveyed their different attitudes to human beings.
>
> In your answer, you could:
> - compare their different attitudes
> - compare the methods they use to convey those attitudes
> - support your ideas with quotations from both texts.
>
> **[16 marks]**

AQA ENGLISH — Grades 3–5

HOMEWORK ACTIVITY: COMPLETE YOUR RESPONSE　　　**TIMING: 30 MINS**

LEARNING OBJECTIVES
- To be able to structure an effective comparison

EQUIPMENT
- Source C: *Earth in the Balance*
- Source F: *A Century of Achievement*

1. **On a separate piece of paper, complete your response to the Paper 2, Section A exam-style question below. Write a further two or three paragraphs.**

> For this question, you need to refer to the whole of Source C: *Earth in the Balance* together with the whole of Source F: *A Century of Achievement*.
>
> Compare how the writers have conveyed their different attitudes to human beings.
>
> In your answer, you could:
> - compare their different attitudes
> - compare the methods they use to convey those attitudes
> - support your ideas with quotations from both texts.
>
> **[16 marks]**

2. **When you have written your response, check you have achieved all of the success criteria below.**

   a) Tick all the criteria you feel you have achieved.

   - ☐ I have identified and compared the writers' attitudes to human beings.
   - ☐ I have supported my points with evidence from the text.
   - ☐ I have analysed and compared how the writers use structure, sentence forms, words, phrases and language features to convey their attitudes.
   - ☐ I have clearly signalled comparisons using conjunctions and adverbials such as *whereas* and *similarly*.
   - ☐ I have written in paragraphs.
   - ☐ I have carefully checked for accurate spelling and punctuation, and clear written expression.

   b) Look at any of the criteria you feel you have not achieved. Add to and improve your response so that you can tick all of them.

ENGLISH
Grades 3-5

20 ANSWERS

STARTER ACTIVITY: REFRESH

1. All the skills will support an effective comparison task; however, the key skills to use when structuring a comparison are: identifying the writers' ideas and perspectives in the texts; comparing the writers' ideas and perspectives in the texts; supporting your ideas with evidence from the texts; analysing the writers' use of language and structure in the texts; comparing the writers' use of language and structure in the texts; using adverbials and conjunctions to guide the reader.

MAIN ACTIVITY: PLANNING A COMPARISON

1. to 5. Examples:

Achievement: 'the violent collision between human civilization and the earth' (Source C); 'The human mind reels when it tries to grasp the stupendous achievements of the Nineteenth Century' (Source F)

Abilities: 'Perhaps we should feel awe for our own power' (Source C); 'men of gigantic intellect… the magicians of to-day' (Source F)

Attitude to planet Earth: 'Why haven't we launched a massive effort to save our environment?' (Source C); 'the spirits of air, water, earth and fire have been made to do man's every bidding' (Source F); 'the materials for which have been hewn in so many forests and quarried from so many mines' (Source F)

MAIN ACTIVITY: A PARAGRAPH OF COMPARISON

1.

Marks	Criteria
13–16 marks	• Clear and detailed analysis of the writers' choices • A carefully selected range of relevant, focused textual evidence from both texts • A developed and considered understanding of the different ideas and perspectives in both texts
9–12 marks	• Clear explanation of the writers' choices • A range of relevant, focused textual evidence from both texts • A clear understanding of the different ideas and perspectives in both texts
5–8 marks	• Some comments on the writers' choices • Relevant and focused textual evidence from one or both texts • Awareness of range of different ideas and perspectives
1–4 marks	• Straightforward comments on the writers' choices • Largely relevant textual evidence • Some awareness of ideas and/or perspectives
No marks	• No creditable response

HOMEWORK ACTIVITY: COMPLETE YOUR RESPONSE

1. See guidance for *A paragraph of comparison* activity.
2. Ensure the student has achieved all, or the majority of, the success criteria.

ENGLISH — Grades 3–5

21 DESCRIPTIVE AND NARRATIVE WRITING: GATHERING IDEAS

LEARNING OBJECTIVES
- To be able to gather ideas for a descriptive writing task
- To be able to gather ideas for a narrative writing task

SPECIFICATION LINKS
- 3.1.2 writing for impact

STARTER ACTIVITY
- **Exploring an image; 5 minutes; page 144**
  Give the student one minute to complete question 1. Then, discuss the range and clarity of their response.

MAIN ACTIVITIES
- **Developing descriptive ideas; 20 minutes; page 145**
  Explain that the exam offers a choice of a descriptive task with an image as stimulus, or a narrative writing task. Point out that, depending on the image, some techniques may be more fruitful than others and therefore planning may appear uneven.
- **Gathering narrative ideas 1; 20 minutes; page 146**
  Explain that, although the exam-style question instructs them to 'describe', this is effectively a narrative task: telling the story of 'an occasion'. Discuss which elements will improve the student's writing and which may be unnecessary and/or detract from it, e.g. to what extent is it necessary to explain how and why you encountered a spider?

PLENARY ACTIVITY
- **Review; 5 minutes**
  Discuss which of the approaches and techniques tackled in this lesson seem the most helpful and productive – and why. Ensure the purpose of the techniques is clear – to generate content and to develop depth in description/narrative technique.

HOMEWORK ACTIVITY
- **Gathering narrative ideas 2; 30 minutes; page 147**
  Explain that gathering ideas and planning are key elements of any writing task, and that practice in these skills is valuable. Discuss briefly whether the most effective elements will differ to those in *Gathering narrative ideas 1*, e.g. would description to set the scene have more relevance and impact here?

SUPPORT IDEA
- **Exploring an image** Prompt the student to think like a camera, moving around and through the image, capturing every detail.

EXTENSION IDEA
- **Gathering narrative ideas 1 and 2** Encourage the student to gather a wealth of ideas and details. The most successful writing is based on careful selection from extensive planning.

PROGRESS AND OBSERVATIONS

ENGLISH
— Grades 3-5 —

AQA

Starter activity: Exploring an image

Timing: 5 mins

Learning objectives
- To be able to gather ideas for a descriptive writing task

Equipment
none

Read this exam-style question. You will see a question similar to this in Section B of Paper 1.

Write a description suggested by this picture:

[40 marks]

1. What is happening in the picture? What could you describe in your response? Write down your ideas.

144

ENGLISH
— Grades 3-5 —

Main activity: Developing descriptive ideas	Timing: 20 mins

Learning objectives	Equipment
• To be able to gather ideas for a descriptive writing task	none

1. **Look again at the image from the exam-style question in the previous activity, then use the spider diagram below to develop your ideas.**

Where are you – the person who will describe this experience? Are you:
- in the picture?
- not in the picture but involved in some way?
- an invisible observer?

What are you and the people in the picture thinking and feeling?

What happened before and after the moment captured in the picture?

Gathering ideas

What can't you see in the picture? What else might be happening – or might have already happened?

It is easy to focus on what you can see in the picture. Think about your other senses. What can you hear, smell, feel and taste?

ENGLISH
Grades 3–5

MAIN ACTIVITY: GATHERING NARRATIVE IDEAS 1   **TIMING: 20 MINS**

LEARNING OBJECTIVES
- To be able to gather ideas for a narrative writing task

EQUIPMENT
none

Look at this exam-style writing task. You will get a question similar to this in Section B of Paper 1.

> Describe an occasion when you faced a fear. Focus on the thoughts and feelings you had at that time.
> **[40 marks]**

1. **What will be the main focus of your writing? The fear that you faced? An animal? A situation? Or something else?**
   a) Note down three possible ideas.

   ....

   ....

   ....

   b) Choose one of your ideas to take forward in this task. Tick it.

2. **Look at this list of elements you may want to include in your response. Tick any that you would like to achieve in your writing.**

   ☐ use description to set the scene   ☐ tension   ☐ action
   ☐ explain the build-up   ☐ describe your thoughts and feelings   ☐ mystery

   ☐ something else ....

3. **Now look closely at the elements you have ticked. How will you achieve them? Write down some ideas.**

   ....

   ....

   ....

   ....

   ....

   ....

   ....

   ....

   ....

AQA ENGLISH — Grades 3–5

HOMEWORK ACTIVITY: GATHERING NARRATIVE IDEAS 2   **TIMING: 30 MINS**

LEARNING OBJECTIVES
- To be able to gather ideas for a narrative writing task

EQUIPMENT
none

Look at this Paper 1, Section B exam-style writing task.

> Write the opening part of a story about an occasion when you saw, or thought you saw, something strange or mysterious.
>
> [40 marks]

1. **What will be the main focus of your writing? The strange or mysterious thing you saw? A creature? An occurrence? Or something else?**

    a) Note down three possible ideas.

    b) Choose one of your ideas to take forward in this task. Tick it.

2. **Look at this list of elements you may want to include in your response. Tick any that you would like to achieve in your writing.**

    - ☐ use description to set the scene
    - ☐ explain the build-up
    - ☐ tension
    - ☐ describe your thoughts and feelings
    - ☐ action
    - ☐ mystery
    - ☐ something else _____

3. **Now look closely at the elements you have ticked. How will you achieve them? Write down some ideas.**

ENGLISH
Grades 3-5

21 ANSWERS

STARTER ACTIVITY: EXPLORING AN IMAGE
1. Clearly visible key elements should be noted, e.g. sky, trees, snow, children, play.

MAIN ACTIVITY: DEVELOPING DESCRIPTIVE IDEAS
1. Look for responses that develop descriptions beyond what is clearly visible: for example, waking up to find it is snowing; sledging; building a snowman, etc.

MAIN ACTIVITY: GATHERING NARRATIVE IDEAS 1
1. Student's own answer
2. Description to set the scene, explanation of build-up and action are the weakest and/or least appropriate elements for this response. In particular, lengthy explanations are least likely to yield effective writing.
3. Student's own answer. Examples: gothic details to set an unsettling scene; the creature approaching to build tension; describing the symptoms of fear (sweating palms, knotted stomach, etc.); the action of the final encounter, etc.

HOMEWORK ACTIVITY: GATHERING NARRATIVE IDEAS 2
1. Student's own answer
2. Explanation of build-up and action are arguably the weakest and/or least appropriate elements for this response. Description to set the scene may contribute to tension, however.
3. Student's own answer

AQA ENGLISH — Grades 3–5

22 Descriptive and Narrative Writing: Structure and Planning

Learning objectives
- To be able to structure and sequence ideas for clarity and impact

Specification links
- 3.1.2 writing for impact

Starter activity
- **Story structure; 5 minutes; page 150**
  Point out that this approach is most relevant to narrative writing, but can be useful when structuring a descriptive task too. Ensure the student understands the difference between descriptive writing and narrative writing.

Main activities
- **Structuring description; 20 minutes; page 151**
  Ensure the student's understanding of the two possible approaches to descriptive writing. Guide them towards the conclusion that the 'moving through time' approach allows them to incorporate the 'moving through the picture' approach and results in a richer, more sophisticated piece of writing.
- **Structuring narrative for impact; 20 minutes; page 152**
  Remind the student to avoid unnecessary material and to focus on engaging the reader's interest and maintaining it.

Plenary activity
- **Review; 5 minutes**
  Ask the student to summarise and evaluate their understanding of how to plan descriptive and narrative writing.

Homework activity
- **Plan your writing; 30 minutes; page 153**
  Emphasise to the student that their response to their chosen task should be original. Discuss which task they will tackle and ask them to summarise the planning process they will follow.

Support idea
- **Structuring description** Encourage the student to focus on the more accessible 'moving through the picture' approach.

Extension idea
- **Plan your writing** Ask the student to write responses to both exam-style writing tasks given on the worksheet.

Progress and observations

ENGLISH
— Grades 3-5 —

Starter activity: Story structure

Timing: 5 mins

Learning objectives
- To be able to structure and sequence ideas for clarity and impact

Equipment
none

One way to plan and structure a piece of narrative or descriptive writing is to think about story structure. Often stories follow the pattern below.

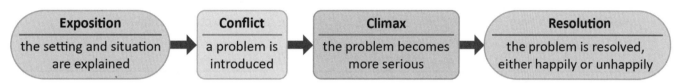

Look at one student's unfinished plan for this Paper 1, Section B exam-style question.

> Write the opening part of a story about an occasion when you saw, or thought you saw, something strange or mysterious.
>
> **[40 marks]**

- sleeping in bed
- woken by strange noise – shadowy figure moving in my room
-

1. Which elements of the typical story structure above has this student used so far? Label them 'exposition', 'conflict', climax' or 'resolution'.

2. How could this student complete their plan and finish their story? Note your ideas below, labelling them 'exposition', 'conflict', 'climax' or 'resolution'.

ENGLISH
— Grades 3-5 —

MAIN ACTIVITY: STRUCTURING DESCRIPTION	TIMING: 20 MINS
LEARNING OBJECTIVES	**EQUIPMENT**
• To be able to structure and sequence ideas for clarity and impact	• *Story structure* Starter activity sheet

Two ways in which you can structure a description based on an image are:
- **moving through the picture**: the narrator is like a camera, describing everything the camera sees as it moves across and through the picture, from left to right and from the horizon to the foreground
- **moving through time**: describing before, during and after the time the picture was taken.

Look at one student's plan for this Paper 1, Section B exam-style task.

Write a description suggested by this picture:

[40 marks]

- wake up – it's snowing
- run outside
- describe trees covered in snow...
- everything white as far as you can see
- snowman
- snowball fight
- sledging
- falling off and crying
- laughter and screaming
- hot chocolate
- cold/shivering
- sun comes out - snowman melting
- next morning everything has gone

1. How could you structure a description that moves through the picture? Tick which ideas you would use, and then number them to show how you would sequence them.

2. How could you structure a description that moves through time? Tick which ideas you would use, and then number them to show how you would sequence them.

3. Which method would make the most effective description? On a separate piece of paper, write a sentence or two explaining your choice.

ENGLISH
— Grades 3–5 —

AQA

| MAIN ACTIVITY: STRUCTURING NARRATIVE FOR IMPACT | TIMING: 20 MINS |

LEARNING OBJECTIVES
- To be able to structure and sequence ideas for clarity and impact

EQUIPMENT
none

When you plan and structure a story, you need to gather as many ideas as you can. You can then choose your strongest ideas and sequence them in the most effective order.

Look at one student's plan for this Paper 1, Section B exam-style writing task.

> Write the opening part of a story about an occasion when you saw, or thought you saw, something strange or mysterious.
>
> **[40 marks]**

Exposition
- brushed my teeth and went to bed
- lay awake
- listening to noises of wind and rain outside my bedroom window, rattling the glass
- worrying about when I need to start revision for my GCSEs
- hear my mum going to bed
- fall asleep

Conflict
- wake up
- hear a strange noise
- open my eyes and hear something moving
- lift my head off the pillow – see a shadowy figure moving in my room
- wardrobe door creaks open
- someone is looking in my wardrobe, opening my drawers and searching the contents

Climax
- heart pounding, can't breathe, want to scream but can't
- sound of grumbling and moaning
- it's coming nearer... leans over me... looks at me... I can see its eyes shining...
- it speaks

Resolution
- It's my mum. She wants to borrow my hairdryer.

1. **How could you select and structure these ideas to engage your reader from the very beginning of your writing and then hold their interest?**

   a) Which of this student's ideas would you use? Tick them.
   b) In what order would you sequence them? Number the ideas you have ticked.

152

ENGLISH
— Grades 3-5 —

| HOMEWORK ACTIVITY: PLAN YOUR WRITING | TIMING: 30 MINS |

LEARNING OBJECTIVES
- To be able to structure and sequence ideas for clarity and impact

EQUIPMENT
none

1. **Plan your response to one of the following writing tasks on a separate piece of paper.**
   Make sure you:
   - gather a range of ideas
   - select the most relevant and effective
   - number them to show how you would sequence them.

> Write the opening part of a story about an occasion when you saw, or thought you saw, something strange or mysterious.
>
> **[40 marks]**

or

> Write a description suggested by this picture:
>
>
>
> **[40 marks]**

22 Answers

STARTER ACTIVITY: STORY STRUCTURE
1. Exposition and conflict
2. Student's own answer

MAIN ACTIVITY: STRUCTURING DESCRIPTION
1. to 3. Student's own answers

MAIN ACTIVITY: STRUCTURING NARRATIVE FOR IMPACT
1. Student's own answers. Arguably, the entire exposition can be cut, as opening the story with waking up in bed implies the relevant expository information.

HOMEWORK ACTIVITY: PLAN YOUR WRITING
1. See marking guidance on pages 251–253.

Glossary

Exposition
The beginning of a story, when the setting and situation are introduced

Conflict
A complication in the plot

Climax
The building of tension, which creates a sense of expectation in the reader

Resolution
The ending, when the action is resolved

ENGLISH — Grades 3-5 —

23 Descriptive and narrative writing: Beginnings and endings

Learning objectives
- To understand key elements of effective beginnings and endings
- To be able to craft effective beginnings and endings

Specification links
- 3.1.2 writing for impact

Starter activity
- **From start to finish; 5 minutes; page 156**
  Discuss the prompt questions on the worksheet and ask the student to note their ideas, placing an emphasis on how writers can achieve these aims. Prompt the student to consider particularly effective beginnings and endings to books and films they know. Remind them of the work they did on openings in the Starter activity in lesson 12.

Main activities
- **Beginnings; 20 minutes; page 157**
  Discuss which elements are most effective in creating engaging beginnings.
- **Endings; 20 minutes; page 158**
  Discuss which approach is most effective in creating a satisfying ending. Point out that the narrative writing task in the exam may ask for a complete story, or just a story opening. Explain that an effective story opening could end on a 'cliffhanger', leaving the reader keen to find out how the situation is resolved.

Plenary activity
- **Gathering ideas; 5 minutes**
  Ask the student to look at the Homework activity and suggest two or three possible beginnings and endings for each task. Suggest that they may want to refer to their planning from the lesson 22 homework.

Homework activity
- **Practise opening and ending; 30 minutes; page 159**
  Highlight the details of the activity: writing an opening and planning two different possible endings.

Support ideas
- **From start to finish** If the student is struggling to complete this activity, return to it as a plenary.
- **Beginnings; Endings** Prompt the student to consider their immediate response to the examples. Which opening makes them want to read on? Which ending would leave them most satisfied or dissatisfied?

Extension idea
- **Beginnings; Endings** What other options are available to writers? Ask the student to write example beginnings or endings based on their suggestions.

Progress and observations

ENGLISH
Grades 3-5

AQA

STARTER ACTIVITY: FROM START TO FINISH **TIMING: 5 MINS**

LEARNING OBJECTIVES
- To understand key elements of effective beginnings and endings

EQUIPMENT
none

Complete the sentences below to help you think about the impact that beginnings and endings in descriptive and narrative writing should have on the reader.

1. When a reader begins a piece of narrative or descriptive writing they should think about…

   ....

   ....

   ....

2. Some of the ways in which writers can achieve this include…

   ....

   ....

   ....

3. When a reader finishes a piece of narrative or descriptive writing they should think or feel…

   ....

   ....

   ....

4. Some of the ways in which writers can achieve this include…

   ....

   ....

   ....

AQA ENGLISH — Grades 3-5

Main activity: Beginnings

Timing: 20 mins

Learning objectives
- To understand key elements of effective beginnings and endings

Equipment
none

There are lots of effective ways to begin a piece of descriptive or narrative writing. For example:

A. Setting the scene The story opens with a description of what is happening or where it is happening.	B. Problems The story opens with a conflict that must be resolved.	C. Questions The reader is prompted to ask questions and continue reading to find out the answers.
D. Action The reader joins the story in the middle of a dramatic event.	E. Dialogue The reader joins the story in the middle of a conversation between two or more characters.	F. Monologue The narrator describes their thoughts and feelings to the reader.

Read the openings below, written in response to this Paper 1, Section B exam-style question.

> Describe an occasion when you faced a fear. Focus on the thoughts and feelings you had at that time.
> **[40 marks]**

i. It was the most terrifying creature I had ever seen. Its long, spindly legs drummed menacingly on the dusty floorboards as it prepared to pounce.

ii. 'You know I hate going down to the cellar,' I shouted. 'You always make me go. It's not fair.'

iii. I was watching the telly, eating a sandwich and looking at my phone. I could hear my mum calling me. 'Jade,' she shouted, 'I need you to go down to the cellar for me!'

iv. I flicked on the light. It flickered and spluttered. I put one foot on the creaking wooden stairs and began to climb down into the dark, damp and dust of the cellar.

1. Which of the techniques above do these openings use? Label them A, B, C, D, E or F according to the descriptions in the table above.

2. Which of the openings is the most effective? Explain your choice.

ENGLISH
— Grades 3–5 —

MAIN ACTIVITY: ENDINGS	TIMING: 20 MINS

LEARNING OBJECTIVES
- To understand key elements of effective beginnings and endings

EQUIPMENT
none

There are lots of effective ways to conclude a piece of descriptive or narrative writing. For example:

A. A happy ending	B. A twist	C. An unhappy ending	D. A cliffhanger
The conflict in the story is successfully resolved and all the reader's questions are answered.	The conflict is resolved in a surprising or unexpected way.	All the reader's questions are answered and the conflict is resolved – but not happily.	The reader's questions are not answered and the conflict is not resolved.

Read the final sentences of four students' responses to this Paper 1, Section B exam-style question.

> Describe an occasion when you faced a fear. Focus on the thoughts and feelings you had at that time.
> **[40 marks]**

i. It wasn't a spider after all. It was a twig. I crept back up the cellar stairs and went quietly to my room.

ii. I haven't been frightened of spiders ever since. In fact, now I've got a pet tarantula called Boris. He sits on my shoulder and we watch TV together.

iii. I was pinned in the corner, me staring at the spider and the spider staring back. I wondered how long it would take my mum to notice I was missing.

iv. I crept back upstairs, still sweating and shaking. I'm still terrified of spiders. And my mum still makes me go down to the cellar because she's too frightened to go down there herself.

1. Which of the techniques above do these endings use? Label them A, B, C or D according to the descriptions in the table above.

2. Which of the endings is the least effective? Explain your choice.

AQA ENGLISH
Grades 3-5

HOMEWORK ACTIVITY: PRACTISE OPENING AND ENDING   TIMING: 30 MINS

LEARNING OBJECTIVES
- To be able to craft effective beginnings and endings

EQUIPMENT
none

Choose one of these Paper 1, Section B exam-style writing tasks.

> Write the opening part of a story about an occasion when you saw, or thought you saw, something strange or mysterious.
>
> [40 marks]

or

> Write a description suggested by this picture:
>
>
>
> [40 marks]

1. On a separate piece of paper, write the opening paragraph of your response.

2. How could you end your story opening or description? On a separate piece of paper, write a summary of two different ways in which you could conclude it.

23 Answers

STARTER ACTIVITY: FROM START TO FINISH

1. and 2. Examples: engaging the reader by prompting questions; appealing characters/settings.
3. and 4. Examples: satisfying or surprising endings that resolve conflicts and answer all questions set up during the story.

MAIN ACTIVITY: BEGINNINGS

1. i) B, C, F; ii) C, E; iii) A, E; iv) A, C, D
2. Opening iii) is arguably the least effective, focusing on irrelevant detail; opening i) launches the reader straight into the action, while openings ii) and iv) use dialogue or description to build an atmosphere of tension.

MAIN ACTIVITY: ENDINGS

1. i) B; ii) A; iii) D; iv) C
2. Openings i) and ii) provide a satisfyingly humorous resolution; opening iv) does not fully resolve the conflict of the story; opening iii) is similarly dissatisfying because it ends on a cliffhanger.

HOMEWORK ACTIVITY: PRACTISE OPENING AND ENDING

1. See marking guidance on pages 251–253.
2. The student should be able to explain their approach and the impact they intend it to have on the reader.

ENGLISH
Grades 3-5

24 DESCRIPTIVE AND NARRATIVE WRITING: USING PARAGRAPHS FOR EFFECT

LEARNING OBJECTIVES
- To be able to use paragraphs accurately
- To be able to structure paragraphs for effect

SPECIFICATION LINKS
- 3.1.2 producing clear and coherent text
- 3.1.2 writing for impact

STARTER ACTIVITY
- **How to paragraph; 5 minutes; page 162**
  Check the student's familiarity with the rules of paragraphing.

MAIN ACTIVITIES
- **Short paragraphs; 20 minutes; page 163**
  Discuss whether overuse weakens the impact of short paragraphs. Emphasise that they should be used carefully to occasionally bend the rules of accurate paragraphing.
- **Hooks and punches; 20 minutes; page 164**
  Discuss a range of possible events that could form the hook or punch at the end of the incomplete paragraph. Emphasise visually the importance of 'punching' and 'hooking' the reader.

PLENARY ACTIVITY
- **Review and plan; 5 minutes**
  Ask the student to summarise and evaluate their understanding of how to paragraph for effect. Discuss how this understanding could be applied to the Homework activity.

HOMEWORK ACTIVITY
- **Paragraphing for effect; 30 minutes; page 165**
  Point out to the student that they should select the key points from the plan and identify which might lend themselves to short paragraphs, hooks or punches *before* they start writing. Emphasise the need to paragraph accurately as well as for effect.

SUPPORT IDEAS
- **How to paragraph** Prompt the student with questions: where does the speech start? Where does the setting or time change?
- **Hooks and punches** Ask the student to write three possible sentences to conclude the paragraph. Discuss whether any of them work as hooks or punches, and, if so, how.

EXTENSION IDEA
- **Hooks and punches** Ask the student to write a number of hooks and punches and then select the most effective ones.

PROGRESS AND OBSERVATIONS

ENGLISH
Grades 3-5
AQA

STARTER ACTIVITY: HOW TO PARAGRAPH **TIMING: 5 MINS**

LEARNING OBJECTIVES
- To be able to use paragraphs accurately

EQUIPMENT
none

You should start a new paragraph whenever:
- the person speaking changes
- the setting changes
- the topic changes
- the time changes.

Look at this student's response to a Paper 1, Section B exam-style writing task.

> Write the opening part of a story about an occasion when you saw, or thought you saw, something strange or mysterious.
>
> [40 marks]

> The lights from the cottage glowed faintly behind me as I headed out into the night and soon they were gone, lost behind trees. Now darkness stretched in every direction. I could see nothing but the stars and the black outline of hills in the distance. I looked up to the stars, scattered like glowing rocks across a blanket of blackness. One star seemed to be moving. I blinked and looked again. It was definitely moving across the sky, getting larger and changing colour from white to red to green. 'What on earth...?' I said aloud. The next thing I knew, I was lying on the ground, shivering in the cold, as the sun rose behind the distant hills. I must have been asleep for hours.

1. Mark the text with a double slash // every time the student should have started a new paragraph.

ENGLISH
Grades 3–5

MAIN ACTIVITY: SHORT PARAGRAPHS   **TIMING: 20 MINS**

LEARNING OBJECTIVES
- To be able to structure paragraphs for effect

EQUIPMENT
none

Look at these paragraphs written in response to the Paper 1, Section B exam-style writing task below. The student has given the final sentence its own paragraph. This is incorrect according to the rules of paragraphing, but they have chosen to do so for effect.

> Write the opening part of a story about an occasion when you saw, or thought you saw, something strange or mysterious.
>
> **[40 marks]**

> Grey clouds swept across the sky and the wind began to blow harder. The light was fading quickly and in the falling darkness splashes of rain began to land on my face. In the distance, I heard a dog barking. It sounded angry. Suddenly the wind dropped and I paused to listen to the stillness and scan the horizon for anything familiar. There was nothing I knew, nothing I recognised at all. I was lost. The dog started barking again, as though it was running. That was when I saw it.
>
> The silhouette of a dog appeared at the top of the hill, running towards me, its teeth bared and its eyes glowing with fury.

1. What is the effect of the student's choice of paragraphing? Write one or two sentences explaining your ideas.

2. Could the writer have achieved a similar effect by giving any of the other sentences its own paragraph?

    a) Underline one sentence in the longer paragraph.

    b) Explain your choice.

ENGLISH
— Grades 3-5 —

| MAIN ACTIVITY: HOOKS AND PUNCHES | TIMING: 20 MINS |

LEARNING OBJECTIVES
- To be able to structure paragraphs for effect

EQUIPMENT
none

You can structure longer paragraphs for effect in a piece of narrative or descriptive writing.

1. **Read the final sentences in each of these paragraphs, written in response to the Paper 1, Section B exam-style writing task below.**

> Write the opening part of a story about an occasion when you saw, or thought you saw, something strange or mysterious.
>
> [40 marks]

> The creature bounded towards me, its short black fur bristling, its eyes burning, its teeth bared and dripping with strands of drool. In the few seconds it took to reach me, I looked around for somewhere to run, somewhere to climb, some way to get away from the monster. There was nowhere to run, nowhere to hide.

> The creature bounded towards me, its short black fur bristling, its eyes burning, its teeth bared and dripping with strands of drool. In the few seconds it took to reach me, I looked around for somewhere to run, somewhere to climb, some way to get away from the monster. Was this how my life would end – my body torn to pieces and devoured?

   a) One paragraph ends with a **hook** to create a feeling of pace and tension, and make the reader want to read on to find out what happens. Label it 'H'.

   b) One paragraph ends with a **punch**. A key idea is put at the end to give it dramatic emphasis. Label it 'P'.

2. **Now read the next paragraph in this student's response.**

> I took a step back and it took a step forward. I took another step back. It took two steps forward. Its eyes burned, staring into mine and it seemed to tense every muscle, as though preparing to attack.

   a) Write a final sentence that would work as a hook at the end of this paragraph.

   ----

   b) Write a final sentence that would work as a punch at the end of this paragraph.

164

AQA ENGLISH — Grades 3-5

Homework activity: Paragraphing for effect

Timing: 30 mins

Learning objectives
- To be able to use paragraphs accurately
- To be able to structure paragraphs for effect

Equipment

none

Look at this student's plan for their response to a Paper 1, Section B exam-style writing task.

> Describe an occasion when you faced a fear. Focus on the thoughts and feelings you had at that time.
> [40 marks]

- in underground cavern
- feeling claustrophobic
- suddenly realise water is dripping
- water starts gushing in
- the cavern is filling up
- the way back and the way ahead are about to disappear beneath the water

1. On a separate piece of paper, write at least three paragraphs in response to the task, using some of the ideas from the student's plan.
   Make sure you:
   - carefully structure longer paragraphs, thinking about hooks and punches
   - use one short paragraph for dramatic effect.

2. Annotate your writing, noting the paragraphing choices you have made and the effect you intend your choices to have on the reader.

ENGLISH
Grades 3-5

24 ANSWERS

STARTER ACTIVITY: HOW TO PARAGRAPH

1. The lights from the cottage glowed faintly behind me as I headed out into the night and soon they were gone, lost behind trees. Now darkness stretched in every direction. I could see nothing but the stars and the black outline of hills in the distance. I looked up to the stars, scattered like glowing rocks across a blanket of blackness. One star seemed to be moving. I blinked and looked again. It was definitely moving across the sky, getting larger and changing colour from white to red to green. // 'What on earth...?' I said aloud. // The next thing I knew, I was lying on the ground, shivering in the cold, as the sun rose behind the distant hills. I must have been asleep for hours.

MAIN ACTIVITY: SHORT PARAGRAPHS

1. Short paragraphs can be used to emphasise key points or add dramatic emphasis.
2. Any one of the final three sentences of the longer paragraph could each be given their own paragraph to create dramatic emphasis.

MAIN ACTIVITY: HOOKS AND PUNCHES

1. a) H – 'There was nowhere to run, nowhere to hide.'
b) P – 'Was this how my life would end – my body torn to pieces and devoured?'
2. a) Hook sentences might focus on an interruption, e.g. a shout or whistle that distracts the creature.
b) Punch sentences might focus on the dog's attack and its consequences.

HOMEWORK ACTIVITY: PARAGRAPHING FOR EFFECT

1. and 2. See marking guidance on pages 251–253. Ensure paragraphs are used accurately or structured for effect, and are annotated to identify that effect.

ENGLISH
Grades 3-5

25 Descriptive and narrative writing: Structuring sentences

Learning objectives
- To develop understanding of clauses
- To be able to structure sentences for clarity

Specification links
- 3.1.2 producing clear and coherent text

Starter activity
- **What is a sentence?; 5 minutes; page 168**
  Use the activity to prompt and assess the student's understanding of sentences. Refer to the Glossary for a clear definition. Note that option B follows a typical sentence structure (subject + verb + object + adverb) but lacks meaning. Option D lacks punctuation, suggesting it is part of a longer sentence.

Main activities
- **Breaking sentences down; 20 minutes; page 169**
  The student can adjust the given sentence or rewrite it.
- **Building sentences up; 20 minutes; page 170**
  Check that the student understands the function of conjunctions and how to form present participles. Encourage them to use each conjunction only once, highlighting the need to avoid repetition.

Plenary activity
- **Rebuilding a sentence; 5 minutes**
  Ask the student to repeat the activity from 'Building sentences up' using conjunctions and present participles to link the clauses differently. If time allows, come up with two versions of each sentence and discuss which has the greatest clarity and fluency.

Homework activity
- **Crafting sentences; 30 minutes; page 171**
  Note that this worksheet uses the same stimulus as the Homework activity in lesson 24. If the student has completed the homework, ask them to rewrite one of their paragraphs from that activity twice.

Support idea
- **Breaking sentences down**; **Building sentences up** Model breaking down and linking up sentences, explaining how you made each decision.

Extension idea
- **Building sentences up** Encourage the student to read their sentence aloud each time they add to it, monitoring for clarity and fluency, and considering other possible choices that could be made.

Progress and observations

ENGLISH
— Grades 3-5 —

STARTER ACTIVITY: WHAT IS A SENTENCE?   **TIMING: 5 MINS**

LEARNING OBJECTIVES

- To develop understanding of clauses

EQUIPMENT

none

1. **Which of the following are sentences? Tick them.**

    ☐   A. Quickly home.
    ☐   B. Cat smiles a home quickly.
    ☐   C. Even under over after on up down.
    ☐   D. there is no place like home
    ☐   E. There is no place like home.

2. **Rewrite those you haven't ticked to make them into sentences. Use as many of the original words as possible.**

ENGLISH
Grades 3-5

MAIN ACTIVITY: BREAKING SENTENCES DOWN

TIMING: 20 MINS

LEARNING OBJECTIVES
- To develop understanding of clauses
- To be able to structure sentences for clarity

EQUIPMENT
none

Look at the sentence below, written in response to a writing task.

> Although it had been cold for several days, with thick grey clouds hanging over our tiny, remote cottage, there had been no sign of snow until one cold, bright morning snowflakes began to fall, rapidly wrapping the earth in a thick, white blanket, covering any sign of the grass or path or road beneath.

1. **Break this sentence down into as many shorter sentences as you can.**
   You will need to:
   - remove single words
   - add single words
   - alter single words
   - add full stops and capital letters.

   ----

2. **Check your answer.**
   Make sure that:
   - you have used accurate punctuation
   - each of your sentences conveys one key piece of information
   - each of your sentences makes clear sense.

ENGLISH
— Grades 3-5 —

| MAIN ACTIVITY: BUILDING SENTENCES UP | TIMING: 20 MINS |

LEARNING OBJECTIVES
- To develop understanding of clauses
- To be able to structure sentences for clarity

EQUIPMENT
none

Read the sentences below.

> We ran to the window.
>
> It floated through the air.
>
> We laughed.
>
> We put on coats and shoes.
>
> We watched the snow.
>
> It settled on the ground.
>
> We quickly hurried to the door.
>
> We ran out into the crisp, cold air.

1. **Link all of the ideas above into one longer sentence.**
   You could link them using:
   - **conjunctions**, for example: *and, but, when, as, because, until, after, before*
   - **present participles**, for example: *running, watching, floating, settling*.

   ----

2. **Check your answer.**
   Make sure that:
   - you have used accurate punctuation
   - your sentence makes clear sense.

ENGLISH
— Grades 3-5 —

HOMEWORK ACTIVITY: CRAFTING SENTENCES	TIMING: 30 MINS

LEARNING OBJECTIVES
- To be able to structure sentences for clarity

EQUIPMENT
none

Look again at this student's plan for their response to a Paper 1, Section B exam-style writing task.

> Describe an occasion when you faced a fear. Focus on the thoughts and feelings you had at that time.
> **[40 marks]**

- in underground cavern
- feeling claustrophobic
- suddenly realise water is dripping
- water starts gushing in
- the cavern is filling up
- the way back and the way ahead are about to disappear beneath the water

1. On a separate piece of paper, write a paragraph in response to the task, using some of the ideas from the student's plan.
   Think about:
   - using shorter sentences containing just one piece of information
   - using longer sentences containing more than one piece of information
   - how you will link the pieces of information in the longer sentences.

2. Rewrite your paragraph, using different choices of sentence structure and methods of linking ideas within sentences.

3. Which version of your paragraph do you prefer? Why? Explain your choice.

ENGLISH
Grades 3-5

25 ANSWERS

STARTER ACTIVITY: WHAT IS A SENTENCE?
1. Option E is the only complete sentence.
2. Student's own answers

MAIN ACTIVITY: BREAKING SENTENCES DOWN
1. Example: It had been cold for several days. Thick grey clouds hung over our tiny, remote cottage. There had been no sign of snow. One cold, bright morning snowflakes began to fall. They rapidly wrapped the earth in a thick, white blanket. They covered any sign of the grass or path or road beneath.
2. Student's own answer

MAIN ACTIVITY: BUILDING SENTENCES UP
1. Example: We ran to the window, watched the snow **float** through the air **until** it settled on the ground, **and** we laughed, quickly **hurrying** to the door, **putting** on coats and shoes, **and running** out into the crisp, cold air.
2. Student's own answer

HOMEWORK ACTIVITY: CRAFTING SENTENCES
1. Student's own answer. Ensure a variety of sentence structures and conjunctions are used. Above all, focus on clarity and fluency.
2. Student's own answer
3. Student's own answer

GLOSSARY

Sentence
A group of words that must contain a subject and a verb – it expresses a complete thought, and can have one or more clauses

Conjunction
A word used to connect clauses or sentences, e.g. *and*, *but*, *when*, *because*

Present participle
A verb form ending in *–ing*, e.g. running, jumping, shouting

Clause
A group of words that contains a subject (noun, pronoun or noun phrase) and a verb; it can be in the active or passive voice and may also contain an object; it is not the same as a sentence, as clauses can be subordinated whereas sentences cannot

ENGLISH
Grades 3–5

26 DESCRIPTIVE AND NARRATIVE WRITING: SENTENCE STRUCTURE FOR EFFECT

LEARNING OBJECTIVES	SPECIFICATION LINKS
• To be able to manipulate sentence structure • To be able to structure sentences for effect	• 3.1.2 writing for impact

STARTER ACTIVITY

- **Short sentences; 5 minutes; page 174**
  Recap lesson 9, if completed, which looks at sentences and their impact on the reader. Also recap lesson 24, which looks at short paragraphs for emphasis. Ask the student to adjust the sentences on the worksheet, removing any conjunctions and adding punctuation and capital letters to clarify the changes.

MAIN ACTIVITIES

- **Ordering clauses; 20 minutes; page 175**
  Point out that chronology plays a part in reordering clauses because events in a sentence in chronological order cannot be resequenced without changing or losing meaning.
- **Experimenting with sentences; 20 minutes; page 176**
  Note that the information positioned at the beginning and, in particular, the end of the sentence tends to have the greatest emphasis.

PLENARY ACTIVITY

- **Review; 5 minutes**
  Ask the student to summarise and evaluate their understanding of how sentences can be structured for effect. Discuss initial ideas for the Homework activity and how this understanding could be applied to it.

HOMEWORK ACTIVITY

- **Crafting sentences for impact; 30 minutes; page 177**
  Ask the student to write one or two paragraphs of five to ten sentences for each response. Emphasise the importance of producing two responses, and experimenting with different sentence structures in each.

SUPPORT IDEA

- **Ordering clauses; Experimenting with sentences** The student may benefit from cutting out and shuffling the pairs of clauses to help them experiment with restructuring.

EXTENSION IDEAS

- **Experimenting with sentences** Encourage the student to be as specific as possible about the variety of effects and impacts that the different sentence structures achieve.
- **Crafting sentences for impact** Ask the student to produce a final draft of their response, compiling the most effective elements of both versions, with annotations to identify their intended impact.

PROGRESS AND OBSERVATIONS

ENGLISH
— Grades 3-5 —

Starter activity: Short sentences

Timing: 5 mins

Learning objectives
- To be able to structure sentences for effect

Equipment
none

Read these long sentences, written in response to a Paper 1, Section B exam-style writing task.

> Write the opening part of a story about an occasion when you saw, or thought you saw, something strange or mysterious.
>
> **[40 marks]**

A. As I looked out of the window at the dark night sky, I noticed a shadowy figure moving across the grass below until, just beneath my window, it stopped and it was looking straight at me.

B. I could see its eyes, dark and menacing, glistening in the light of the moon like two pools of the blackest oil and I tried to turn away but I could not because it felt as though I was rooted to the floor.

1. Which parts of these sentences could you separate into their own shorter sentences to give them greater emphasis? Underline them.

MAIN ACTIVITY: ORDERING CLAUSES   **TIMING: 20 MINS**

LEARNING OBJECTIVES
- To be able to manipulate sentence structure

EQUIPMENT
- scissors

In some sentences, the different parts – or clauses – can be swapped around without changing the meaning.

| I fell over | and | hurt myself. | → | I hurt myself | and | fell over. | ✗ |
| I hurt myself | when | I fell over. | → | When | I fell over, | I hurt myself. | ✓ |

1. Which of these sentences can be reordered without changing their meaning or losing sense? Tick them.

A. { I could hear footsteps on the stairs } { so I shut and locked my door. }

B. { I knew the thing was coming for me, } { although I didn't know why. }

C. { I could hear the footsteps coming closer to my door } { and } { I froze. }

D. { The thing hammered at my door, } { groaning and muttering my name. }

E. { I backed away from the door, } { shivering in terror. }

2. Look at the sentences you have ticked. Write a new version underneath each one, with the two halves of the sentence swapped around.

3. Which version of each sentence do you prefer? Mark it with an asterisk *.

ENGLISH
Grades 3-5

MAIN ACTIVITY: EXPERIMENTING WITH SENTENCES **TIMING: 20 MINS**

LEARNING OBJECTIVES
- To be able to structure sentences for effect

EQUIPMENT
- scissors

All the elements in the sentences below can be moved around, repositioned and sequenced differently.

A. { I watched in terror } { as the key in the lock } { turned } { slowly } { as though by itself. }

B. { The door handle turned } { as I backed away from the door } { in trembling terror. }

C. { There } { stood } { the most frightening thing I have ever seen } { in the doorway. }

1. Rewrite each sentence two or three times, on a separate piece of paper, experimenting with sequencing its elements in different ways.

2. Think about the impact of the sentence structures you have used and which ideas they emphasise.

    a) Label the structures that emphasise what is happening 'Action'.
    b) Label the structures that emphasise the feelings of the narrator 'Feeling'.
    c) Label the structures that emphasise tension by holding back key information 'Tension'.

ENGLISH
— Grades 3-5 —

AQA

HOMEWORK ACTIVITY: CRAFTING SENTENCES FOR IMPACT   TIMING: 30 MINS

LEARNING OBJECTIVES
- To be able to structure sentences for effect

EQUIPMENT
none

1. Write the first three sentences of your response to this Paper 1, Section B exam-style writing task.

   > Write the opening part of a story about an occasion when you saw, or thought you saw, something strange or mysterious.
   >
   > **[40 marks]**

2. Rewrite your response, thinking carefully about how you could add impact by restructuring your sentences.
   You could:
   - use a short sentence to add dramatic impact
   - rearrange the elements of longer sentences to alter their emphasis or to add tension.

ENGLISH
Grades 3-5

26 ANSWERS

STARTER ACTIVITY: SHORT SENTENCES

1. 'it was looking straight at me'; 'it felt as though I was rooted to the floor'

MAIN ACTIVITY: ORDERING CLAUSES

1. Sentences B, D and E can be reordered.
2. and 3. Student's own answer

MAIN ACTIVITY: EXPERIMENTING WITH SENTENCES

1. and 2. Examples: Action – As I backed away from the door in trembling terror, the door handle turned.
Feeling – There, in the doorway, stood the most frightening thing I have ever seen.
Tension – I watched in terror as the key in the lock, as though by itself, slowly turned.

HOMEWORK ACTIVITY: CRAFTING SENTENCES FOR IMPACT

1. Student's own answer
2. Ensure that the student writes at least two versions of the opening, using a variety of carefully considered sentence structures.

GLOSSARY

Clause
A group of words that contains a subject (noun, pronoun or noun phrase) and a verb; it can be in the active or passive voice and may also contain an object; it is not the same as a sentence, as clauses can be subordinated whereas sentences cannot

ENGLISH
Grades 3-5

27 DESCRIPTIVE AND NARRATIVE WRITING: SELECTING VOCABULARY

LEARNING OBJECTIVES	SPECIFICATION LINKS
• To be able to select vocabulary for concision and precision • To be able to consider connotation	• 3.1.2 writing for impact

STARTER ACTIVITY
- **Overdoing description; 5 minutes; page 180**
  Discuss the effectiveness of the sentence, focusing on unnecessary use of modification (e.g. light, bright, pure white) and verbs (e.g. fell and fluttered and wandered and drifted and floated). Emphasise the importance of making concise, precise vocabulary choices.

MAIN ACTIVITIES
- **Concision and precision; 20 minutes; page 181**
  Ensure that the student understands the need to balance conciseness and precision. Ask them to complete the questions, reviewing their choices after each one.
- **Connotation; 20 minutes; page 182**
  Remind the student of their work on connotation in lesson 7. Emphasise the link between their intention as a writer (the impact/effect/mood they want to create) and choosing vocabulary for its connotations.

PLENARY ACTIVITY
- **Review; 5 minutes**
  Ask the student to summarise and evaluate their understanding of vocabulary choice. Discuss initial ideas for the Homework activity and the decisions they will need to make.

HOMEWORK ACTIVITY
- **Crafting vocabulary; 30 minutes; page 183**
  Ask the student to write one or two paragraphs in response to the exam-style writing task. Emphasise the importance of reviewing and revising their vocabulary choices, and of making these revisions clear.

SUPPORT IDEA
- **Crafting vocabulary** Suggest that the student first identify vocabulary that could be improved, then gather three or four possible choices and, finally, choose the most effective option.

EXTENSION IDEA
- **Connotation** Encourage the student to come up with a range of connotations and to give precise explanations for which option they would choose and why.

PROGRESS AND OBSERVATIONS

ENGLISH
— Grades 3–5 —

AQA

| STARTER ACTIVITY: OVERDOING DESCRIPTION | TIMING: 5 MINS |

LEARNING OBJECTIVES
- To be able to select vocabulary for concision and precision

EQUIPMENT
none

Look at the sentence below, written in response to the following Paper 1, Section B exam-style writing task.

Write a description suggested by this picture:

[40 marks]

> Tiny little delicate flakes of light, bright, pure white snow fell and fluttered and wandered and drifted and floated slowly, gracefully in ever changing patterns and swirls, landing and settling quietly and gently on the ground.

1. **Which vocabulary choices could you cut out of this sentence to improve it without losing its meaning or impact? Cross them out.**

ENGLISH
Grades 3-5

AQA

MAIN ACTIVITY: CONCISION AND PRECISION   **TIMING: 20 MINS**

LEARNING OBJECTIVES
- To be able to select vocabulary for concision and precision

EQUIPMENT
none

Read the sentences below.

We ~~went out quickly~~ into the ~~snowy outdoors~~.

Anwar was ~~laughing excitedly~~ until a snowball ~~hit him hard~~ in his face.

'That hurt!' he ~~said loudly~~.

He ~~looked angrily~~ at everyone around him.

'This is war,' he ~~said quietly to himself under his breath~~.

1. Replace each crossed out phrase with a single word, without changing or losing its meaning.

2. Write two or three sentences describing someone building a snowman. Make sure your vocabulary choices are as concise and precise as possible.

....

....

....

....

....

....

....

3. Look again at your sentences for question 2. Could you make your vocabulary choices even more precise and concise?

ENGLISH
— Grades 3-5 —

AQA

MAIN ACTIVITY: CONNOTATION   **TIMING: 20 MINS**

LEARNING OBJECTIVES

- To be able to consider connotation

EQUIPMENT

none

1. Read the sentence below from one student's response to a descriptive writing task.

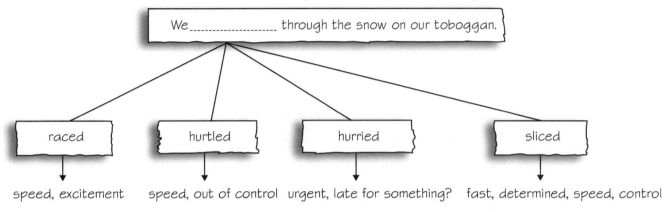

a) The student has noted some possible vocabulary choices and their connotations. Which one would you choose? Tick it.

b) Write a sentence or two explaining your choice.

----

2. Read the sentences below.

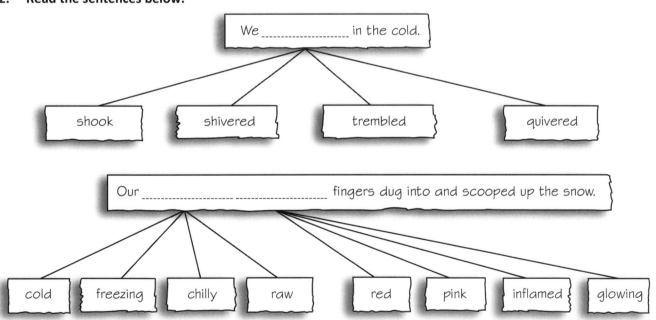

a) Discuss the connotations of each vocabulary choice with your tutor.

b) Which option would you choose in each case? Tick them.

182

ENGLISH
— Grades 3-5 —

| HOMEWORK ACTIVITY: CRAFTING VOCABULARY | TIMING: 30 MINS |

LEARNING OBJECTIVES
- To be able to select vocabulary for concision and precision
- To be able to consider connotation

EQUIPMENT
none

1. On a separate piece of paper, write the opening paragraph of your response to this Paper 1, Section B-style writing task.

Write a description suggested by this picture:

2. Look carefully at your vocabulary choices.

   a) Could any of your vocabulary be more concise and precise? Identify, review and revise any that could, using a thesaurus or online dictionary where necessary.
   b) Could any of your choices be replaced with vocabulary that has more effective connotations? Identify, review and revise them.

Remember to clearly show all the options you consider, and all the choices you make as you review and revise your writing.

ENGLISH
— Grades 3-5 —

27 ANSWERS

STARTER ACTIVITY: OVERDOING DESCRIPTION
1. Example: ~~Tiny little~~ delicate flakes of ~~light, bright,~~ pure white snow ~~fell and~~ fluttered ~~and wandered and drifted and floated slowly, gracefully~~ in ever changing patterns ~~and swirls, landing and~~ settling ~~quietly and~~ gently on the ground.

MAIN ACTIVITY: CONCISION AND PRECISION
1. Examples: We ~~went out quickly~~ hurried into the ~~snowy outdoors~~ snow.
Anwar was ~~laughing excitedly~~ giggling until a snowball ~~hit him hard~~ smashed in his face.
'That hurt!' he ~~said loudly~~ bellowed.
He ~~looked angrily~~ scowled at everyone around him.
'This is war,' he ~~said quietly to himself under his breath~~ muttered.
2. Student's own answer
3. Student's own answer

MAIN ACTIVITY: CONNOTATION
1. Student's own answer
2. Examples: shook/quivered – excitement; shivered – cold; trembled – fear; cold – unhappiness, lack of emotion; freezing – extreme cold, pain; chilly – bearable coldness; raw – pain; red/inflamed – anger, pain; glowing/pink – comfortable, bearable coldness.

HOMEWORK ACTIVITY: CRAFTING VOCABULARY
1. See marking guidance on pages 251–253. Look for responses that aim to achieve an engaging, descriptive opening.
2. Ensure clear evidence of review and revision is shown.

GLOSSARY

Connotation
The ideas and feelings that a word or phrase can suggest to the reader

Precision
Writing precisely means choosing the most appropriate vocabulary to illustrate a point. This involves choosing precise vocabulary, such as *postpone* rather than *put off* and *was purchased* rather than *got bought*.

Concision
Concise writing uses the fewest number of words possible, without sacrificing the intended meaning or effect.

AQA ENGLISH — Grades 3–5

28 Descriptive and narrative writing: Consolidation

LEARNING OBJECTIVES	SPECIFICATION LINKS
• To be able to plan and write an effective piece of descriptive or narrative writing	• 3.1.2 producing clear and coherent text • 3.1.2 writing for impact

Starter activity

- **The map; 5 minutes; page 186**
  Explain to the student that this lesson will consolidate all of their learning on descriptive and narrative writing. Emphasise that this activity will be the 'map' they will follow as they craft their response to the writing task.

Main activities

- **Planning; 20 minutes; page 187**
  Reiterate the importance of planning over the need to 'just get on with the writing'.

- **Beginning writing; 20 minutes; page 188**
  If the previous activity goes over time, focus this activity on the opening sentence or two of the response. Note that it is probably advisable for students at this level to review their writing as a whole, rather than after the opening paragraph; however, this is a valuable exercise for students of all levels. Identify opportunities for revision and note possible changes.

Plenary activity

- **Review; 5 minutes**
  Work with the student to review the impact of their opening, focusing on choices and possible revisions to paragraphing, sentence structure and vocabulary choice.

Homework activity

- **Complete your response; 30 minutes; page 189**
  Emphasise the importance of following the 'map' from the Starter activity.

Support idea

- **Planning** Encourage the student to verbalise their thinking. Prompt where necessary.

Extension idea

- **Planning; Beginning writing** Encourage the student to constantly review and revise throughout the planning and writing process, focusing on how effectively their response will achieve their intention.

Progress and observations

ENGLISH
Grades 3-5

AQA

STARTER ACTIVITY: THE MAP

TIMING: 5 MINS

LEARNING OBJECTIVES

- To be able to plan and write an effective piece of descriptive or narrative writing

EQUIPMENT

none

You are going to write your response to this Paper 1, Section B exam-style writing task.

> Describe an occasion when you accidentally overheard a conversation - and wished you had not heard it. Focus on the thoughts and feelings you had at that time.
>
> [40 marks]

1. Below is a list of the steps for crafting an effective response. At what stage and in what order will you complete them?

    a) Tick to show whether you will complete each step *before*, *during* or *after* writing.

    b) Number the steps to show the order in which you will complete them.

	Before	During	After	Number
Think carefully about the beginning and ending.	☐	☐	☐	☐
Review and revise your choices of paragraph structure, sentence structure and vocabulary.	☐	☐	☐	☐
Structure and sequence your ideas.	☐	☐	☐	☐
Identify the central idea your writing will focus on.	☐	☐	☐	☐
Structure your sentences for clarity and impact.	☐	☐	☐	☐
Identify your intention (the impact you want your writing to have on the reader).	☐	☐	☐	☐
Select precise vocabulary for impact.	☐	☐	☐	☐
Check your spelling, punctuation and grammar.	☐	☐	☐	☐
Think about how you will use paragraphs.	☐	☐	☐	☐
Gather a range of ideas.	☐	☐	☐	☐

AQA ENGLISH
Grades 3–5

MAIN ACTIVITY: PLANNING **TIMING: 20 MINS**

LEARNING OBJECTIVES

- To be able to plan and write an effective piece of descriptive or narrative writing

EQUIPMENT

none

1. Use the questions below to help you plan a response to this Paper 1, Section B exam-style writing task.

> Describe an occasion when you accidentally overheard a conversation - and wished you had not heard it. Focus on the thoughts and feelings you had at that time.
>
> **[40 marks]**

The central idea

a) What did you overhear? How did you feel? Try to think of two different ideas, and then choose the strongest.

....

....

....

The intention

b) How do you want your reader to respond to your writing? For example, with shock, sympathy, disgust, humour or something else?

....

....

....

The details

c) Note down the ideas, events and details you will include in your response.

....

....

....

The order

d) Write out your ideas in order, thinking carefully about the beginning and ending in particular.

....

....

....

ENGLISH
Grades 3-5

AQA

| MAIN ACTIVITY: BEGINNING WRITING | TIMING: **20** MINS |

LEARNING OBJECTIVES
- To be able to plan and write an effective piece of descriptive or narrative writing

EQUIPMENT
none

> Describe an occasion when you accidentally overheard a conversation - and wished you had not heard it. Focus on the thoughts and feelings you had at that time.
>
> **[40 marks]**

1. Write the first two or three sentences of your response to the Paper 1, Section B exam-style writing task.

2. **Pause to review your writing so far.**
   Think about:

   Structure
   - Will your opening effectively engage and interest the reader?

   Paragraphs
   - Could you use a short paragraph to add impact to your writing?
   - Could you add a 'hook' or 'punch' to the end of a paragraph?

   Sentence structure
   - Are your sentences carefully structured to express your ideas clearly and fluently?
   - Could you use a short sentence to add dramatic impact?
   - Could you rearrange the elements of any longer sentences to alter their emphasis or add tension?

   Vocabulary
   - Could any of your vocabulary choices be more concise or precise?
   - Could any of your vocabulary choices have more effective connotations?

AQA ENGLISH — Grades 3-5

HOMEWORK ACTIVITY: COMPLETE YOUR RESPONSE	TIMING: 30 MINS

LEARNING OBJECTIVES
- To be able to plan and write an effective piece of descriptive or narrative writing

EQUIPMENT
none

1. Complete your response to this Paper 1, Section B exam-style writing task.

> Describe an occasion when you accidentally overheard a conversation - and wished you had not heard it. Focus on the thoughts and feelings you had at that time.
>
> **[40 marks]**

2. When you have completed your response, review and revise it.
   Think about your choices of:
   - whole text structure
   - paragraph structure
   - sentence structure
   - vocabulary.

28 Answers

STARTER ACTIVITY: THE MAP

1. a) and b) Before writing:
1. Identify the central idea your writing will focus on
2. Identify your intention (the impact you want your writing to have on the reader)
3. Gather a range of ideas
4. Structure and sequence your ideas
5. Think carefully about the beginning and ending.
During writing:
6. Think about how you will use paragraphs
7. Structure your sentences for clarity and impact
8. Select precise vocabulary for impact.
After writing:
9. Review and revise your choices of paragraph structure, sentence structure and vocabulary
10. Check your spelling, punctuation and grammar.

MAIN ACTIVITY: PLANNING

1. Check that enough material has been gathered and sequenced to ensure successful completion of the writing task.

MAIN ACTIVITY: BEGINNING WRITING

1. and 2. Ensure the student's review is thorough and carefully considered.

HOMEWORK ACTIVITY: COMPLETE YOUR RESPONSE

1. See marking guidance on pages 251–253. Look for responses that focus on the narrator's thoughts and feelings.
2. Ensure the student's review and revision are thorough and carefully considered.

AQA ENGLISH — Grades 3-5

29 Writing to present a viewpoint: Gathering ideas

Learning objectives
- To be able to identify the appropriate form, purpose and audience for a writing task
- To be able to gather ideas to present a viewpoint

Specification links
- 3.1.2 producing clear and coherent text
- 3.1.2 writing for impact

Starter activity
- **Reading the task; 5 minutes; page 192**
  Remind the student that they will tackle a similar writing task in Paper 2 of the exam. Emphasise the importance of identifying the key words and phrases in the task before planning or writing anything.

Main activities
- **Know your own mind; 20 minutes; page 193**
  Remind the student of relevant texts they read in earlier lessons that may prompt ideas, e.g. Source C: *Earth in the Balance* (page 19) and Source F: *A Century of Achievement* (page 22). Support them with discussion. Point out that considering others' points of view is a technique that can be used to develop one's own, even if these views are not referred to in their final response.
- **Question the question; 20 minutes; page 194**
  Note that some ideas may be repeated in questions 1 and 2. Explain to the student that the challenge of gathering ideas in two different ways can help them to broaden their thinking.

Plenary activity
- **Select and reject; 5 minutes**
  Ask the student to review the ideas they gathered in the previous activity. Which are the strongest? Which will form the basis of a powerful response to the writing task? Which might be combined to form a more developed argument? Which should be rejected?

Homework activity
- **Gathering ideas; 30 minutes; page 195**
  Ensure the student understands the sequence of steps used in the lesson to gather a range of ideas, and emphasise that these should also be followed in the Homework activity.

Support ideas
- **Know your own mind** Prompt the student to consider which people might have a point of view, e.g. scientists, environmentalists, the owners of science and technology companies, etc.
- **Question the question** The student may find one method more accessible than another; if so, focus on that one.

Extension idea
- **Question the question** Encourage the student to gather the widest possible range of ideas. Explain that a process of selection and rejection will follow.

Progress and observations

ENGLISH — Grades 3-5

AQA

STARTER ACTIVITY: READING THE TASK

TIMING: 5 MINS

LEARNING OBJECTIVES

- To be able to identify the appropriate form, purpose and audience for a writing task

EQUIPMENT

none

Read the Paper 2, Section A exam-style writing task below.

> 'Humankind is destroying the Earth. Science and technology is doing more harm than good. We need to act now before it's too late.'
>
> Write an article for a broadsheet newspaper in which you explain your point of view on this statement.
>
> **[40 marks]**

1. **Underline and label the key words or phrases in the task.**
   - Use 'form' to label words or phrases that tell you about the form in which you should write, for example a letter or an article.
   - Use 'purpose' to label the words or phrases that tell you the purpose of your writing.
   - Use 'audience' to label the words or phrases that tell you about the audience you are writing for.
   - Use 'idea' to label the central idea that you must respond to in your writing.

2. **Use the table below to note down some of the key features you need to remember when writing in this form, for this purpose and for this audience.**

Formality	Presentation and layout	Techniques

AQA ENGLISH — Grades 3–5

MAIN ACTIVITY: KNOW YOUR OWN MIND	TIMING: 20 MINS

LEARNING OBJECTIVES
- To be able to gather ideas to present a viewpoint

EQUIPMENT
none

Look again at the Paper 2, Section B exam-style writing task from the Starter activity.

> 'Humankind is destroying the Earth. Science and technology is doing more harm than good. We need to act now before it's too late.'
>
> Write an article for a broadsheet newspaper in which you explain your point of view on this statement.
>
> **[40 marks]**

1. **Who might have a strong opinion on this topic? Think of four types of people and write their job titles or backgrounds in the boxes below.**
   Think about:
   - people you know
   - people in your local area
   - people you hear and see on the news
   - anyone else.

2. What opinions might these people have? Note their thoughts in the thought bubbles.
3. Look at the different opinions you have noted. Do you agree with any of them? Note your point of view in one or two sentences.

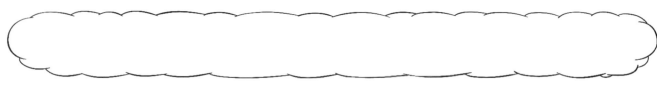

ENGLISH
Grades 3–5

MAIN ACTIVITY: QUESTION THE QUESTION **TIMING: 20 MINS**

LEARNING OBJECTIVES

- To be able to gather ideas to present a viewpoint

EQUIPMENT

none

One way to develop your point of view is to return to the task and question it. You could ask:

What?   When?   Who?   Why?   Where?   How?

Here are some questions a student has asked about the task.

How are we destroying the Earth?

Why is it doing harm?

> 'Humankind is destroying the Earth. Science and technology is doing more harm than good. We need to act now before it's too late.'

What do we need to do?

1. Note down the ideas that these questions give you.

....

....

....

....

....

....

Another way to develop your ideas is to think about the problems raised by the statement in the writing task, and the solutions you could suggest.

2. Note your ideas in the table below.

Problems	Solutions

AQA ENGLISH — Grades 3–5

Homework activity: Gathering ideas

Timing: 30 mins

Learning objectives
- To be able to identify the appropriate form, purpose and audience for a writing task
- To be able to gather ideas to present a viewpoint

Equipment

none

You are going to gather a range of ideas in response to this Paper 2, Section B exam-style writing task.

> 'Our towns and cities are out of control. We need to work together as a community to solve our community's problems.'
>
> Write a letter to your local newspaper in which you explain your point of view on this statement.
>
> **[40 marks]**

1. Annotate the task, identifying the form, purpose, audience and central idea.

2. Note your opinion on this topic.

   ....
   ....
   ....
   ....

3. Develop your ideas by questioning the question and/or thinking about problems and solutions.

   ....
   ....
   ....
   ....
   ....
   ....
   ....
   ....
   ....
   ....

4. Review your ideas. Which could you use in your response to the task above? Tick them.

ENGLISH
Grades 3–5

29 Answers

Starter activity: Reading the task

1. Form: newspaper article; Purpose: explain your point of view; Audience: readers of a broadsheet newspaper; Idea: Humankind is destroying the Earth. We need to act now.
2. Examples: formal register, headline, rhetorical devices, counter-argument.

Main activity: Know your own mind

1. Ensure a range of relevant parties are identified, e.g. scientists, environmentalists, owners of science or technology companies.
2. Student's own answer
3. Student's own answer

Main activity: Question the question

1. and 2. Student's own answer. Ensure the student identifies at least five key ideas, allowing them to select the strongest and reject the weakest.

Homework activity: Gathering ideas

1. Form: letter to newspaper
Purpose: explain your point of view
Audience: readers of a local newspaper
Idea: Towns and cities out of control; work together to solve community's problems
2. and 3. Student's own answers
4. Ensure at least five key ideas are identified, and at least three significant points selected.

AQA ENGLISH — Grades 3-5

30 Writing to present a viewpoint: Structure and planning

LEARNING OBJECTIVES
- To understand how to structure an argument text
- To be able to plan and shape an argument

SPECIFICATION LINKS
- 3.1.2 producing clear and coherent text
- 3.1.2 writing for impact

STARTER ACTIVITY
- **Know your intentions; 5 minutes; page 198**
  Explain to the student that they are going to focus on the exam-style writing task they worked on for homework in lesson 29. Ask the student to complete the question as fully but as succinctly as possible.

MAIN ACTIVITIES
- **Structure; 15 minutes; page 199**
  Ask the student to complete question 1, pointing out that some elements (e.g. key idea/evidence) will appear three or more times in a typical argument. Note that not every row on the mapping table needs to be filled in. In question 2, focus the student's attention on why these elements are key to an effective argument.
- **Sequence and shape; 25 minutes; page 200**
  Ask the student to map their ideas in response to question 1 onto their structure from the Starter activity. It is a good idea to use adhesive putty so that they can experiment with arranging their ideas in different orders. Discuss each addition to the plan, focusing on the extent to which it achieves the contribution noted in the table. Explain that any gaps that become apparent, e.g. evidence, will be completed in the Homework activity, and that you will be exploring introductions and conclusions in more depth in the next lesson.

PLENARY ACTIVITY
- **Review; 5 minutes**
  Ask the student to review their plan: does it achieve the intention they identified in the Starter activity? Ask them to consider any gaps in their planning, and explain that they will fill these in for homework.

HOMEWORK ACTIVITY
- **Complete your plan; 30 minutes; page 201**
  The student can use glue to attach their ideas to the plan. Encourage them to focus on selecting the sort of evidence that will be available under exam conditions, e.g. facts that they already know (but probably not statistics), personal experiences etc.

SUPPORT IDEA
- **Structure** If the student is unfamiliar with writing arguments, you may need to provide an appropriate structure.

EXTENSION IDEA
- **Sequence and shape** Encourage the student to experiment with different sequences, shaping their response to achieve their intention as fully as possible.

PROGRESS AND OBSERVATIONS

ENGLISH
— Grades 3-5 —

AQA

STARTER ACTIVITY: KNOW YOUR INTENTIONS

TIMING: 5 MINS

LEARNING OBJECTIVES
- To be able to plan and shape an argument

EQUIPMENT
none

You are going to develop your planning in response to this Paper 2, Section B exam-style writing task.

> 'Our towns and cities are out of control. We need to work together as a community to solve our community's problems.'
>
> Write a letter to your local newspaper in which you explain your point of view on this statement.
>
> **[40 marks]**

Before you begin your plan, it is important to be clear on the intention you want to achieve in your response.

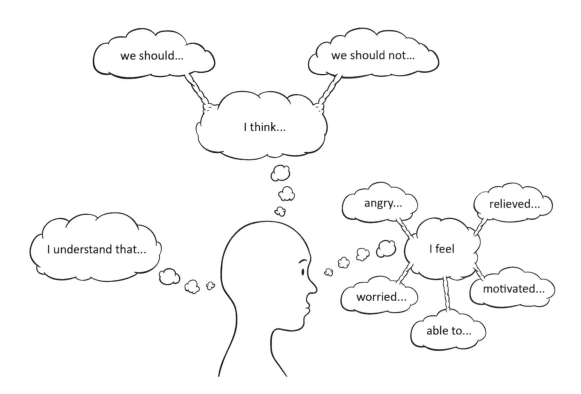

1. What do you want your reader to think, feel and/or know when they have finished reading your response to the above writing task? Summarise your intention in one or two sentences.

ENGLISH
— Grades 3-5 —

MAIN ACTIVITY: STRUCTURE **TIMING: 15 MINS**

LEARNING OBJECTIVES

- To understand how to structure an argument text

EQUIPMENT

none

Look at the typical elements of a text that presents the writer's viewpoint.

{ introduction } { conclusion } { counter argument } { key ideas } { supporting evidence }

1. Add the elements to the table below to map out an effective argument text. You may need to use some elements more than once.
2. What should each element contribute to the text and your intention? Add your ideas to the table.

	Element	Contribution
1		
2		
3		
4		
5		
6		
7		
8		
9		
10		

ENGLISH
— Grades 3-5 —

MAIN ACTIVITY: SEQUENCE AND SHAPE **TIMING: 25 MINS**

LEARNING OBJECTIVES
- To be able to plan and shape an argument

EQUIPMENT
- sticky notes

1. On separate sticky notes, write all the key ideas you could use in your response to the Paper 2, Section B exam-style writing task below.

> 'Our towns and cities are out of control. We need to work together as a community to solve our community's problems.'
>
> Write a letter to your local newspaper in which you explain your point of view on this statement.
>
> [40 marks]

2. Match each sticky note to your structure from the previous activity. Experiment with sequencing your ideas in different ways in the space below to produce the most effective plan.

AQA ENGLISH — Grades 3–5

HOMEWORK ACTIVITY: COMPLETE YOUR PLAN **TIMING: 30 MINS**

LEARNING OBJECTIVES
- To be able to plan and shape an argument

EQUIPMENT
- glue

> 'Our towns and cities are out of control. We need to work together as a community to solve our community's problems.'
>
> Write a letter to your local newspaper in which you explain your point of view on this statement.
>
> **[40 marks]**

1. Copy and complete the final plan of your response to the Paper 2, Section B exam-style writing task above.

	Element	Contribution
1		
2		
3		
4		
5		
6		
7		
8		
9		
10		

ENGLISH
— Grades 3-5 —

30 ANSWERS

STARTER ACTIVITY: KNOW YOUR INTENTIONS
1. Ensure that the student identifies a specific intention that clearly defines the impact they wish to make on the reader; do not accept vague aims such as *to get my point of view across*.

MAIN ACTIVITY: STRUCTURE
1. and 2. Examples:
Introduction: to establish the current situation and the argument, engaging the reader
Key ideas: explore an aspect of the problem/situation in order to support and develop the writer's point of view
Supporting evidence: an example to support this key idea
Counter argument: an opposing argument, undermined to reinforce the writer's point of view
Conclusion: a final summary of the writer's point of view to drive the argument home to the reader

MAIN ACTIVITY: SEQUENCE AND SHAPE
1. and 2. Ensure the student chooses an appropriate idea for each part of the structure, e.g. an engaging idea in the introduction, a concise idea that distils the writer's point of view for the conclusion etc.

HOMEWORK ACTIVITY: COMPLETE YOUR PLAN
1. Ensure that the student completes all of the given elements of the plan.

GLOSSARY

Counter argument
An argument that opposes the writer's point of view – writers often include a counter argument in order to highlight its failings and therefore reinforce the strength of their own point of view

Intention
The impact the writer wants a text to have on the reader

ENGLISH
Grades 3-5

31 WRITING TO PRESENT A VIEWPOINT: INTRODUCTIONS AND CONCLUSIONS

LEARNING OBJECTIVES
- To be able to craft an effective introduction and conclusion

SPECIFICATION LINKS
- 3.1.2 producing clear and coherent text
- 3.1.2 writing for impact

STARTER ACTIVITY
- **And the winner is…; 5 minutes; page 204**
  Discuss what makes an effective introduction (e.g. engaging and involving the reader) and an effective conclusion (e.g. leaving the reader with a call to action or clear image of the consequences of accepting or rejecting the writer's viewpoint).

MAIN ACTIVITIES
- **Introductions; 20 minutes; page 205**
  Discuss with the student why the three suggested elements of an introduction are effective. Discuss images and ideas that could be included in their introduction, e.g. highlighting how life has changed around the world because of science and technology.
- **Conclusions; 20 minutes; page 206**
  Discuss with the student why the three suggested elements of a conclusion are effective. Discuss the possible benefits or consequences of agreeing or disagreeing with the writer's point of view.

PLENARY ACTIVITY
- **Review; 5 minutes**
  Ask the student to review and evaluate their understanding of how to tackle writing an effective introduction and conclusion, and the impact that they can have on a reader.

HOMEWORK ACTIVITY
- **An introduction and conclusion; 30 minutes; page 207**
  Advise the student to look back at the plan they wrote for this writing task in lesson 30.

SUPPORT IDEA
- **Introductions; Conclusions** Encourage the student to concentrate on understanding the suggested approach and developing relevant ideas, rather than writing full responses to the tasks.

EXTENSION IDEA
- **Introductions; Conclusions** Encourage the student to develop a range of possible ideas and consider whether to include one, some or all of them.

PROGRESS AND OBSERVATIONS

ENGLISH
Grades 3-5

AQA

STARTER ACTIVITY: AND THE WINNER IS...

TIMING: 5 MINS

LEARNING OBJECTIVES
- To be able to craft an effective introduction and conclusion

EQUIPMENT
none

1. Look at these three opening sentences written by students in response to a Paper 2, Section B exam-style writing task.

> 'Humankind is destroying the Earth. Science and technology is doing more harm than good. We need to act now before it's too late.'
>
> Write an article for a broadsheet newspaper in which you explain your point of view on this statement.
>
> **[40 marks]**

A. In this newspaper article, I am going to write about how we are destroying the Earth and we need to do something about it.

B. Imagine how the world might look in the year 2100.

C. In the last forty years, thousands of animals and plants all around the world have become extinct, lost forever.

   a) Which sentence is the most effective? Tick it.
   b) Which is the least effective? Circle it.

2. Look at these three closing sentences written by students in response to the exam-style writing task.

A. So as I have already said, we need to recycle more, use less and look after the planet.

B. If we do not act now, what kind of life will your grandchildren have on this bare, colourless, polluted planet?

C. It's not too late to change everything but we need to start now, today.

   a) Which sentence is the most effective? Tick it.
   b) Which is the least effective? Circle it.

AQA ENGLISH — Grades 3–5

Main activity: Introductions

Timing: 20 mins

Learning objectives
- To be able to craft an effective introduction and conclusion

Equipment
none

Below is Student C's introduction to their response to the Paper 2, Section B exam-style writing task from the Starter activity, and some notes about the elements they wanted to include to make it more effective.

> In the last forty years, thousands of animals and plants all around the world have become extinct, lost forever. This is not an accident – it is the result of humankind caring more about making money and living comfortable lives than the planet on which we live. Perhaps it is already too late, but it is not too late to start trying to undo all the damage we have done.

Engage the reader with a shocking or surprising image/idea

Explain the background to the issue I am exploring

Introduce (but do not explain) my point of view

1. Underline where in their introduction Student C has achieved some of the elements they noted. Draw lines linking the relevant annotation to the text you have underlined.

2. Imagine you are planning to write a response to the same writing task, arguing that:
   - science and technology have transformed our lives for the better
   - we have damaged the environment but can use our scientific and technological skills to repair it.

   a) Write a sentence containing a shocking or surprising image or idea you could include in your introduction.

   ....

   ....

   ....

   b) Write a sentence explaining the background to your argument.

   ....

   ....

   ....

   c) Write a sentence introducing (but not explaining) your argument.

   ....

   ....

   ....

ENGLISH
Grades 3-5

MAIN ACTIVITY: CONCLUSIONS **TIMING: 20 MINS**

LEARNING OBJECTIVES
- To be able to craft an effective introduction and conclusion

EQUIPMENT
none

Effective conclusions often:
   A – summarise the writer's argument
   B – emphasise the benefits of agreeing with and/or acting on the writer's argument
   C – highlight the consequences of ignoring the writer's argument.

1. Which of these features do these sentences from one student's conclusion achieve? Label them A, B or C.

   i. Imagine the world if we do nothing: trees, grass, animals, humans, all slowly choking and dying in a polluted desert filled with unrecycled, rotting rubbish.

   ii. If we can stop, or even reverse, the damage we have done to our planet, the Earth may recover and heal.

   iii. If we do not act now, what kind of life will your grandchildren have on this bare, colourless, polluted planet?

   iv. It's not too late to change everything but we need to start now, today.

   v. If we can walk more, drive less, recycle more, use less and be happy with what we have got, we may still have a planet to live on in a hundred years.

2. Which of these sentences would you include in a conclusion? Tick them.

3. Look again at the sentences you have ticked. What order would you sequence them in? Number them.

4. Imagine you are planning to write a response to the same writing task, arguing that:
   - science and technology have transformed our lives for the better
   - we have damaged the environment but can use our scientific and technological skills to repair it.

5. What are the benefits of agreeing with this point of view? What are the consequences of ignoring this argument? Write one or two sentences summarising the benefits and consequences.

206

AQA ENGLISH — Grades 3-5

HOMEWORK ACTIVITY: AN INTRODUCTION AND CONCLUSION TIMING: 30 MINS

LEARNING OBJECTIVES
- To be able to craft an effective introduction and conclusion

EQUIPMENT
none

1. On a separate piece of paper, write the introduction and conclusion of your response to this Paper 2, Section B exam-style writing task.

> 'Our towns and cities are out of control. We need to work together as a community to solve our community's problems.'
>
> Write a letter to your local newspaper in which you explain your point of view on this statement.
>
> **[40 marks]**

2. Annotate your introduction.

    Identify where you have:
    - engaged the reader with a shocking or surprising image or idea
    - explained the background to the issue you are exploring
    - introduced (but not explained) your point of view.

3. Annotate your conclusion.

    Identify where you have:
    - summarised your argument
    - emphasised the benefits of agreeing with and/or acting on your argument
    - highlighted the consequences of ignoring your argument.

31 Answers

STARTER ACTIVITY: AND THE WINNER IS...

1. a) Sentences B and C are effective
b) Sentence A is the least effective because it repeats the question and adds little to the argument.
2. a) Sentences B and C are effective
b) Sentence A is the least effective because it simply repeats the arguments already expressed.

MAIN ACTIVITY: INTRODUCTIONS

1. Engages the reader: 'In the last forty years, thousands of animals and plants all around the world have become extinct, lost forever.'
Explains the background: 'This is not an accident – it is the result of humankind caring more about making money and living comfortable lives than the planet on which we live.'
Introduces the writer's point of view: 'Perhaps it is already too late, but it is not too late to start trying to undo all the damage we have done.'
2. Student's own answer

MAIN ACTIVITY: CONCLUSIONS

1. i) C; ii) B; iii) C; iv) A; v) A and B
2. All of the sentences are arguably effective.
3. Examples: i, ii, iv; v, ii, iii, etc.
4. Examples: benefits – we can continue to develop and benefit from scientific and technological innovation; consequences – the problems we have caused could remain unresolved with disastrous consequences.

HOMEWORK ACTIVITY: AN INTRODUCTION AND CONCLUSION

1. See marking guidance on pages 251–253.
2. and 3. Ensure a significant number of elements are used (and annotated) to create an effective introduction and conclusion.

AQA ENGLISH — Grades 3–5

32 Writing to present a viewpoint: Building paragraphs

LEARNING OBJECTIVES

- To understand how to structure paragraphs in an argument text
- To be able to link ideas using cohesive devices

SPECIFICATION LINKS

- 3.1.2 producing clear and coherent text

STARTER ACTIVITY

- **What's missing?; 5 minutes; page 210**
  Draw the student's attention to the lack of content and cohesion in the example.

MAIN ACTIVITIES

- **Build a paragraph; 20 minutes; page 211**
  Explain that an expert may be someone the student knows, e.g. a teacher could give an expert opinion on education; a parent could give an expert opinion on parenting, etc.
- **Linking your ideas; 20 minutes; page 212**
  Check the student understands what cohesion is and why it is necessary. In question 2 the student can either rewrite their own sentences and structure them in a cohesive paragraph, or adjust the original versions on the worksheet *Build a paragraph*.

PLENARY ACTIVITY

- **Review; 10 minutes**
  Review the cohesive elements the student added to their writing in the previous activity. Build a repertoire of cohesive adverbials by asking them to suggest possible alternatives.

HOMEWORK ACTIVITY

- **Write a cohesive response; 30 minutes; page 213**
  The student should complete at least two paragraphs following on from the introduction they wrote for homework in lesson 31. Remind them to make use of the plan they completed for homework in lesson 30.

SUPPORT IDEA

- **What's missing?** Encourage the student to identify and label elements in the paragraph that achieve the given criteria. Prompt them to question how effectively the identified elements achieve those criteria.

EXTENSION IDEA

- **Linking your ideas** Ask the student to suggest ways in which the exemplar paragraph could be improved, e.g. using synonyms to replace the repeated noun 'town's'

PROGRESS AND OBSERVATIONS

ENGLISH
Grades 3–5

STARTER ACTIVITY: WHAT'S MISSING?

TIMING: 5 MINS

LEARNING OBJECTIVES
- To understand how to structure paragraphs in an argument text
- To be able to link ideas using cohesive devices

EQUIPMENT
none

An effective paragraph in an argument text is likely to:
- state a key idea in the argument
- support it with evidence
- explain how the idea and any evidence support the argument
- link the ideas within the paragraph to each other and to the previous paragraph.

Look at this paragraph from one student's response to this Paper 2, Section B exam-style writing task.

> 'Our towns and cities are out of control. We need to work together as a community to solve our community's problems.'
>
> Write a letter to your local newspaper in which you explain your point of view on this statement.
>
> **[40 marks]**

> Teenagers often have nothing to do and they get bored very easily. Teenagers cause trouble and they get a bad reputation. Somebody should do something.

1. **What is missing from the response?**

....

....

....

....

....

ENGLISH
Grades 3-5

MAIN ACTIVITY: BUILD A PARAGRAPH **TIMING: 20 MINS**

LEARNING OBJECTIVES
- To understand how to structure paragraphs in an argument text

EQUIPMENT
none

You are going to rebuild this paragraph so that it makes an effective contribution to the student's argument.

> Teenagers often have nothing to do and they get bored very easily. Teenagers cause trouble and they get a bad reputation. Somebody should do something.

To help the reader understand your key idea, you need to express it as clearly as possible.

1. What key idea is the student attempting to convey in this paragraph? Write one or two sentences expressing it as clearly as possible.

_____

_____

_____

_____

To help the reader appreciate your key idea, you need to support it with evidence or an example, such as:
- a fact
- an opinion expressed by an expert
- your own personal experience.

2. What evidence could you use to support the key idea? Write one or two sentences presenting your evidence.

_____

_____

_____

_____

To develop the reader's understanding of your key idea, you need to explain why your evidence is significant.

3. What does your evidence prove? How does it contribute to your argument? Write one or two sentences explaining its significance.

_____

_____

_____

_____

ENGLISH
— Grades 3-5 —

| Main activity: Linking your ideas | Timing: 20 mins |

Learning objectives	Equipment
• To be able to link ideas using cohesive devices	none

You can use cohesive devices to link your ideas and give your writing **cohesion**.

Pronouns/determiners	Adverbials	Synonyms
it	however	words with a similar meaning, used to avoid repetition
them	moreover	
this	similarly	
these	for example	

1. Look carefully at the cohesive devices in this paragraph from one student's response to a Paper 2, Section B exam-style writing task.

> 'Our towns and cities are out of control. We need to work together as a community to solve our community's problems.'
>
> Write a letter to your local newspaper in which you explain your point of view on this statement.
>
> **[40 marks]**

> Teenagers often have nothing to do and they get bored very easily. This can lead to them causing trouble and getting a bad reputation. For example, a group of young people in the town recently brought the traffic to a standstill by playing football in the middle of the road. These problems could easily be resolved by providing relatively cheap activities for the town's youth using the town's resources, such as organised sports teams training in the town's sports centre.

   a) Circle any synonyms for the word 'teenager'.

   b) Underline any pronouns or determiners that refer back to ideas in the previous sentences.

   c) Draw a box around any adverbials that link sentences and ideas.

2. Look again at the sentences you wrote in the activity *Build a paragraph*. On a separate piece of paper, experiment with different ways of linking the ideas in your sentences to create a cohesive paragraph.

3. When you have finished, look at the cohesive devices you have used.

   a) Circle any synonyms you have used to avoid repetition.

   b) Underline any pronouns or determiners that refer back to ideas in the previous sentences.

   c) Draw a box around any adverbials that link sentences and ideas.

AQA ENGLISH
Grades 3-5

| HOMEWORK ACTIVITY: WRITE A COHESIVE RESPONSE | TIMING: 30 MINS |

LEARNING OBJECTIVES
- To understand how to structure paragraphs in an argument text
- To be able to link ideas using cohesive devices

EQUIPMENT
none

1. Write two carefully structured, cohesive paragraphs in response to this Paper 2, Section B exam-style writing task.

   > 'Our towns and cities are out of control. We need to work together as a community to solve our community's problems.'
   >
   > Write a letter to your local newspaper in which you explain your point of view on this statement.
   >
   > [40 marks]

2. Use this checklist to make sure you have structured your paragraphs effectively.

   ☐ I have stated a key idea from my argument.
   ☐ I have supported it with evidence.
   ☐ I have explained how the idea and evidence support my argument.

3. Now look at the cohesive devices you have used to link the ideas in your paragraphs.

   a) Circle any synonyms you have used to avoid repetition.

   b) Underline any pronouns or determiners that refer back to ideas in the previous sentences.

   c) Draw a box around any adverbials that link sentences and ideas.

ENGLISH
Grades 3-5

32 ANSWERS

STARTER ACTIVITY: WHAT'S MISSING?
1. Supporting evidence/examples, adequate explanation of this idea's relevance to the argument, cohesive features linking the ideas expressed

MAIN ACTIVITY: BUILD A PARAGRAPH
1. Look for responses that identify boredom due to a lack of facilities and organised activities as the cause of poor behaviour in teenagers.
2. Answers may identify an event (e.g. the loss of a local amenity), or a personal experience or anecdote of poor behaviour in teenagers.
3. Answers should suggest a solution to the problem, e.g. something the local community can do to resolve the issue.

MAIN ACTIVITY: LINKING YOUR IDEAS
1. a) synonyms: teenagers, young people, the town's youth; b) pronouns/determiners: this, these; c) adverbials: for example, such as
2. and 3. Student's own answers

HOMEWORK ACTIVITY: WRITE A COHESIVE RESPONSE
1. See marking guidance on pages 251–253.
2. Student's own answer. Ensure all, or the majority, of the success criteria are achieved.
3. Student's own answers. Ensure they have correctly identified their use of synonyms, pronouns, determiners and adverbials.

GLOSSARY

Adverbial
A word or phrase that modifies a verb, adjective or another adverbial – adverbial conjuncts, such as *similarly*, *however* and *for example*, are used to link clauses within sentences and to make links between sentences

Cohesion
A cohesive device is a word or phrase used to link ideas within and across paragraphs. It is used to show how parts of the text fit together, creating cohesion. For example, the use of adverbials such as *on the one hand* and *in contrast*

Pronoun
A word that can be substituted for a noun or noun phrase, e.g. *I, you, we, he, this, these*

Determiner
A word that introduces and modifies a noun or noun phrase, e.g. *the, a, this, these*

ENGLISH
Grades 3-5

33 WRITING TO PRESENT A VIEWPOINT: USING STRUCTURE FOR EFFECT

LEARNING OBJECTIVES

- To understand that a writer's choices at text and sentence level can influence the reader's response
- To be able to manipulate paragraph and sentence structure for effect

SPECIFICATION LINKS

- 3.1.2 writing for impact

STARTER ACTIVITY

- **Stories and viewpoints; 5 minutes; page 216**
  Remind the student of their work on paragraph and sentence structure in lessons 24–26. Discuss how these techniques can be used in narrative and descriptive writing, and how they could also be applied when writing to present a viewpoint.

MAIN ACTIVITIES

- **Short sentences and paragraphs; 20 minutes; page 217**
  Remind the student that short sentences and paragraphs are most effective when used sparingly.
- **Experimenting with sentences; 20 minutes; page 218**
  Point out to the student that the information positioned at the beginning and, in particular, the end of the sentence tends to have the greatest emphasis.

PLENARY ACTIVITY

- **Review; 5 minutes**
  Ask the student to summarise and evaluate their understanding of how paragraphs and sentences can be structured for effect when writing to present a viewpoint. Discuss initial ideas for the Homework activity and how this understanding could be applied to it.

HOMEWORK ACTIVITY

- **Crafting for impact; 30 minutes; page 219**
  If the student completed the Homework activity in lesson 32, they can redraft these paragraphs. Encourage them to focus on revisions to sentence and paragraph structure for effect.

SUPPORT IDEA

- **Experimenting with sentences** Reading aloud may help the student to identify nuances of emphasis in different sentence structures.

EXTENSION IDEA

- **Crafting for impact** Encourage the student to experiment with their sentences. Encourage them to write several different versions of their response and select the strongest elements from each to produce a final draft.

PROGRESS AND OBSERVATIONS

ENGLISH
— Grades 3-5 —

STARTER ACTIVITY: STORIES AND VIEWPOINTS **TIMING: 5 MINS**

LEARNING OBJECTIVES
- To understand that a writer's choices at text and sentence level can influence the reader's response

EQUIPMENT
none

These two statements are true of narrative and descriptive writing.

> Short sentences and paragraphs can add dramatic emphasis and impact.

> Longer sentences and paragraphs can be restructured to alter their emphasis or impact.

1. Which of the above statements are also true when you are writing to present a viewpoint?

....

....

....

....

....

....

AQA ENGLISH
Grades 3-5

MAIN ACTIVITY: SHORT SENTENCES AND PARAGRAPHS   **TIMING: 20 MINS**

LEARNING OBJECTIVES
- To be able to manipulate paragraph and sentence structure for effect

EQUIPMENT
none

Read this paragraph, written in response to the Paper 2, Section B exam-style writing task below. It consists entirely of longer sentences.

> 'Humankind is destroying the Earth. Science and technology is doing more harm than good. We need to act now before it's too late.'
>
> Write an article for a broadsheet newspaper in which you explain your point of view on this statement.
>
> **[40 marks]**

> Every day of every year we are bombarded with adverts for new mobile phones, new televisions, new gadgets to replace our old ones that are still working perfectly, and this needs to stop. Technology is no longer working hard to improve our lives, instead it's simply trying to get hold of our money by selling us things to replace other things we don't need to replace and we fall for it every time. We are filling the Earth with rubbish and soon it will be full.

Breaking some of these longer sentences into shorter sentences would make the response more effective by:
- making the sentences clearer
- adding emphasis to the most important ideas.

1. **Add full stops, capital letters and make any other necessary changes to improve the clarity and impact of this writer's sentences.**

2. **Look again at the short sentences you have created in the paragraph above. Which one would be most effective if you emphasised it by making it into short paragraph? Underline it.**

ENGLISH
— Grades 3-5 —

MAIN ACTIVITY: EXPERIMENTING WITH SENTENCES **TIMING: 20 MINS**

LEARNING OBJECTIVES

- To be able to manipulate paragraph and sentence structure for effect

EQUIPMENT

none

The elements in the sentences below can be moved around, repositioned and reordered.

1. Rewrite each sentence two or three times, experimenting with ordering the elements in different ways.

a) | We will make our planet uninhabitable | soon | if we continue like this. |

b) | Perhaps | we should do something | now | rather than waiting for the worst to happen. |

c) | Science and technology | are starting to destroy us | now | although | we thought that | they | could save us | once upon a time. |

2. Which version of each sentence gives the greatest impact and emphasis to its ideas? Tick it.

218

AQA ENGLISH — Grades 3-5

HOMEWORK ACTIVITY: CRAFTING FOR IMPACT **TIMING: 30 MINS**

LEARNING OBJECTIVES
- To be able to manipulate paragraph and sentence structure for effect

EQUIPMENT
none

> 'Our towns and cities are out of control. We need to work together as a community to solve our community's problems.'
>
> Write a letter to your local newspaper in which you explain your point of view on this statement.

1. Write one paragraph in response to the Paper 2, Section B exam-style writing task above.

2. Rewrite your paragraph, thinking carefully about how you could add impact by changing paragraph and sentence structure.
   You could:
   - use a short sentence
   - add a short paragraph
   - reorder the elements of longer sentences.

33 ANSWERS

STARTER ACTIVITY: STORIES AND VIEWPOINTS

1. Paragraph and sentence structure can be manipulated to create similar effects when writing to present a viewpoint.

MAIN ACTIVITY: SHORT SENTENCES AND PARAGRAPHS

1. and 2. Example: Every day of every year we are bombarded with adverts for new mobile phones, new televisions, new gadgets to replace our old ones that are still working perfectly. This needs to stop. Technology is no longer working hard to improve our lives, instead it's simply trying to get hold of our money by selling us things to replace other things we don't need to replace. We fall for it every time. We are filling the Earth with rubbish. <u>And soon it will be full.</u>

MAIN ACTIVITY: EXPERIMENTING WITH SENTENCES

1. Examples: a) If we continue like this, we will soon make our planet uninhabitable.
b) Rather than waiting for the worst to happen, we should perhaps do something now.
c) Although once upon a time we thought that science and technology would save us, now they are starting to destroy us.
2. Student's own answer

HOMEWORK ACTIVITY: CRAFTING FOR IMPACT

1. See marking guidance on pages 251–253. Look for responses that explain and support a point of view, focusing on the issue raised by the statement in the task.
2. Ensure that the student completes at least two versions of the response, using a variety of carefully considered paragraph and sentence structures.

ENGLISH
— Grades 3-5 —

34 Writing to present a viewpoint: Selecting vocabulary

LEARNING OBJECTIVES
- To be able to select vocabulary for precision and impact

SPECIFICATION LINKS
- 3.1.2 producing clear and coherent text
- 3.1.2 writing for impact

STARTER ACTIVITY
- **Review and revise; 5 minutes; page 222**
  Point out to the student that they have two chances to select effective vocabulary: during and after writing. Reviewing writing at the end of the exam is not simply an opportunity to correct spelling and punctuation; it should also be used to review and revise vocabulary and sentence structure choices.

MAIN ACTIVITIES
- **Precision; 20 minutes; page 223**
  Highlight to the student the problems of using a thesaurus, and particularly the risk of misusing unfamiliar words. Explain how the approach in this activity allows them to use their own personal thesaurus by trawling the vocabulary they already have. Once the student has completed the activity they should review their decisions.
- **Emotive impact; 20 minutes; page 224**
  Once the student has completed the activity they should review their decisions.

PLENARY ACTIVITY
- **Vocabulary review; 5 minutes**
  Ask the student to write one sentence in response to the exam-style writing task in the Homework activity, then review and revise their vocabulary choices for precision and impact.

HOMEWORK ACTIVITY
- **Crafting vocabulary; 30 minutes; page 225**
  Ask the student to write one or two paragraphs in response to the exam-style writing task. Emphasise the importance of reviewing and revising vocabulary choices, and marking their revisions clearly.

SUPPORT IDEA
- **Precision; Emotive impact** Focus the student on just one or two of the sentences or vocabulary choices.

EXTENSION IDEA
- **Precision; Emotive impact** Ask the student to gather the widest possible range of vocabulary choices before selecting the most effective ones. Discuss why their choices are the most effective, considering connotation, implication, etc.

PROGRESS AND OBSERVATIONS

ENGLISH
— Grades 3-5 —

STARTER ACTIVITY: REVIEW AND REVISE

TIMING: 5 MINS

LEARNING OBJECTIVES
- To be able to select vocabulary for precision and impact

EQUIPMENT
none

Read these sentences from a student's response to a Paper 2, Section B exam-style writing task.

> Things are not as bad as they might seem. The news and the papers make everything sound bad and make people worried about going out but there are lots of good things happening in the world.

1. How effective is the student's vocabulary choice? Circle any words or phrases that you feel could be improved

AQA ENGLISH — Grades 3–5

MAIN ACTIVITY: PRECISION

TIMING: 20 MINS

LEARNING OBJECTIVES
- To be able to select vocabulary for precision and impact

EQUIPMENT
none

Look again at the sentences below.

Some of the student's vocabulary choices are very vague. You are going to improve them to make them more precise.

1. **Read the questions around the sentences and note at least three possible vocabulary choices to replace each underlined word or phrase.**

Which things? ....

What do you mean by bad? ....

How could this be expressed more precisely? ....

What kinds of things? What do you mean by bad? ....

Things are not as bad as they might seem. The news and the papers make everything sound bad and make people worried about going out but there are lots of good things happening in the world.

How worried are they? ....

How many? ....

What kinds of good things? ....

223

ENGLISH
— Grades 3-5 —

AQA

MAIN ACTIVITY: EMOTIVE IMPACT   **TIMING: 20 MINS**

LEARNING OBJECTIVES
- To be able to select vocabulary for precision and impact

EQUIPMENT
- green and orange highlighter pens

Read the sentences below.

1. **Look at the vocabulary choices to fill each gap.**
   - Highlight in orange the choices that are not emotive enough.
   - Highlight in green the choices that are appropriately emotive.

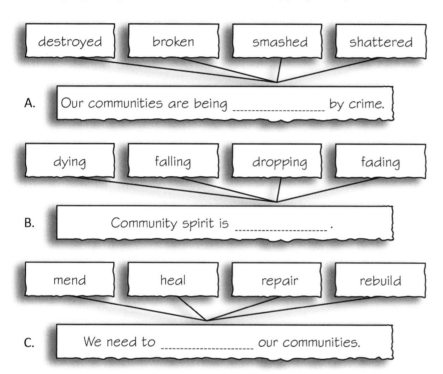

2. How could you make the circled vocabulary choices in the sentence below more emotive? Note two or three possible choices to replace each one. Tick your preferred choice in each case.

> Old people will no longer feel too (scared) to go out, young people will learn to (like) their town again, and the whole community will feel (like new).

scared

like

like new

224

ENGLISH
Grades 3–5

HOMEWORK ACTIVITY: CRAFTING VOCABULARY **TIMING: 30 MINS**

LEARNING OBJECTIVES
- To be able to select vocabulary for precision and impact

EQUIPMENT
none

1. **Write the opening of your response to this Paper 2, Section B exam-style writing task.**

   > 'Humankind is destroying the Earth. Science and technology is doing more harm than good. We need to act now before it's too late.'
   >
   > Write an article for a broadsheet newspaper in which you explain your point of view on this statement.
   >
   > **[40 marks]**

   ----

2. **Look carefully at your vocabulary choices.**

   a) Could any of your vocabulary choices be more precise? Identify, review and revise them.

   b) Could any of your vocabulary choices be more emotive? Identify, review and revise them.

   Remember to make your revisions clear and show all of the options you consider.

34 ANSWERS

STARTER ACTIVITY: REVIEW AND REVISE
1. Examples: things, bad, worried, lots, good things.

MAIN ACTIVITY: PRECISION
1. Examples: things: the situation in our community, the state of our towns; bad: worrying, disturbing; the news and the papers: the media; everything sound bad: emphasise the negative side of life, highlight the more shocking events in our country; worried: concerned, anxious; lots: a significant number, hundreds; good things: acts of kindness, positive events.

MAIN ACTIVITY: EMOTIVE IMPACT
1. Responses will vary.
A: 'shattered' or 'destroyed' are arguably the most appropriate, 'broken' and 'smashed' are not emotive enough
B: 'dying' or 'falling' are arguably the most appropriate, 'dropping' and 'fading' are not emotive enough
C: 'heal' or 'rebuild' are arguably the most appropriate, 'mend' and 'repair' are not emotive enough.
2. Example: Old people will no longer feel too terrified to go out, young people will learn to love their town again, and the whole community will feel reborn.

HOMEWORK ACTIVITY: CRAFTING VOCABULARY
1. See marking guidance on pages 251–253. Look for responses that introduce a point of view, focusing on the issue raised by the statement in the task.
2. Ensure clear evidence of review and revision is shown.

GLOSSARY

Emotive language
Language intended to prompt an emotional response in the reader

AQA ENGLISH — Grades 3–5

35 WRITING TO PRESENT A VIEWPOINT: WRITING A RESPONSE

LEARNING OBJECTIVES
- To be able to plan and write an effective argument to present a viewpoint

SPECIFICATION LINKS
- 3.1.2 producing clear and coherent text
- 3.1.2 writing for impact

STARTER ACTIVITY
- **The map; 10 minutes; page 228**
  Explain that this lesson will consolidate the student's learning on writing to present a viewpoint. Emphasise that this first activity will produce a map for them to follow as they craft their response to the writing task. Note the similarities between this map and the map for descriptive and narrative writing in lesson 28.

MAIN ACTIVITIES
- **Planning; 20 minutes; page 229**
  Reiterate the importance of planning over the need to 'just get on with the writing'. Remind the student that a good way to develop a point of view is to focus on the problems and possible solutions raised by the issue in the task.
- **Beginning writing; 15 minutes; page 230**
  If the previous activity goes over time, focus this activity on the opening sentence or two of the response. Note that it is probably advisable for students at this level to review their writing as a whole, rather than after the opening paragraph; however, this is a valuable exercise for students of all levels.

PLENARY ACTIVITY
- **Review; 5 minutes**
  Work with the student to review the impact of their opening to the writing task, focusing on possible revisions to paragraphing, sentence structures and vocabulary choices.

HOMEWORK ACTIVITY
- **Complete your response; 30 minutes; page 231**
  Emphasise the importance of following the map created in the Starter activity.

SUPPORT IDEA
- **Planning** Encourage the student to verbalise their thinking. Prompt where necessary.

EXTENSION IDEA
- **Planning; Beginning writing** Encourage the student to review and revise throughout the planning and writing process, focusing on how effectively their response will achieve their intention.

PROGRESS AND OBSERVATIONS

ENGLISH
— Grades 3-5 —

STARTER ACTIVITY: THE MAP

TIMING: 10 MINS

LEARNING OBJECTIVES
- To be able to plan and write an effective argument to present a viewpoint

EQUIPMENT
none

You are going to write your response to this Paper 2, Section B exam-style writing task.

> 'Exams are pointless. They are a test of how much you can remember, not how intelligent you are or how hard you work. There must be a better way to show employers, colleges and universities what students are like.'
>
> Write an article for a broadsheet newspaper in which you explain your point of view on this statement.
>
> **[40 marks]**

1. Below is a list of the steps for crafting an effective response. At what stage and in what order will you complete them?

    a) Tick to show whether you will complete each step **before**, **during** or **after** writing.

    b) Number the steps to show the order in which you will complete them.

	Before	During	After	Number
Identify your own opinion and think about the problems and solutions you could explore in your response.	☐	☐	☐	☐
Structure and sequence your ideas.	☐	☐	☐	☐
Review and revise your choices of paragraph and sentence structure, and vocabulary.	☐	☐	☐	☐
Think carefully about your introduction and conclusion.	☐	☐	☐	☐
Identify the form, purpose, audience and central idea of your writing.	☐	☐	☐	☐
Structure your sentences for clarity and impact.	☐	☐	☐	☐
Check your spelling, punctuation and grammar.	☐	☐	☐	☐
Select precise vocabulary for impact.	☐	☐	☐	☐
Think about how you will use paragraph structure.	☐	☐	☐	☐
Gather a range of ideas.	☐	☐	☐	☐

AQA ENGLISH
Grades 3–5

MAIN ACTIVITY: PLANNING **TIMING: 20 MINS**

LEARNING OBJECTIVES
- To be able to plan and write an effective argument to present a viewpoint

EQUIPMENT
none

> 'Exams are pointless. They are a test of how much you can remember, not how intelligent you are or how hard you work. There must be a better way to show employers, colleges and universities what students are like.'
>
> Write an article for a broadsheet newspaper in which you explain your point of view on this statement.
> **[40 marks]**

1. Use the questions below to plan your response to the Paper 2, Section B exam-style writing task above.

The central idea
  a) What is the central idea?

....

....

....

My opinion
  b) What do you think about exams? Are they pointless?

....

....

....

....

....

Problems and solutions
  c) Identify the problem and some solutions. Are exams a problem? If so, why – and what is the solution? If not, why not?

....

....

....

....

The order
  d) Finally, sequence your ideas, thinking carefully about your introduction and conclusion in particular.

ENGLISH
— Grades 3–5 —

MAIN ACTIVITY: BEGINNING WRITING **TIMING: 15 MINS**

LEARNING OBJECTIVES
- To be able to plan and write an effective argument to present a viewpoint

EQUIPMENT
none

1. **Write the opening of your response to the Paper 2, Section B exam-style writing task below.**

   > 'Exams are pointless. They are a test of how much you can remember, not how intelligent you are or how hard you work. There must be a better way to show employers, colleges and universities what students are like.'
   >
   > Write an article for a broadsheet newspaper in which you explain your point of view on this statement.
   >
   > **[40 marks]**

2. **Pause to review your writing so far.**
   Think about:

   Structure
   - Will your opening effectively engage and interest the reader?

   Paragraphs
   - Could you use a short paragraph to add impact?

   Sentence structure
   - Are your sentences carefully structured to express your ideas clearly and fluently?
   - Could you use a short sentence to add dramatic impact?
   - Could you rearrange the elements of any longer sentences to add emphasis to your argument?

   Vocabulary
   - Could any of your vocabulary choices be more precise?
   - Could any of your vocabulary choices be more emotive?

ENGLISH
Grades 3–5

HOMEWORK ACTIVITY: COMPLETE YOUR RESPONSE

TIMING: 30 MINS

LEARNING OBJECTIVES
- To be able to plan and write an effective argument to present a viewpoint

EQUIPMENT
none

1. Complete your response to the Paper 2, Section B exam-style writing task below.

> 'Exams are pointless. They are a test of how much you can remember, not how intelligent you are or how hard you work. There must be a better way to show employers, colleges and universities what students are like.'
>
> Write an article for a broadsheet newspaper in which you explain your point of view on this statement.
>
> **[40 marks]**

2. When you have completed your response, review and revise your writing.
   Think about your choices of:
   - whole text structure
   - paragraph structure
   - sentence structure
   - vocabulary.

ENGLISH
— Grades 3-5 —

35 Answers

STARTER ACTIVITY: THE MAP

1. a) and b) Before writing:
1. Identify the form, purpose, audience and central idea of your writing.
2. Identify your own opinion and think about the problems and solutions you could explore in your response.
3. Gather a range of ideas.
4. Structure and sequence your ideas.
5. Think carefully about your introduction and conclusion.
During writing:
6. Think about how you will use paragraph structure.
7. Structure your sentences for clarity and impact.
8. Select precise vocabulary for impact.
After writing:
9. Review and revise your choices of paragraph and sentence structure, and vocabulary.
10. Check your spelling, punctuation and grammar.

MAIN ACTIVITY: PLANNING

1. Student's own answers. Look for responses that outline and justify an argument for or against exams, and identify potential solutions. Check that enough material has been gathered and sequenced to ensure successful completion of the writing task.

MAIN ACTIVITY: BEGINNING WRITING

1. See exam-style mark scheme on pages 251–253.
2. Ensure review of paragraph, sentence and vocabulary choices is thorough and carefully considered.

HOMEWORK ACTIVITY: COMPLETE YOUR RESPONSE

1. See marking guidance on pages 251–253.
2. Ensure review and revision of whole text, paragraph, sentence and vocabulary choices is thorough and carefully considered.

ENGLISH
— Grades 3-5 —

36 SPaG: Basic punctuation

LEARNING OBJECTIVES
- To be able to use full stops accurately
- To be able to use commas accurately
- To be able to use apostrophes accurately

SPECIFICATION LINKS
- 3.1.2 producing clear and coherent text

STARTER ACTIVITY
- **What's missing?; 5 minutes; page 234**
  Explain that the emphasis on and reward for accurate punctuation have increased in the exam mark scheme. Fold the worksheet in half along the dotted line to hide the correct answers. Ask the student to complete the activity, focusing on full stops, then commas, then apostrophes. Note how difficult it is to make sense of the text without punctuation.

MAIN ACTIVITIES
- **Full stops and commas; 20 minutes; page 235**
  (Note: These two questions could be used as short, starter-style activities in other lessons.)
  Question 1: confirm understanding of comma splices. Fold the sheet along the dotted line to hide the correct answer. The student could begin by numbering the six clauses or pieces of information. Reveal the answers and discuss them to identify areas for improvement.
  Question 2: encourage the student to include at least one list. Allow them one opportunity to check their use of commas.
- **Apostrophes; 20 minutes; page 236**
  (Note: These two questions could be used as short, starter-style activities in other lessons.)
  Question 1: fold the sheet along the dotted line to hide the correct answer. Highlight that apostrophes replace omitted letters, not spaces and explain that contractions are not appropriate for more formal writing. Reveal the answers and discuss them to identify areas for improvement.
  Question 2: note that some nouns ending in *-s* are plurals, some are proper nouns, and others are singular common nouns. Explain to the student that listening to the word can help them decide whether to add an additional *-s* when creating the possessive. If adding *-s* changes the sound, then it is probably necessary, e.g. *Lewis'* needs an extra *-s*, but *boys'* does not. Discuss the answers to identify areas for improvement.

PLENARY ACTIVITY
- **Review; 5 minutes**
  Ask the student to summarise the function of full stops, commas and apostrophes, and the rules for using them.

HOMEWORK ACTIVITY
- **Test writing; 30 minutes; page 237**
  Advise the student to write three or four sentences for each part of the test.

SUPPORT IDEA
- **Full stops and commas** Advise the student to check every time they use a comma that it should not be a full stop.

EXTENSION IDEA
- **Throughout** Ask the student to verbalise their thought processes as they punctuate, explaining the reasons for their choices and the rules behind them.

PROGRESS AND OBSERVATIONS

ENGLISH
Grades 3-5

AQA

| STARTER ACTIVITY: WHAT'S MISSING? | TIMING: 5 MINS |

LEARNING OBJECTIVES
- To be able to use full stops accurately
- To be able to use commas accurately
- To be able to use apostrophes accurately

EQUIPMENT
none

1. **Add the correct punctuation to the sentences below.**
   Think about:
   - full stops
   - capital letters
   - commas
   - apostrophes.

---

id love to get a dog but my mum says we shouldnt she says her friend jos has a dog if you take joss dog for a walk its not long before its lost its collar gone missing or got covered in mud

---

------fold------

I'd love to get a dog but my mum says we shouldn't. She says her friend Jos has a dog. If you take Jos's dog for a walk, it's not long before it's lost its collar, gone missing or got covered in mud.

234

ENGLISH
— Grades 3-5 —

MAIN ACTIVITY: FULL STOPS AND COMMAS	TIMING: 20 MINS

LEARNING OBJECTIVES
- To be able to use full stops accurately
- To be able to use commas accurately

EQUIPMENT
none

Full stops and comma splices
- You can link two sentences with a conjunction, for example: *and, but, when*.
- You can separate two sentences with a full stop.
- You cannot link two sentences with a comma.

1. **Read the text below. It contains six clauses or pieces of information.**
   Turn it into six short sentences by:
   - adding full stops and capital letters
   - deleting the conjunctions.

> Although it was raining, we went to town and we visited all the shops but we didn't buy much because there was nothing we wanted and we didn't have much money.

----------fold----------

> It was raining. We went to town. We visited all the shops. We didn't buy much. There was nothing we wanted. We didn't have much money.

Commas
You use commas to separate items, events or information in a list. For example:
> I bought a top, some trousers, shoes and a scarf.

You also use commas to separate clauses and phrases that precede the main clause in a sentence, for example:
> When we had finished dinner, I washed up.

2. **On a separate piece of paper, complete the sentences below, describing what you did this morning.**
   a) When…
   b) Because…
   c) After…
   d) Before…
   e) Suddenly…

3. **Check you have used commas correctly in each of your sentences.**

ENGLISH
Grades 3-5

AQA

| MAIN ACTIVITY: APOSTROPHES | TIMING: 20 MINS |

LEARNING OBJECTIVES
- To be able to use apostrophes accurately

EQUIPMENT
none

Apostrophes for contractions

Apostrophes are used to replace omitted letters in contractions, for example:

Do not → Don't   I am → I'm

1. **How many contractions can you create in these sentences? Underline the words you want to replace, and write the contraction above them.**

> I am good at punctuation because I do not hurry when I am checking my writing. I would not be so good at it if I had not done so much practice. What is surprising is that there are so many apostrophes in these sentences. Who would have thought it?

--fold--

> I'm good at punctuation because I don't hurry when I'm checking my writing. I wouldn't be so good at it if I hadn't done so much practice. What's surprising is that there're so many apostrophes in these sentences. Who'd have thought it?

Apostrophes for possession

Possession is where something belongs to someone or something. To show possession, add an apostrophe and *s* to the owner. For example:

the house in which Jamie lives → Jamie's house
the first chapter of the book → the book's first chapter

Some people think that, if the owner ends in an 's', there is no need to add an 's', just an apostrophe. Some people think you should add the 's' even if the owner already ends in an 's'. For example:

Mr Jones' class
Mr Jones's class

In your exam, you can choose to do either, as long as you are consistent in your choice.

2. **Complete the text below by adding apostrophes to show possession.**

> The boys match was meant to kick off at 2pm but the referees whistle had gone missing. The boys all stood around chatting. Kwame and Scotts conversation was about last nights match. Avinash told Josh about his dads new car. Ten minutes later the whistle was still missing. Lewis lost his temper. Lewis temper was shocking.

ENGLISH
— Grades 3-5 —

| HOMEWORK ACTIVITY: TEST WRITING | TIMING: 30 MINS |

LEARNING OBJECTIVES
- To be able to use full stops accurately
- To be able to use commas accurately
- To be able to use apostrophes accurately

EQUIPMENT
none

1. On a separate piece of paper, create a test with four separate sections to assess a student's understanding of:
   - **full stops**
   - **commas**
   - **apostrophes in contractions**
   - **apostrophes for possession.**

The test should take a student approximately ten minutes to complete.

2. **On another piece of paper, create an answer sheet showing the correct answers to your test.**

36 Answers

Starter activity: What's missing?
1. See activity sheet for answers.

Main activity: Full stops and commas
1. See activity sheet for answers.
2. Ensure commas are correctly positioned. Example:
a) When I got up, I brushed my teeth.
b) Because it was cold, I put on two pullovers.
c) After breakfast, I put on my shoes.
d) Before I left the house, I said goodbye to my mum.
e) Suddenly, I realised I was late.
3. Student's own answer

Main activity: Apostrophes
1. See activity sheet for answers.
2. The boys' match was meant to kick off at 2pm but the referee's whistle had gone missing. The boys all stood around chatting. Kwame and Scott's conversation was about last night's match. Avinash told Josh about his dad's new car. Ten minutes later the whistle was still missing. Lewis lost his temper. Lewis's temper was shocking.

Homework activity: Test writing
1. Student's own answer
2. Student's own answer. Ensure all test answers are correct.

Glossary

Comma splice
When a comma is incorrectly used to join two sentences that should be separated by a full stop, it is called a comma splice

ENGLISH
Grades 3–5

37 SPaG: Advanced punctuation

Learning objectives	Specification links
• To be able to use speech punctuation accurately • To be able to use colons and semi-colons accurately	• 3.1.2 producing clear and coherent text

Starter activity
- **What's wrong?; 5 minutes; page 240**
  Explain that the emphasis on and reward for accurate punctuation have increased in the exam mark scheme. Fold the worksheet in half along the dotted line to hide the correct answers. Ask the student to complete the activity. Reveal the answers and discuss them to identify areas for improvement.

Main activities
- **Speech punctuation; 20 minutes; page 241**
  Ensure that the student understands the rules of speech punctuation, using commas and full stops at the end of speech.
- **Colons and semi-colons; 20 minutes; page 242**
  (Note: These two questions could be used as short, starter-style activities in other lessons.)
  Question 1: focus on the phrases that are made redundant through the use of a colon, e.g. 'for example'. Note that this is not a 'rule': colons should only be used with careful attention to clarity of meaning. Discuss the answers to identify areas for improvement.
  Question 2: emphasise that semi-colons cannot replace all conjunctions, and should be used sparingly. Again, point out that it is important to pay careful attention to clarity of meaning.

Plenary activity
- **Review; 5 minutes**
  Ask the student to summarise the function of speech punctuation, colons and semi-colons, and the rules for using them.

Homework activity
- **Test writing; 30 minutes; page 243**
  Advise the student to write three or four sentences for each part of the test.

Support idea
- **Speech punctuation** Ask the student to write the conversation without worrying about the punctuation, and then focus on checking its accuracy, concentrating on one success criterion at a time.

Extension idea
- **Colons and semi-colons** Prompt the student to consider the impact of using a colon or semi colon, e.g. concision of expression and/or emphasis on the idea or information that follows it.

Progress and observations

ENGLISH
Grades 3-5

Starter activity: What's wrong?

Timing: 5 mins

Learning objectives
- To be able to use speech punctuation accurately
- To be able to use colons and semi-colons accurately

Equipment
none

1. **Add the correct punctuation to the sentences below.**
   Think about:
   - speech punctuation
   - colons and semi-colons.

> Parents nag you all the time. Examples include; what I eat, how much homework I do and what time I have to be home. 'You need vegetables to keep you fit and healthy' she says. 'there's a reason your teachers give you homework' she says. 'home by ten o'clock' she says 'and that's my final word'

------------------------------fold------------------------------

> Parents nag you all the time. Examples include**:** what I eat, how much homework I do and what time I have to be home. 'You need vegetables to keep you fit and healthy**,**' she says. '**T**here's a reason your teachers give you homework**,**' she says. '**H**ome by ten o'clock**,**' she says**,** 'and that's my final word**.**'

240

ENGLISH
— Grades 3-5 —

MAIN ACTIVITY: SPEECH PUNCTUATION

TIMING: 20 MINS

LEARNING OBJECTIVES
- To be able to use speech punctuation accurately

EQUIPMENT
none

Look at the correct speech punctuation in the sentences below.

'You need vegetables to keep you fit and healthy,' she says.

'There's a reason your teachers give you homework,' she says.

'Home by ten o'clock,' she says, 'and that's my final word.'

There is always a punctuation mark at the end of speech, before the closing speech marks:

- a *comma* if the sentence continues
- a *full stop* if the sentence does not continue.

Notice there is also often a punctuation mark after the *identifier* (he said, she said, etc.).

1. **Write a short conversation between two people in which each person speaks at least twice.**
   Make sure you include:
   - speech marks
   - identifiers (for example: he said, she shouted, I muttered)
   - accurately positioned full stops and commas.

   ....

   ....

   ....

   ....

   ....

   ....

2. **Use this checklist to make sure your speech is punctuated correctly.**

   ☐ I have used speech marks around each piece of speech.
   ☐ I have used the correct punctuation mark before each closing speech mark.
   ☐ I have used the correct punctuation mark after each identifier.

ENGLISH
— Grades 3-5 —

| MAIN ACTIVITY: COLONS AND SEMI-COLONS | TIMING: 20 MINS |

LEARNING OBJECTIVES
- To be able to use colons and semi-colons accurately

EQUIPMENT
none

Colons
Colons can be used to introduce a quotation, a list of information or an explanation.

1. Improve the sentences below by adding a colon and removing any unnecessary words.

A. Mercutio curses the Montagues and Capulets. For example, 'A plague o' both your houses.'

B. There are three main ways to access the internet. These are computers, tablets and smartphones.

C. The smartphone is an amazing invention. This is because it incorporated a huge number of gadgets all in one tiny package.

Semi-colons
Semi-colons can replace conjunctions to show a strong relationship between two pieces of information. For example:

    The show ended and we went home.   The show ended; we went home.

Conjunctions help to make the relationship between two pieces of information clearer. When replacing a conjunction with a semi-colon, make sure you are not weakening the connection between the information.

2. In which of these sentences could you remove the underlined conjunction and replace it with a semi-colon without weakening its meaning? Tick them.

A. I love lettuce <u>because</u> it's so crunchy and refreshing.

B. I love football <u>although</u> I am not very good at it.

C. I loved judo <u>when</u> I was much younger.

D. I used to like skateboarding <u>but</u> I hate it now.

242

ENGLISH
Grades 3-5

AQA

HOMEWORK ACTIVITY: TEST WRITING   **TIMING: 30 MINS**

LEARNING OBJECTIVES
- To be able to use speech punctuation accurately
- To be able to use colons and semi-colons accurately

EQUIPMENT
none

1. **On a separate piece of paper, create a test with three separate sections to assess a student's understanding of:**
   - **speech punctuation**
   - **colons**
   - **semi colons.**

The test should take a student approximately ten minutes to complete.

2. **On another piece of paper, create an answer sheet showing the correct answers to your test.**

ENGLISH
Grades 3-5

37 ANSWERS

STARTER ACTIVITY: WHAT'S WRONG?
1. See activity sheet for answers

MAIN ACTIVITY: SPEECH PUNCTUATION
1. Student's own answer
2. Student's own answer. Ensure all the success criteria are achieved.

MAIN ACTIVITY: COLONS AND SEMI-COLONS
1. a) Mercutio curses the Montagues and Capulets: 'A plague o' both your houses.'
b) There are three main ways to access the internet: computers, tablets and smartphones.
c) The smartphone is an amazing invention: it incorporated a huge number of gadgets all in one tiny package.
2. The conjunction can be successfully replaced with a semi-colon in sentences A and D. It cannot be replaced in sentence C. A semi-colon would weaken but not destroy meaning in sentence B.

HOMEWORK ACTIVITY: TEST WRITING
1. Student's own answer
2. Student's own answer. Ensure all test answers are correct.

AQA ENGLISH Grades 3-5

38 SPaG: Spelling and Proofreading

Learning Objectives
- To develop awareness of homophones
- To be able to proofread thoroughly

Specification Links
- 3.1.2 producing clear and coherent text

Starter Activity
- **Error hunt; 10 minutes; page 246**
  Remind students that the emphasis on and reward for accurate spelling, punctuation and grammar have increased in the exam mark scheme. Fold the worksheet in half along the dotted line to hide the correct answers. Ask the student to complete the activity. Reveal the answers and discuss to identify areas for improvement.

Main Activities
- **Homophones; 15 minutes; page 247**
  As the student completes the activity, note any homophones that present difficulty.
- **Proofreading; 20 minutes; page 248**
  Fold the worksheet along the dotted line to hide the correct answers. Ask the student to focus on one category of error at a time. Reveal the correct answers. Reflect on and identify those categories that the student finds most challenging.

Plenary Activity
- **Review; 5 minutes**
  As a preliminary activity to the homework, review the lesson and identify key areas to add to the proofreading checklist.

Homework Activity
- **Proofreading checklist; 30 minutes; page 249**
  Explain to the student that this activity will make them more aware of the errors they are prone to making and/or overlooking. It will act as a summary of the elements of writing that they need to pay special attention to when proofreading. Suggest that they focus on five pieces of writing completed for homework over the last few weeks.

Support Ideas
- **Error hunt** Suggest the student focus on one category of error at a time, e.g. spelling first, then punctuation, etc.
- **Homophones** Encourage the student to use a process of elimination.

Extension Idea
- **Proofreading checklist** Ask the student to compile a list of common spelling errors made in their writing. Encourage them to learn and self-test using the look-say-cover-write-check method.

Progress and Observations

ENGLISH
— Grades 3-5 —

Starter activity: Error hunt

Timing: 10 mins

Learning objectives
- To be able to proofread thoroughly

Equipment
none

This student's writing contains:
- spelling errors
- punctuation errors
- sense errors.

1. How many errors can you find? Underline and correct them.

> More than a century ago, the car was invented, at the time it would of seemed like the greatest invention of all time. Now are lives depend on on them and their are far to many petrol and diesel engines pumping out toxic fumes that are slowly but surely destroying the Earth's atmosphere.

-----------------------------------fold-----------------------------------

> More than a century ago, the car was invented<u>.</u> <u>At</u> the time it would <u>have</u> seemed like the greatest invention of all time. Now <u>our</u> lives depend <u>on</u> ~~on~~ them and <u>there</u> are far <u>too</u> many petrol and diesel engines pumping out toxic fumes that are slowly but surely destroying the Earth's atmosphere.

ENGLISH — Grades 3-5

Main activity: Homophones

Timing: 15 mins

Learning objectives
- To develop awareness of homophones

Equipment
none

1. Look at the groups of homophones below. Write the correct spelling in each gap.

A.
| Has a similar meaning and spelling to 'here' — **there** | → | Can it be broken down into *they are*? — **they're** | → | Means belonging to them — **their** |

_____ going over _____ with _____ friends.

B.
| Means belonging to you — **your** | → | Can it be broken down into *you are*? — **you're** |

_____ going to be late for _____ lesson.

C.
| Can it be broken down into *it is*? — **it's** | → | Means belonging to it — **its** |

Look at the dog! _____ chasing _____ own tail!

D.
| Going to / Have to — **to** | → | Too many? Too much? Too many 'o's! — **too** | → | Is it a number? — **two** |

_____ burgers are _____ much for me _____ eat.

E.
| Is it a *wh-* question word, like *when* and *what*? — **where** | → | Can it be broken down into *we are*? — **we're** | → | Is it the past tense of are? — **were** |

They didn't know _____ they _____ . 'Help! _____ lost!' they shouted.

F.
| You are / We are — **are** | → | Does it belong to us? — **our** |

_____ friends _____ here!

247

ENGLISH
Grades 3–5

AQA

MAIN ACTIVITY: PROOFREADING   **TIMING: 20 MINS**

LEARNING OBJECTIVES
- To be able to proofread thoroughly

EQUIPMENT
none

1. Amend the mistakes in the paragraph below. Use the checklist to help you find all the mistakes.

   ☐ Missing full stops and/or comma splices
   - Check every comma in the text. Should it be a full stop?
   - Read the text aloud or carefully in your head. Stop and look for missing full stops when you feel it doesn't make sense.

   ☐ Missing commas
   - Look for lists and sentences that begin with conjunctions or adverbials, such as *although, when, however*.

   ☐ Spellings: homophone errors
   - Look out for the most common homophones, such as *there/their/they're, your/you're, too/to/two*.

   ☐ Spellings: common errors
   - Do any words look wrong? Try spelling them two or three different ways in the margin. Which way looks correct?

   ☐ Missing or repeated words
   - Slowly read the text aloud or carefully in your head.

Sport is definatley one way in which community spirit can be built. Our local council took disicion to reduce the times the leisure centre is open becuase they needed to save money. However they now do many more classes and sports activities for local people, this includes football netball basketball and fitness classes for all different ages and fitness levels for a a lot of people are leisure centre has become the heart of the community, people are are even having there weddings their.

--------fold--------

Sport is <u>definitely</u> one way in which community spirit can be built. Our local council took <u>the decision</u> to reduce the times the leisure centre is open <u>because</u> they needed to save money. However<u>,</u> they now do many more classes and sports activities for local people<u>.</u> <u>T</u>his includes football<u>,</u> netball<u>,</u> basketball and fitness classes for all different ages and fitness levels<u>.</u> <u>F</u>or <u>a</u> lot of people <u>our</u> leisure centre has become the heart of the community<u>.</u> <u>P</u>eople <u>are</u> even having <u>their</u> weddings <u>there</u>.

248

ENGLISH
Grades 3-5

HOMEWORK ACTIVITY: PROOFREADING CHECKLIST	TIMING: 30 MINS

LEARNING OBJECTIVES	EQUIPMENT
• To be able to proofread thoroughly	none

1. Look carefully through your work from this lesson. Which errors do you find hardest to spot? Note them in your proofreading checklist below.

2. Thoroughly proofread your five most recent pieces of writing. What errors can you find? Note them in your proofreading checklist below.

Spelling

Punctuation

Grammar and sense

38 ANSWERS

STARTER ACTIVITY: ERROR HUNT

1. See activity sheet for answers.

MAIN ACTIVITY: HOMOPHONES

1. A. They're going over there with their friends.
B. You're going to be late for your lesson.
C. Look at the dog! It's chasing its own tail!
D. Two burgers are too much for me to eat.
E. They didn't know where they were. 'Help! We're lost!' they shouted.
F. Our friends are here!

MAIN ACTIVITY: PROOFREADING

1. See activity sheet for answers.

HOMEWORK ACTIVITY: PROOFREADING CHECKLIST

1. Student's own answer
2. Compare the student's checklist with the pieces of writing they reviewed. Ensure all common and frequent errors are included.

GLOSSARY

Homophone
A word with the same pronunciation as, but a different spelling and meaning to, another word

AQA ENGLISH — Grades 3–5

WRITING MARKING GUIDANCE: CONTENT AND STRUCTURE

Marks	Criteria
22–24 marks	• Register is skilfully controlled and fully appropriate for audience. • Purpose is confidently achieved. • Language is crafted with sophistication, and a considerable variety of vocabulary and language devices is used to fully achieve purpose and intention. • Structural choices are varied and skilfully managed. • A range of complex, developed ideas skilfully engages and directs the reader's response. • Paragraphing and discourse markers are skilfully managed for clarity and fluency.
19–21 marks	• Register is fully appropriate for audience. • Purpose is fully achieved. • Language is deliberately crafted for effect and impact, and a considerable variety of vocabulary and language devices is used. • Structural choices are effective and varied. • A range of clearly linked and developed ideas engage the reader. • Paragraphing is consistently effective, with fluent use of discourse markers.
16–18 marks	• Register is consistently appropriate for audience. • Purpose is consistently achieved. • A broad vocabulary and a range of language devices are clearly chosen for effect. • Structural choices are effective. • A range of clearly linked ideas engages the reader. • Paragraphing is effective, with a range of discourse markers.
13–15 marks	• Register is broadly appropriate for audience. • Purpose is broadly achieved. • Vocabulary and language devices are clearly chosen for effect. • Structural choices are broadly effective. • A range of linked ideas engage the reader. • Paragraphing is usually effective, with a range of discourse markers.
10–12 marks	• Register is frequently appropriate for audience. • Purpose is frequently achieved. • Vocabulary and language devices are sometimes deliberately chosen for effect. • Structural choices are sometimes significant. • A growing range of relevant, linked ideas is presented. • Paragraphing is generally accurate, with largely appropriate use of discourse markers.
7–9 marks	• Register is inconsistently appropriate for audience. • Purpose is inconsistently achieved. • There is some variety in vocabulary and language devices. • There is some awareness of structural conventions. • A range of relevant, linked ideas is presented. • Paragraphing is inaccurate, with inconsistently appropriate use of discourse markers.
4–6 marks	• There is some awareness of audience. • There is some awareness of purpose. • Straightforward vocabulary and language devices are used. • There is some evidence of structural choices. • One or two relevant ideas are linked. • Paragraphing is inaccurate.

ENGLISH
Grades 3-5

WRITING MARKING GUIDANCE: CONTENT AND STRUCTURE

1–3 marks	• There is a limited sense of audience.
	• There is a limited sense of purpose.
	• Limited, basic vocabulary is used.
	• There is little or no evidence of structural choices.
	• Limited, unlinked ideas are presented.
	• No paragraphing is used.
No marks	• No creditable response

Actual AQA mark schemes and specifications can be found on the AQA website.

AQA ENGLISH — Grades 3-5

Writing marking guidance: Spelling, punctuation and grammar

Marks	Criteria
13–16 marks	<ul><li>Sentence demarcation is consistently accurate.</li><li>Meaning is fully supported with a range of punctuation, used highly accurately.</li><li>Sentence forms are highly varied and crafted for effect.</li><li>Standard English is used consistently and appropriately, with secure management of grammatical structures.</li><li>Vocabulary choices are sophisticated.</li><li>Spelling is highly accurate.</li></ul>
9–12 marks	<ul><li>Sentence demarcation is usually accurate.</li><li>Meaning is usually supported with a range of punctuation, used with some accuracy.</li><li>Sentence forms are varied and crafted for effect.</li><li>Standard English is used generally accurately, with largely accurate management of grammatical structures.</li><li>A broad range of vocabulary choices is used.</li><li>Less common words are generally accurately spelled.</li></ul>
5–8 marks	<ul><li>Sentence demarcation is largely accurate.</li><li>Meaning is largely supported with a range of punctuation.</li><li>Some variety of sentence forms is used.</li><li>Standard English is sometimes used, with some inaccuracies in agreement.</li><li>Vocabulary choices are varied.</li><li>Less common words are often accurately spelled</li></ul>
1–4 marks	<ul><li>Sentence demarcation is infrequent.</li><li>There is limited evidence of deliberate punctuation.</li><li>A limited range of sentence forms is used.</li><li>There is limited use of Standard English, with frequent inaccuracies in agreement.</li><li>Common words are accurately spelled.</li><li>Vocabulary choices are straightforward.</li></ul>
No marks	<ul><li>No creditable response</li></ul>

ENGLISH
Grades 3-5

PROGRESS AND OBSERVATIONS

Published by Pearson Education Limited, 80 Strand, London, WC2R 0RL.

www.pearsonschools.co.uk

Text © Pearson Education Limited 2018
Series consultant: Margaret Reeve
Edited by Elektra Media Ltd
Designed by Andrew Magee
Typeset by Elektra Media Ltd
Produced by Elektra Media Ltd
Original illustrations © Pearson Education Limited 2018
Illustrated by Elektra Media Ltd
Cover design by Andrew Magee

The rights of David Grant to be identified as author of this work has been asserted by him in accordance with the Copyright, Designs and Patents Act 1988.

First published 2018
21 20 19 18
10 9 8 7 6 5 4 3 2 1

British Library Cataloguing in Publication Data
A catalogue record for this book is available from the British Library

ISBN 9781292195377

Copyright notice
All rights reserved. The material in this publication is copyright. Activity sheets may be freely photocopied for use by the purchasing tutor. However, this material is copyright and under no circumstances may copies be offered for sale. If you wish to use the material in any way other than that specified you must apply in writing to the publishers.

The ActiveBook accompanying this book contains editable Word files. Pearson Education Limited cannot accept responsibility for the quality, accuracy or fitness for purpose of the materials contained in the Word files once edited. To revert to the original Word files, download the files again.

Printed in the United Kingdom by Ashford Colour Press Ltd

Acknowledgements
The authors and publisher would like to thank the following individuals and organisations for their kind permission to reproduce copyright material:
Page 17: Reprinted by permission of HarperCollins Publishers Ltd © 2012, Ben Macintyre; The Napoleon of Crime: The Life and Times of Adam Worth, the Real Moriarty by Ben Macintyre © 1997. Reprinted by kind permission of Ben Macintyre. Page 18: Reproduced with the permissions of Yale University Press. Page 19: Excerpt from EARTH IN THE BALANCE by Al Gore. Copyright © 1992 by Senator Al Gore. Reprinted by permission of Houghton Mifflin Harcourt Publishing Company. All rights reserved. Page 20: "Prologue" from THE SECRET HISTORY by Donna Tartt, copyright © 1992 by Donna Tartt. Used by permission of Alfred A. Knopf, an imprint of the Knopf Doubleday Publishing Group, a division of Penguin Random House LLC. All rights reserved; Reproduced with the permission of ROGERS, COLERIDGE & WHITE LTD. Page 21: From THE ESSEX SERPENT BY SARAH PERRY. Copyright © 2016 by Sarah Perry. Reprinted by permission of Harper Collins Publishers; Reproduced with the permissions of Profile Books ltd.

We would like to thank Tutorful for its invaluable help in the development and trialling of this course.

Photographs
Photodisc: Steve Mason 144, 151, 180; **Shutterstock:** Anemone 153, 159, 183
All other images © Pearson Education

Notes from the publisher
Pearson has robust editorial processes, including answer and fact checks, to ensure the accuracy of the content in this publication, and every effort is made to ensure this publication is free of errors. We are, however, only human, and occasionally errors do occur. Pearson is not liable for any misunderstandings that arise as a result of errors in this publication, but it is our priority to ensure that the content is accurate. If you spot an error, please do contact us at resourcescorrections@pearson.com so we can make sure it is corrected.

Contents

Introduction

Content table including main teaching points	6
Cross-referencing tables – Pitmans and Wordpower	8

Student writing and exercises

1.	Neighbours	12
2.	Indian marriage	16
3.	Going to English classes	20
4.	How I left my country	24
5.	My poor friend Zehra	28
6.	My favourite person	32
7.	In this city	36
8.	A town that I know well	40
9.	Sunday	44
10.	China	48
11.	The fox and the stork	52
12.	Banging on the floor	56
13.	A visit to my friend	60
14.	Family life in Morocco	64
15.	Escape from Vietnam	68
16.	My husband's ex-wife	72
17.	The cooking pot	76
18.	Education in China	80
19.	Pakistani customs	84
20.	Future plans	88
21.	The man and the monkey	92
22.	Christmas and new year in Vietnam	96
23.	I left my country with sadness	100
24.	Growing and learning together	104
25.	When will you grow up?	108
26.	Somali tradition	112
27.	We want this!	116
28.	A woman's place?	120
29.	My grandmother's life	124
30.	The runaway	128

THE LONDON LANGUAGE AND LITERACY UNIT

Acknowledgements

The editors would like to thank the following

- all the members of the original ESL Publishing Group: Lesley Agnew, Rakesh Bhanot, June Garbutt, Johannes Hailemariam, Patty Hemingway, Janet Herman, Jane McLaughlin, Julia Naish, Jan Thompson, Margaret Twaddle, Helen Waites, Rosemary Warhurst, Adrian Whittaker and Cary Whitworth

- all the illustrators of the original booklets: Johannes Hailemariam, Rosmond M. Milner, Jane Richbell, Chele Sykes, and Cary Whitworth

- Margaret Folarin for illustrations new to this edition and CopyArt for providing copyright free illustrations

- Ruth Atkinson and Penny Weaver for the Wordpower Cross Referencing

- Foufou Savitzky for proof-reading and suggestions

- Lesley Jacobs for her administrative support, and Rachel Fletcher for the design.

WE WOULD ESPECIALLY LIKE TO THANK ALL THE STUDENTS WHO CONTRIBUTED WORK, AND WITHOUT WHOM THERE WOULD BE NO BOOK.

ISBN 1 872972 49 7

London Language & Literacy Unit 1997

Permission is given to photocopy for educational purposes within the purchasing institution.

Friends, Families and Folk Tales

Introduction

Background to the current edition

This is a re-edited compilation taken from five booklets of students' writing which were originally published by the ILEA ESL Publishing Group in the mid-1980s, under the title Collections of Student Writing (1. Festivals, Folk Tales and Stories 2. Families and Friends 3. Changes 4. More Festivals, Folk Tales and Stories 5. Refugee Writings.) In the original collections all the writings came from ESOL students attending classes in ILEA Adult Education Institutes. The current collection also has some work by students at Richmond Adult and Community College, and Southwark College. We wish to thank all the students whose work appears here and apologise to those we were unable to contact to ask for permission to use their work again. We would also like to say a collective thank you to all the ILEA ESL teachers and the members of the ESL Publishing group (whose names appear on page 3 of this book) who had the foresight, and who worked so hard and voluntarily, to produce the original collections.

The Original Publications

As the Teachers' Notes which accompanied the first publications stated,

> "In these books, there is a wealth of custom, tradition and story from all over the world. There is also a wealth of personal experience as families and individuals have uprooted themselves and moved to a totally new environment...... These writings draw on experience and tradition and will enable the work of ESL students to be known and read far beyond the classroom and will prove interesting to the general reader. We also hope they will prove to be a valuable reading resource for teachers of English."

A decade on, and with little writing from ESOL students available, other than through local schemes, we felt it was a good time to make part of this valuable body of work available once more.

The Current Edition

We have re-edited the collection, chosen and graded 30 texts and added reading, writing and grammar exercises for each piece of writing. The first ten stories are at beginner/elementary level and from then on, the stories become progressively more complex, in terms of structure and vocabulary. Each story stands in its own right and there is no obvious advantage to working through them chronologically. A content table or book map shows the reading and writing skills practised in the exercises, the grammar point focused on and the genre of each story.

The Format

A similar format is taken for each piece of writing:
- the text is introduced to the reader with an illustration and discussion questions.
- reading, grammar and writing exercises follow in that order, always ending with a free writing activity.

New Tutors

There is a range of ways in which the stories can be used and we would like to suggest a number of points for all tutors, but particularly those who are new to ESOL work, to bear in mind.

1. This is a collection of student writing and not a course book. There is no underlying grammatical progression or infrastructure. The grammar exercises which accompany each story were those which seemed most aptly to apply to the texts themselves. Therefore, there are a number of grammatical points which recur – for example, practising the correct form of the past simple tense,

while other structures are never introduced. It was the language in the stories which prompted the grammatical activities.

2. We imagine that teachers wishing to focus on the structures highlighted in the texts might employ the stories to illustrate the grammar point(s) in a written, communicative context – a good example of language in use. The exercises would then provide teachers with controlled practice activities (both oral and written) as well as ideas for free writing practice. The structures practised in the exercises are detailed in the content table.

3. Many of the exercises involve students using inductive approaches – rules are not given, but concept questions are asked to help people work out patterns and rules for themselves. We believe students should be encouraged to interact with each other and the teacher to work out how the language is organised. Students could also be encouraged to access grammar reference materials to test out their theories and to compare their first languages with English, language and literacy level allowing.

4. A large number of ESOL students now work towards some kind of accreditation – Open College profiling, Pitmans ESOL exams, Wordpower etc. In designing the reading, writing and grammar activities, we have considered the need to develop students' study skills, as well as the literacy and grammatical content of the most common accreditation currently in use. This does not mean that we recommend any particular accreditation scheme. We also believe the exercises will give students useful practice and experience of the process of using language towards specific objectives – whether task or skills based. We would emphasise the importance of this process. This is particularly relevant at a time when product appears to be given priority over process.

5. Teachers will need to ensure that they have pre-taught the language of instructions which are embedded in the exercise instructions – eg match, fill in gaps, discuss etc. Much of this vocabulary will be useful for students aiming to pass exams.

Dyslexic Students

Some ESOL and literacy classes will have dyslexic learners. The holistic, context-bound approach to teaching skills that we have taken in this book should work with all students, but be particularly suitable for those with dyslexia or specific learning difficulties. The inductive approach to grammar, the attention to inference in the reading exercises, and to spelling and text organisation in the writing exercises, should all be beneficial to dyslexic learners. However, there are one or two types of exercises that dyslexic learners may have difficulty with. One of these is where students have to put in order sentences or words from the story that have been muddled up. This will be less problematical if the sentences or words are cut up, and the learner can physically move them around. Again, where students have to make sentences from substitution tables, dyslexic learners may find it easier if the words in each column are in a different colour, and again are cut up, and can be sorted out physically.

Genre

Texts produced in similar contexts with similar purpose share important textual features and patterns. We have included the genre of each text in the content table. We hope this will prove a useful tool for teachers, particularly as a knowledge of genre is empowering for students and is "fundamental to the construction of modern knowledge and the power that goes with it." (Genre and Process, Rob McCormac, ALBSU Newsletter 37, 1990.)

We hope you will enjoy working with this collection of stories, born of personal experience and traditions from all over the globe and that it may act as a catalyst for future publications from ESOL students.

Marina Spiegel
Helen Sunderland
June 1997

Friends, Families and Folk Tales

Content table including main teaching points

STORY	READING TEACHING POINT	GENRE	GRAMMAR TEACHING POINT	WRITING TEACHING POINT	TYPE OF FREE WRITING
1. Neighbours	reading common words	description of person	word order have/be – present simple	punctuation – capitals & full stops	description of person
2. Indian marriage	reading for specific information	description of a custom	present simple – 3rd person singular	proof-reading – spelling and punctuation	description of a custom
3. Going to English classes	reading for specific information reading common words	personal narrative	reg/irreg present and past simple time phrases & words	punctuation – capitals and full stops / months of the year	personal narrative
4. How I left my country	paragraph/sentence ordering, sequencing, time markers	personal narrative	past/present simple	spelling 'igh' pattern scanning	personal narrative
5. My poor friend Zehra	reading for specific information	description of person	word order with adjectives	punctuation – commas (listing) spelling 'ie' pattern	description of person
6. My favourite person	whole word recognition reading for specific information	description of person	present simple + negative – 3rd person singular	numbers 1 – 10	description of person
7. In this city	scanning segmenting	description of feelings	there is/there are	'th' – θ ð discrimination spelling – anagrams	description of place
8. A town that I know well	reading for specific information using context to understand new words	description of place	past & present simple of 'to be'	numbers & dates paragraphing	description of place
9. Sunday	reading for specific information	description of way of life	prepositions of time, past, future & present simple tenses	days of the week, punctuation – full stops, capitals, commas	description of way of life
10. China	reading for specific information alphabetical ordering dictionary skills	description of place	comparatives – 'er' and 'more'	punctuation – capitals postcard format	postcard
11. The fox and the stork	reading intensively using context to understand new words	narrative	conjunctions – and/but/so/because	time markers	narrative
12. Banging on the floor	reading for specific information, distinguishing between fact/opinion	description of person	word order do not/does not	paragraphing / punctuation – commas in phrases	description of person
13. A visit to my friend	reading for specific information, dictionary skills	personal narrative	some/any object pronouns	letter writing – (invitation) formal/informal register	letter of invitation
14. Family life in Morocco	reading for specific information, reading intensively	description of way of life	adverbs of frequency	spelling – common words planning a narrative – selecting & ordering ideas	personal narrative
15. Escape from Vietnam	reading for chronology, scanning for synonyms	personal narrative	reg/irreg present and past simple modals – could, had to	summaries, paragraphing spelling 'ould' pattern	description of journey

Content table including main teaching points

STORY	READING TEACHING POINT	GENRE	GRAMMAR TEACHING POINT	WRITING TEACHING POINT	TYPE OF FREE WRITING
16. My husband's ex-wife	reading intensively scanning word-building	description of person	word order / present perfect adverbs of frequency	spelling describing a person – beginnings & endings	description of person
17. The cooking pot	ordering	narrative	'wh' questions / present perfect – questions + negative	punctuation – direct speech	description of event
18. Education in China	reading for specific information	description of way of life	there is/are, and question form past simple	months of the year letter of enquiry	personal narrative or description of way of life
19. Pakistani customs	reading for detail and with accuracy	description of way of life	cohesion and logical sequencing active & passive	guided description planning a piece of writing	description of customs
20. Future plans	reading for facts and inference understanding vocabulary from context	discursive narrative	gerund after prepositions past/present and future simple	planning a piece of writing	future plans
21. The man and the monkey	ordering	narrative	prepositions articles	ordering a narrative	narrative
22. Christmas and New Year in Vietnam	reading for specific information & inference – synonyms	description of way of life	passive	planning a narrative	comparison of customs
23. I left my country with sadness	reading for detail and intensively	personal narrative	direct/indirect speech	ordering a narrative proofreading	narrative
24. Growing and learning together	reading for gist reading for inference & detail synonyms	description of way of life	English in Use relative pronoun – which	proof reading alphabetical ordering	description of way of life
25. When will you grow up?	scanning and use of context reading for specific information	personal narrative	prepositions conditionals – 1st & 2nd	letter writing – writing to school	formal letter
26. Somali tradition	reading for specific information synonyms	description of way of life	first conditional negative conditional	proofreading writing from notes	description of custom
27. We want this!	scanning, synonyms	expressing opinion	prepositions, parts of speech – noun, adjective, adverb	summarising	expressing opinion
28. A woman's place	differentiating between fact & opinion	expressing opinion	conjunctions – but, although, however, phrasal verbs with 'look'	letter writing planning/paragraphing	expressing opinion
29. My grandmother's life	reading for specific information synonyms	description of person	relative clauses (defining & non-defining)	discourse markers – beginnings & endings planning writing	description of person
30. The runaway	predicting, reading for inference & with accuracy	personal narrative	tenses – perfect/simple/continuous, direct/indirect speech	style – use of tenses letter writing	formal letter

THE LONDON LANGUAGE AND LITERACY UNIT

Friends, Families and Folk Tales

Pitmans ESOL Exams

A cross-referenced table showing stories and exercises which can give practice for specific parts of the examinations.

	USE OF ENGLISH		READING	
BASIC	Story 1	ex. G2, W2	Story 1	ex. R1
	Story 2	ex. G3, W1	Story 2	ex. R1, R2
	Story 6	ex. G1, G2	Story 6	ex. R1
	Story 7	ex. G1, G2, G3	Story 7	ex. R1
	Story 8	ex. G1, G2	Story 8	ex. R1
	Story 9	ex. G1, G2, G3	Story 9	ex. R1
	Story 17	ex. G1		
ELEMENTARY	Story 3	ex. G2	Story 3	ex. R1, R2
	Story 4	ex. R1	Story 5	ex. R1
	Story 5	ex. G1	Story 7	ex. R1
	Story 7	ex. G1, G2, G3	Story 8	ex. R1, W1
	Story 8	ex. G1, G2	Story 10	ex. R1
	Story 11	ex. G1, G2, G3	Story 12	ex. R1, R2
	Story 16	ex. G2	Story 13	ex R1
	Story 17	ex. G1	Story 16	ex. R1, R2
	Story 18	ex. G1, G2, W2	Story 19	ex. R1
	Story 20	ex G1, G2	Story 20	ex. R1
	Story 21	ex. G1, G2	Story 26	ex. R1
INTERMEDIATE	Story 14	ex. R1	Story 14	ex. R2
	Story 18	ex. G1, G2, G3	Story 18	ex. R1, R2
	Story 24	ex. G1	Story 19	ex. R2
	Story 25	ex. G1	Story 22	ex. R1
	Story 27	ex. G1	Story 23	ex. R2, W1
	Story 28	ex. G2	Story 24	ex. R2
	Story 30	ex. W1	Story 25	ex. R1
			Story 28	ex. R1
			Story 29	ex. R1, R3
			Story 30	ex. R2

Key

R: Reading Exercises
G: Grammar Exercises
W: Writing Exercises

So that G1 refers to the first grammar exercise, R2 to the second reading exercise, and so on.

	READING AND WRITING		WRITING	
BASIC	Story 10	ex. W2	Story 1	ex. W1, W3
	Story 13	ex. W2, R1	Story 2	ex. W3
			Story 6	ex. W3
			Story 7	ex. W3
			Story 8	ex. W3
			Story 9	ex. W2, W3
			Story 10	ex. W1
			Story 12	ex. W3
			Story 16	ex. W2
ELEMENTARY	Story 10	ex. W2	Story 3	ex. W2, W3
	Story 13	ex. R1, W1	Story 4	ex. W3
	Story 18	ex. W1	Story 5	ex. W1, W3
			Story 7	ex. W3
			Story 8	ex. W2, W3
			Story 11	ex. W3
			Story 12	ex. W1, W2, W3
			Story 15	ex W3
			Story 16	ex. W2
			Story 17	ex W3
			Story 18	ex. W2, W3
			Story 20	ex. W1, W2
			Story 24	ex. W3
			Story 26	ex. W3
			Story 29	ex. W5
INTERMEDIATE	Story 18	ex. W1	Story 14	ex. W2, W3
	Story 25	ex. W1	Story 18	ex. W2, W3
	Story 28	ex. W1	Story 19	ex. W2
	Story 30	ex. W2	Story 20	ex. W1, W2
			Story 21	ex. W4
			Story 22	ex. W4
			Story 23	ex. W1, W2, W3, W4, W5
			Story 24	ex. W3
			Story 26	ex. W2, W3
			Story 27	ex. W2, W3
			Story 28	ex. W3
			Story 29	ex. W1, W2, W3, W4, W5

Friends, Families and Folk Tales

Wordpower

A cross-referenced table mapping the student writings with Wordpower Units and Elements

TEXT	EXERCISE	UNIT	ELEMENT
1. Neighbours	discussion R1, R2 W3	303 301 302	1 1 3
2. Indian marriage	discussion R1 W3	303 301 302	1 1 3
3. Going to English classes	discussion W4	303 302	1 3
4. How I left my country	discussion R1, R2 W3	303 301 302	1 1 3
5. My poor friend Zehra	discussion R1 W3	303 301 302	1 1 3
6. My favourite person	discussion W3	303 302	1 3
7. In this city	discussion W3	303 302	1 3
8. A town that I know well	discussion R1, R2 W1, W2 W3	303 301 301 302	1 1 1 3
9. Sunday	discussion R1, R2 W3	303 301 302	1 1 3
10. China	discussion R1, R2 W2	303 301 302	1 1 2
11. The fox and the stork	discussion R1 W2a	303 301 303/302	1 1 1/3
12. Banging on the floor	discussion R1 W1 W3	303 301 301 302	1 1 1 3
13. A visit to my friend	discussion R1 W1 W2	306 304 304 305	1 1 1 2
14. Family life in Morocco	discussion R2 W2 W3	306 304 304 305	1 1 1 3
15. Escape from Vietnam	discussion R1, R2 W1 W3	303 301 301 302	1 1 1 3

TEXT	EXERCISE	UNIT	ELEMENT
16. My husband's ex-wife	discussion R1 W2B	303 301 302	1 1 3
17. The Cooking Pot	discussion R1 W3	303 301 302	1 1 2
18. Education in China	discussion	306	1
19. Pakistani customs	discussion R1, R2 G1, W1, W2, W3	306 304 305	1 1 3
20. Future plans	discussion W1, W2	303 302	1 3
21. The man and the monkey	discussion R1 W2, W4	306 304 305	1 1 3
22. Christmas and New Year in Vietnam	discussion W3 W4	306 304 305/306	1 1 3/1
23. I left my country with sadness	discussion R1, R2 W2 W3	306 304 306 305	1 1 1 3
24. Growing and learning together	discussion R1, R2, R3 W3	306 304 305	1 1 2
25. When will you grow up	discussion R1 W1	306 304 305	1 1 2
26. Somali tradition	discussion R1 W3	303 301 302	1 1 3
27. We want this	discussion R1, R2 W1, W2, W3	306 304 305	1 4 3
28. A woman's place	discussion R1 W1 W2, W3	306 304 305 305	1 1 2 3
29. My grandmother's life	discussion R3 W5	306 304 305	1 1 3
30. The runaway	discussion R1, R2 W2	306 304 305	1 1 2

Friends, Families and Folk Tales

1 Neighbours

¹ My neighbour's name is Miriam.

Miriam is from Somalia.

She is tall. She has black hair. She has black skin. She has black eyes.

⁵ She is nice.

Hadas from Eritrea

¹ My neighbour is a very good person.

All my neighbours are very old people.

It is a very good area, and I like it very much.

Sometimes I leave my money to pay the milkman on the
⁵ window in an envelope – no problem.

Ghirmay from Eritrea

Discussion questions	
a) Where do people in your class come from?	d) Where do you live?
b) Who are you sitting next to?	e) Do you know your neighbours? Do you like them?
c) What does this person look like?	

Neighbours

Reading Exercises

1. Read the story again. Circle true or false.

eg) Miriam is from Somalia (true)/ false

a) Miriam is not tall. true / false

b) She has brown eyes. true / false

c) She is nice. true / false

d) She has black hair. true / false

e) Hadas is from Somalia. true / false

2. Find these words in the box and circle them.

eg) tall
all
area
an
on
no
people
person
pay
problem
money
good
window
area

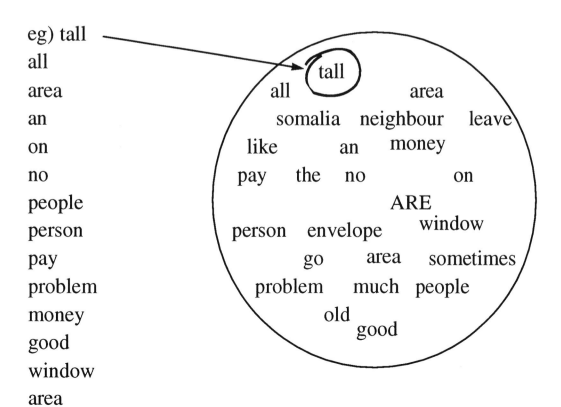

THE LONDON LANGUAGE AND LITERACY UNIT   13

Friends, Families and Folk Tales

Grammar Exercises

1. Put the words in the right order.

eg) nice She is
   She is nice.

a) eyes has black She
   ___ ___ ___ ___

b) from Miriam is Somalia
   ___ ___ ___ ___

d) name My is neighbour's Miriam
   ___ ___ ___ ___ ___

e) much I it very like
   ___ ___ ___ ___ ___

2. Circle the right word.

eg.) she am tall.
         (is)

a) She have / has black eyes.

b) Miriam is / are from Somalia.

c) She have / has black skin.

d) They is / are all of them old.

e) It is / are a very good area.

f) She have / has black eyes.

THE LONDON LANGUAGE AND LITERACY UNIT

Neighbours

Writing Exercises

1. **Write the sentences again, putting in full stops and using capital letters.**

   eg) she is tall   *She is tall.*

   a) miriam is from somalia

   _____ ___ _____ _____

   b) she has black skin

   ____ ____ _____ _____

   c) my neighbour's name is miriam

   ___ _____ _____ ___ _____

   d) they are all very old people

   _____ ____ ___ _____ ____ _____

2. **Read the story again.**
   Fill in the gaps in the sentences. Use the words in the box.

   eg) My *neighbour's* name is Miriam

   a) _____ has black hair.

   b) My _____ is a very good person.

   c) I _____ it very much.

she
money
neighbour
like
sometimes
window

   d) _____ I leave my _____ on the _____.

3. a) Describe a neighbour – here or in another country.
   b) Describe your area.

THE LONDON LANGUAGE AND LITERACY UNIT

Friends, Families and Folk Tales

2 Indian Marriage

¹ She wears a sari.
She wears lots of bangles.
He gives a sari.
He puts a chain of flowers round her neck.
⁵ She puts a chain of flowers round his neck.

Rodha from India

Discussion questions

a) Talk about weddings in a country you have lived in.

b) What do people wear when they get married?

c) What do people do at weddings?

Indian Marriage

Reading Exercises

1. **Read the story. Tick true or false.**

	True	False
eg) He wears a sari.		✔
a) This is a Somali marriage.		
b) She wears a dress.		
c) He wears lots of bangles.		
d) He puts flowers round her neck.		
e) She puts flowers round her neck.		

2. **Match the words to the picture.**

eg) ring

neck

sari

bangles

chain of flowers

Friends, Families and Folk Tales

Grammar Exercises

1. **Read these sentences.**
   I wear a dress but **she** wear**s** a sari.
   We give you flowers and **he** give**s** you a sari.
   What happens to the verbs (wear, give) when used with *he* or *she* in the present?

singular	I	give	her	flowers
	You	give	her	flowers
	He	gives	her	flowers
	She	gives	her	flowers
plural	We	give	her	flowers
	You	give	her	flowers
	They	give	her	flowers

2. **Read this table with a partner.**
   Work with a partner. Make lots of sentences in the present, using *I, you, he, she, we, they* with these verbs: *wear, like, put, live, speak*.

3. **Circle the right word.**

   eg) I (put)/puts a chain of flowers round her neck.

   a) You gives/give a sari.

   b) She wear/wears lots of bangles.

   c) He likes/like flowers.

   d) He wears/wears Indian clothes.

   e) They live/lives in India.

Indian Marriage

Writing Exercises

1. **Fill in the gaps in the sentences. Choose from the words in the box.** eg) <u>She</u> wears a sari.

   a) She wears lots of _____.

   b) He puts ___ _____ ___ _____ round her neck.

   c) She puts a chain of flowers round _____ neck.

   d) She wears a _____.

   e) _____ gives a sari.

   | a bicycle   bangles   He   him   his   dress   sari |
   | a chain of flowers   She |

2. **Look at these sentences. Correct the spelling and the punctuation and write the sentence again.**

   eg) he. gives a Sari   *He gives a sari.*

   a) She Wears a sari. _____

   b) She puts. a Chin of flowers round his nek. _____

   c) SHe wears lot of bangles, _____

   d) he gaves a sari _____

3. **Write 5 sentences about marriage in a country you have lived in.**

THE LONDON LANGUAGE AND LITERACY UNIT

Friends, Families and Folk Tales

3 Going to English Classes

¹ I started English classes last year, in October.
I had never learned English before.
I wanted to learn very much and very fast because my boys understood more English than me, but it was difficult for
⁵ me.

The first lesson, I did not understand what was going on.
I was so upset and I worried about it. After a few months, I understood more but still not enough.

I like this school very much. I enjoy my English class.

Barbara from Poland

Discussion questions

a) How long have you been learning English?
b) Did you learn English or other languages in your country?
c) How did you feel when you first came to English classes?
d) What do you find most difficult and what do you find easiest?

Going to English Classes

Reading Exercises

1. Read these sentences. Choose the correct one and circle a, b, or c.

eg) a) Barbara started English classes in November.
    b) Barbara started English classes in September.
    (c) Barbara started English classes in October.

(i) a) Barbara had learnt English in Poland.
    b) Barbara had not learnt English before.
    c) Barbara had learnt English in England before.

(ii) a) Her sons understood more English than her.
     b) She understood more than her sons.
     c) She did not understand her sons.

(iii) a) She enjoyed her first lesson.
      b) She was upset after her first lesson.
      c) She hates her lessons now.

2. a) Find the following words in the story and underline them.
school, October, English, before, very, than, what, months, enjoy.

b) Match the words.

eg) SCHOOL   what   enjoy   VERY
    OCTOBER months   than   WAS
    ENGLISH   October before THAN
    MONTHS   school   very   ENJOY
    WHAT   English   was   BEFORE

THE LONDON LANGUAGE AND LITERACY UNIT

Friends, Families and Folk Tales

Grammar Exercises

1. **Read the story again and underline all the words and phrases of time,** eg) *before.*
   How many did you find? _____

2. **Fill in the gaps with time words and phrases. Use the words in the box below:**
   eg)   I never learned English *before.*

   a)   I started English classes _____ _____ , in _____.

   b)   I wanted to learn very _____.

   c)   The _____ lesson, I could not understand what was going on.

   d)   _____ a few _____ I understood more.

   e)   _____ I like this school very much.

now fast last year after October first months

3. **Fill in the missing verbs in this table.**

	Present Simple	Past Simple
eg)	*start*	started
		wanted
		understood
		was
		could not
		worried
		learned

Writing Exercises

1. **Read the story again. Discuss with a partner the words that use capitals. Why do they have capitals? Which other kinds of words use capitals?**

2. **Here is some of the story without full stops and capitals. Put in the missing punctuation. Use a red pen.**

   i started english school last year, in october i never learned english before i wanted to learn very much and very fast because my boys understood more english than me, but it was difficult for me

   the first lesson, i did not understand what was going on i was so upset and i worried about it after a few months i understood more but still not enough

3. **a) Read the months of the year.**
   January, February, March, April, May, June, July, August, September, October, November, December.
   b) Write the months of the year in your language, and put the English word next to it.

your language	English	your language	English
eg *enero (Spanish)*	*January*		
1.		7.	
2.		8.	
3.		9.	
4.		10.	
5.		11.	
6.		12.	

3. **Write about your first day in English classes.**

Friends, Families and Folk Tales

4 How I Left My Country

1 In Afghanistan in 1979 the political situation got worse because the Russians attacked my country. We decided to leave in June 1985.

There was a war on. We felt very frightened. First, we took
5 a taxi from Kabul to the bus station. Then, we went to a village. All my family wore peasant clothes. We rode on horseback and after that, we went on foot for about eight hours.

We climbed over the Shamshad mountains. Then, we
10 crossed the border. We took a van and finally arrived in the town of Peshawar in Pakistan.

M. Rahim from Afghanistan

Discussion questions

a) How did you leave your country – by plane, train, road or on foot?

b) Did you have to leave in a hurry?

c) Did you leave alone, or with family or friends?

d) How did you feel – frightened, sad, excited?

How I Left My Country

Reading Exercises

1. **Read the story, and fill in the gaps.**
   Use the words in the box below.

   In Afghanistan in _____ the political situation got worse because the Russians attacked my country. We decided to leave in June _____.

   There was a war on. We felt very frightened. _____, we took a taxi from Kabul to the bus station. _____, we went to a village. All my family wore peasant clothes. We rode on horseback and _____ _____, we went on foot for about eight hours.

   We climbed over the Shamshad mountains. _____, we crossed the border. We took a van and _____ arrived in the town of Peshawar in Pakistan.

then 1979 finally then first after that 1986

2. **Put the sentences in the right order to re-tell the story.**
   Number the sentences.
   - [ ] There was a war on. We felt very frightened.
   - [ ] We took a van and finally arrived in the town of Peshawar in Pakistan.
   - [ ] We decided to leave in June 1985.
   - [ ] Then, we went to a village.
   - [ ] All my family wore peasant clothes.
   - [ ] We climbed over the Shamshad mountains.
   - [ ] In Afghanistan in 1979 the political situation got worse because the Russians attacked my country.
   - [ ] Then, we crossed the border.
   - [ ] First, we took a taxi from Kabul to the bus station.
   - [ ] We rode on horseback and after that, we went on foot.

Friends, Families and Folk Tales

Grammar Exercises

1. All the verbs in the story are in the past simple tense. Read the story again and underline all the verbs.

2. Write the present simple tense for these verbs in the box. Look at the example:

	past simple tense	present simple tense
eg)	decided	*decide*
	climbed	
	crossed	
	arrived	
	went	
	got	
	was	
	took	
	wore	
	rode	

Writing Exercises

1. **Match the right spelling, in the first column, with the correct spelling in one of the other boxes.**

2.

eg (very)	vair	veri	berry	(very)
because	becos	because	becuase	becose
hours	hours	ours	hour	awer
then	than	they	then	hen
there	their	then	these	there
went	want	went	when	whent

Look at these words. Underline the spelling pattern.
frightened
high
eight

Think of more words that have this spelling pattern, eg) *light*.

_____

_____

_____

3. **Write about your journey to England.**

Friends, Families and Folk Tales

5 My Poor Friend Zehra

¹ My friend's name was Zehra. She had blonde hair, brown eyes, and fair skin. She was thin. She was a very kind and nice girl.

I liked her because we were very good friends and we grew ⁵ up together.

The day she died we went to a wedding party. We were playing then we ran into the road. There was a car – it was coming very fast. She did not see it, they were English soldiers, and they could not stop. They hit her and she died.

¹⁰ She was seven years old.

I still think about her because we were best friends.

Shoray from Cyprus

Discussion questions	
a) Did you have a best friend when you were a child?	c) Do you still see or write to your friend?
b) What can you remember about her or him?	d) If not, why did you stop being friends?

My Poor Friend Zehra

Reading Exercises

1. **Read the story again. Tick true or false.**

	True	False
eg) My friend's name was Zehra.	☐	✔
a) She had brown hair.	☐	☐
b) She was kind.	☐	☐
c) I did not like her.	☐	☐
d) She was at a birthday party.	☐	☐
e) A car hit her.	☐	☐

2. **Make full sentences. Look at the example.**

eg) She was a very kind and → nice girl.

a) I liked her because — we went to a wedding party.

b) The day she died — and she died.

c) We were playing, — we were very good friends.

d) They hit her — then we ran into the road.

Friends, Families and Folk Tales

Grammar Exercises

1. Write the sentence again, put in the adjective in the right place.

eg) She had hair   (blonde)
She had blonde hair.

a) She had eyes   (brown)
_____

b) We were friends   (best)
_____

c) We went to a party   (wedding)
_____

2. Look at this sentence.
We were good friends.
Now write it in your language and number the words.

_____

3 Now fill in this table, and tell a partner about your language:

	In English	In _____
a) How many words are there?		
b) Where does the adjective go?		
c) Are there any other differences? What are they?		

THE LONDON LANGUAGE AND LITERACY UNIT

Writing Exercises

1. Put the commas into these sentences. Use a red pen.

eg) She had blonde hair brown eyes and fair skin.
She had blonde hair, brown eyes and fair skin.

a) He had brown hair green eyes and dark skin.

b) She was thin tall beautiful and very unhappy

c) She was short fat plain and very happy.

d) The town is modern noisy and rather busy.

e) I need eggs fish apples and oranges.

2. Look at these words from the story and underline the spelling pattern.

    friend
soldier
    died

Think of more words that have this spelling pattern.   eg) *tie*

_____

_____

_____

3. Describe a good friend of yours or write about something that happened when you were a child.

Friends, Families and Folk Tales

6 My Favourite Person

¹ My favourite person is my mum. I admire my mum, and I love her very much. Her name is Foyje and she is about 32 years old. She looks very beautiful. She has got black eyes and long black hair, and she has got two or three freckles
⁵ on her face.

My mum is a quiet person. She does not talk too much and she always says, "Never tell a lie." I like my mum. She always gives us good advice about everything. She is a pious and thoughtful person.

¹⁰ Her mother is dead. She has three brothers and one sister. They are very friendly with each other. I like the family.

Shobnum from Bangladesh

Discussion questions
a) Who is your favourite person?
b) What is this person like?
c) Why is he or she your favourite person?

My Favourite Person

Reading Exercises

1. **Read the story again. Then, read these sentences. How many are true?**
   a) Foyje looks very beautiful.
   b) She has many freckles.
   c) She is old.
   d) Foyje has brothers and a sister.
   e) She is a quiet person.

2. **Read these sentences. Circle the correct spelling.**

eg)   favorite
My   favourit   person is my mum.
      (favourite)

a) She looks very   beautiful / beeutiful / beutifull.

b) My mum is a   quite / quiet / quit   person.

c) She   dose not / does not / dos not   talk too much.

d) She always gives us good advice about   evrything / everything / evreything.

e) They are very   friendly / friendley / frendly   with each other.

THE LONDON LANGUAGE AND LITERACY UNIT

Friends, Families and Folk Tales

Grammar Exercises

1. a) **Find these verbs in the story. Underline them.**
   is   looks   has got   says   gives   has

   b) **Fill in the gaps in the sentences. Do not forget the final -s.**
   eg) She *has got* black eyes.

   1. She always _____ us good advice.

   2. She _____ very beautiful

   3. She _____ 3 brothers.

   4. She always _____, "Never tell a lie."

   5. She _____ about 32 years old.

2. **Read these 3 sentences.**

   She does not talk too much.
   She doesn't talk too much.
   He talks a lot.

   When do you use *does not* and when do you use *doesn't*?
   Make up 5 groups of sentences with a partner.
   Use doesn't and does not.
   eg) She doesn't smoke.
   She does not smoke.
   He smokes 20 a day.
   Use these verbs: *like, drink, eat, watch, play.*

My Favourite Person

Writing Exercises

1. **Read and match the numbers and then write them in the correct order.**

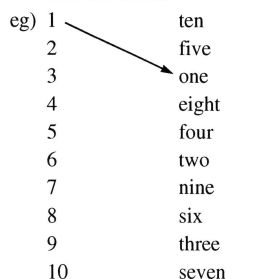

eg) 1	ten	1	*one*
2	five	2	_____
3	one	3	_____
4	eight	4	_____
5	four	5	_____
6	two	6	_____
7	nine	7	_____
8	six	8	_____
9	three	9	_____
10	seven	10	_____

2. **Fill in the gaps with a number. Write the numbers in words.**

eg) I have *two* eyes.

   a) There are _____ fingers on each hand.

   b) We have _____ toes on our feet.

   c) A week has _____ days.

   d) _____ and two make ten.

   e) The word 'man' has _____ letters.

   f) If you take _____ from ten you get nine.

   h) The number after eight is _____.

3. **Write about a member of your family or describe a good friend.**

THE LONDON LANGUAGE AND LITERACY UNIT

Friends, Families and Folk Tales

7   In This City

¹ In this city, there is a street.
In this street, there is a house.
In this house, there is a room.
And in this room an old man is sitting.
⁵ Sitting and crying, for someone.
For someone who has just
Gone through the door.
And who has just
Switched off the light
¹⁰ While forgetting
He was there.

Zainab from Singapore

Discussion questions

a) Do you live in a city or in the countryside?

b) Which do you prefer and why?

c) Where did you live in your country – in the city or in the countryside?

d) What are the problems of living in a city?

In This City

Reading Exercises

1. **Read the text and fill in the gaps.
   Use the words in the box below.**

   In this _____, there is a street.

   In this _____, there is a house.

   In this house, there is a _____.

   And in this room, an old _____ is sitting.

   Sitting and _____ for someone.

   For someone who has just

   Gone through the _____

   And _____ has just

   Switched off the _____

   While forgetting

   _____ was there.

   | room he city light crying street man who door |

2. Join two parts to make whole words.

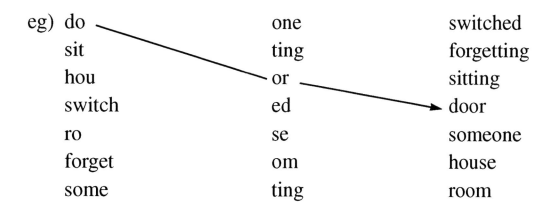

Friends, Families and Folk Tales

Grammar Exercises

1. **Look at these two sentences.**
   In this city there is a street.   (only one)
   In this room there are a lot of chairs.   (many)
   Put in *there is* or *there are* in the gaps.

   eg) *There are* seven days in a week.

   a) In the park _____ _____ a lot of trees.

   b) _____ _____ a book on the table.

   c) _____ _____ eleven players in a football team.

   d) I am watching t v tonight, _____ _____ a good film on.

   e) _____ _____ eight students in this class.

2. **Correct the mistakes in these sentences. Use a red pen. Write the correct sentence on a separate piece of paper.**

   eg) There is 28 letter in the English alphabet
   There are 28 letters in the English alphabet.

   a) Are there a book on the table?

   b) There is two cards parked outside.

   c) There are four man in the shop.

   d) Is there a trains at 10.00 a.m.?

   e) In my city there is many building and peoples.

Writing Exercises

1. **Find the words *through* and *this* in the story and underline them. Are they pronounced in the same way?**
   Through makes a θ sound. *This* makes a δ sound.

   Read the following words aloud.
   there, them, thin, think, that, thanks, thought, these, though
   Put them into the table.

θ	δ
through	*this*

2. **The letters in the words from the story are muddled up. Put the letters in the correct order.**

   ohsue _____   tcyi _____

   omro _____   dewithcs _____

   tseert _____   fof _____

   ghhrtuo _____   lehwi _____

   enomeos _____   reeht _____

3. **Write about your favourite room.**

Friends, Families and Folk Tales

8 A Town That I Know Well

¹ I was born in Skopje. Skopje is the capital city of Macedonia. It is not a big city. Its population is only 850,000 (eight hundred and fifty thousand).

In 1963 there was an earthquake and many buildings ⁵ collapsed. For many people this was a frightening and difficult time.

Now Skopje is a very beautiful city. It has many new buildings and a historical bridge and castle that the Turkish soldiers built very many years ago.

¹⁰ My family live near Skopje in a village called Drazevo.

Ghengis from Macedonia

Discussion questions

a) Where were you born?
b) Was it in a town or in the countryside?
c) What is it like?
d) How old is it?
e) Does it have a special history?

Reading Exercises

1. Read the story again. Circle true or false.

eg) Genghis was born in London.   True / ~~False~~

a) Skopje is the capital city of America.   True / False

b) 850,000 people live in Skopje.   True / False

c) There was an earthquake in 1995.   True / False

d) People were not frightened.   True / False

e) Skopje is a beautiful city.   True / False

2. Read these words, and match them to the definitions.

eg) capital ——— a small group of houses in the countryside

a) earthquake   the number of people who live in a place

b) population   fallen down, broken

c) historical   a time when the earth suddenly shakes

d) collapsed   something from the past

e) village   the most important city in a country

Friends, Families and Folk Tales

Grammar Exercises

1. This story uses the present simple and past simple of the verb *to be*

Present simple	Past simple
I am	I was
You are	You were
He is	He was
She is	She was
It is	It was
We are	We were
You are	You were
They are	They were

   Fill the gaps with the right word.

   I _____ born in Skopje. Skopje _____ the capital city of Macedonia. It __ not a big city. Its population _____ only 850,000 (eight hundred and fifty thousand).

   In 1963 there _____ an earthquake and many buildings collapsed. For many people this _____ a frightening and difficult time.

   Now Skopje _____ a very beautiful city. It has many new buildings and a historical bridge and castle that the Turkish soldiers built very many years ago.

   My family live near Skopje in a village called Drazevo.

2. With a partner, make up 5 sentences with *am, is* and *are*. Then make up 5 sentences with *was* and *were*.

Writing Exercises

1. **Write out the numbers and dates in words.**

eg)	850,000	*eight hundred and fifty thousand*
	630,000	
	245,300	
	7,350	

eg)	1968	*nineteen hundred and sixty eight*
	1990	
	1996	
	1981	

2. **This story has 4 paragraphs.**
   Match the label with the right paragraph.

eg) The earthquake

Ghengis's family home

Description of Skopje

Facts about Skopje

I was born in Skopje. Skopje is the capital city of Macedonia. It is not a big city. Its population is only 850,000 (eight hundred and fifty thousand).

In 1963 there was an earthquake and many buildings collapsed. For many people this was a frightening and difficult time.

Now Skopje is a very beautiful city. It has many new buildings and a historical bridge and castle, that the Turkish soldiers built very many years ago.

My family live near Skopje in a village called Drazevo.

3. **Now write about a town or village that you know well.**

Friends, Families and Folk Tales

9 Sunday

¹ The best day of the week for me is Sunday. I have more time for resting on Sunday.

Because I work and study from Monday to Friday, I have to shop, clean and wash on Saturday. I am very busy during ⁵ the week.

On Sunday there is no work and everywhere is quiet and peaceful. I can watch t.v. and enjoy the family.

The children do not like to stay at home, but me and my husband prefer to do so. Sometimes we can do that, and ¹⁰ sometimes we go out because of the children.

Maryam from Iran

Discussion questions

a) Do you have a busy life?
b) Which is your favourite day of the week and why?
c) What do you usually do on Saturdays and Sundays?

Sunday

Reading Exercises

1. **Read the story and fill in the table. What does the writer do on which days? Use the words in the box.**

	Monday to Friday	Saturday	Sunday
eg)			*goes to the park*

watches tv, shops, studies, rests, works, washes, goes out with the children, walks by the river, stays at home, cleans

2. **Find the days of the week. Circle the words.**

eg) Monday

Tuesday

Wednesday

Thursday

Friday

Saturday

Sunday

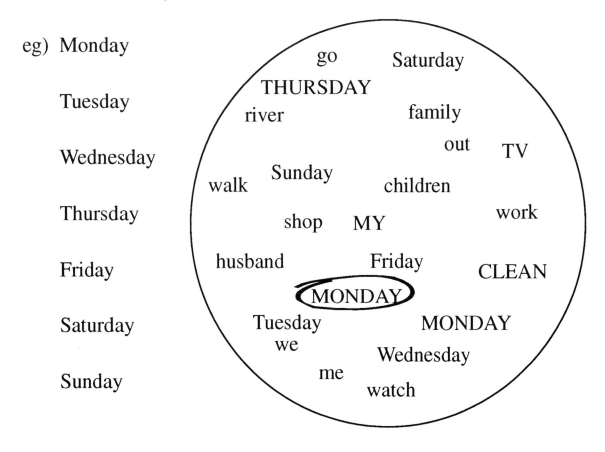

THE LONDON LANGUAGE AND LITERACY UNIT

Friends, Families and Folk Tales

Grammar Exercises

1. **Find these prepositions of time in the story and underline them.**
   <u>on</u> Sunday, <u>from</u> Monday <u>to</u> Saturday, <u>during</u> the week.

2. **Fill in the gaps using *on, from, to, during*.**

   eg) I work from Monday to Friday.

   a) I see my sister _____ Tuesdays.

   b) I will stay there _____ Friday _____ Sunday evening.

   c) _____ Monday I am going to the dentist.

   d) Where were you _____ the film?

   e) I'll talk to you _____ the coffee break.

3. **Put these verbs into the past simple and future simple tense.**

present simple	past simple	future simple
eg) clean	*cleaned*	*will clean*
have to		
work		
can		
go out		
walk		
enjoy		

Writing exercises

1. **Write the days of the week in your language and then write them in English.**

your language	English
eg) (Spanish) lunes	Monday

2. **Read the story again and cover it. Now put in all the capitals, full stops and commas. Use a red pen.**

   the best day of the week for me is sunday i have more time for resting on sunday because i work from monday to friday i have to shop clean and wash on saturdays i am very busy during the week

3. **Write about your favourite day of the week or write about a day in the week you do not like.**

Friends, Families and Folk Tales

10 China

My name is Heng. I come from China. China is in the east of Asia. The weather is hotter than in London, but the north of China is cold in the winter.

China has got forests, sea coast, big cities and many mountains. China has got the Great Wall and a long river – the Yellow River. The mountains are the highest in the world, and the rivers are very long.

Life in general is much faster than in England, people are very busy. China's food is more delicious and very much cheaper than England's. The buildings are modern.

China is a very grand and beautiful country.

by Heng from China

Discussion questions

a) Which country do you come from?

b) Are there mountains in your country?

c) Are there sea coasts in your country?

d) Is your country like England? If not, how is it different?

China

Reading Exercises

1. Read the story again. Tick true or false. True False

eg) China is in the north of Asia. ☐ ✔

a) The north of China is warm in the winter. ☐ ☐

b) The Yellow River is long. ☐ ☐

c) Life in England is faster than in China. ☐ ☐

d) All the buildings in China are old. ☐ ☐

e) Heng is proud of her country. ☐ ☐

2. Read these words.
a) Put them in alphabetical order.

forest   1. _____

delicious 2. _____

building   3. _____

modern   4. _____

coast   5. _____

grand   6. _____

b) Look the words up in a dictionary.
c) Write the definition, or a translation, next to the word.

THE LONDON LANGUAGE AND LITERACY UNIT

Friends, Families and Folk Tales

Grammar Exercises

1. **Look at these 2 sentences.**
   The weather in China **is hotter than** in England.
   Rice **is cheaper than** meat.

   Work with a partner. Make up five sentences comparing your country and England.
   Here are some words you can use:
   big, busy, noisy, clean, cheap, cold, fat, wet.

2. **Look at these sentences.**
   China's food **is more delicious than** England's.
   Fish is **more expensive than** chicken.
   Writing is **more difficult than** reading.

   Think of 2 more sentences like these.

   The sentences in exercises 1 and 2 both compare two things. Work with a partner.
   Discuss when you use *more .... than,* **and when you use** *.....er than.*

is cheaper than.....	is more delicious than....
is hotter than.....	is more expensive than....

You use ....er than when	You use more .... than when
_____	_____
_____	_____
_____	_____

50   THE LONDON LANGUAGE AND LITERACY UNIT

China

Writing Exercises

1. **Here is the story without capital letters.**
   Re-write the sentences and put in the capital letters.

   eg) i come from india.
   I come from India.

   a) my name is heng.
   b) i come from china.
   c) china is in the east of asia.
   d) the weather is hotter than in london.
   e) china has got the great wall and a long river – the yellow river.

   When do you use capital letters? Work with a partner and make a list. Is it the same as in your language?

   Greetings from China!
   Having a wonderful time. China is very beautiful, and the Great Wall really is great!
   Love Heng.

   Helen Sunderland
   6 Buckland House
   Balham Park Estate
   London SW11 4TH.

   2. Read the postcard from China
   Imagine you are on holiday in your country. Write a postcard to your friend.

THE LONDON LANGUAGE AND LITERACY UNIT

Friends, Families and Folk Tales

11 The Fox and The Stork

¹ One day the fox met his friend the stork in the forest and he invited him for dinner. The fox promised that he would make a special dinner to celebrate their meeting. The stork accepted the invitation.

⁵ The next day the stork went to the fox's house. The fox put the special food (which was soup) into a saucer but the stork could not eat it and the fox ate all the soup. After a few hours the stork left.

The time came for the fox to go to the stork's house for
¹⁰ dinner. The fox went but he could not eat because the stork put his food in a very long narrow jar. So the stork ate all the food, and after he finished he said to the fox, "Now it's my turn to laugh."

Stelios from Greece

Discussion questions

a) When you were a child, what was your favourite story?

b) Do you remember who told it or read it to you?

c) Where do folktales in your country come from?

d) Can you tell one of these stories?

The Fox and The Stork

Reading Exercises

1. Put these sentences in the right order to re-tell the story.

a) The fox put the soup in a saucer.
b) The stork put his food in a jar.
c) The fox met his friend the stork in the forest.
d) The stork went to the fox's house.
e) It was the stork's turn to laugh.
f) The fox went to the stork's house.
g) The fox invited the stork for dinner.
h) The fox could not eat, and the stork ate all the food.
i) The stork put the soup in a saucer.

2. Match the word with its definition.

eg) invitation	a small plate for a cup to stand on
narrow	to take what is given to you
celebrate	a container, usually glass
special	an offer to visit someone
saucer	not wide
jar	different from any other
accept	to do special things to show you are happy

Friends, Families and Folk Tales

Grammar Exercises

1. Read the story again. Underline these words:
   and, so but, because
   Discuss with a partner why the writer uses these words.

2. Join the sentences together with the words *and, so, but* or *because*. Write the new sentances on a separate sheet.

eg) The fox met the stork.   He invited him to dinner.
   The fox met the stork and he invited him to dinner.

a)	The stork could not eat	The fox ate all the soup.
b)	The fox went to the stork's house.	He could not eat.
c)	The stork put his food in a jar.	The fox could not eat any.
d)	The fox could not eat	The stork put the food in a very long, narrow jar.

e) I like chocolate   It makes me fat.

f) I cannot eat cheese and chocolate   They give me headaches.

3. Look at these words with a partner. What is the plural?

	singular	plural
eg)	day	*days*
	fox	
	leaf	
	man	
	child	
	potato	

Think of other irregular plurals and write them down.

THE LONDON LANGUAGE AND LITERACY UNIT

The Fox and The Stork

Writing Exercises

1. Read the story again. Underline the phrases that show time.
eg) <u>One day</u>

2. Work with a partner and tell the story again. Use the phrases you have underlined and use *but, and, because* and *so*. You may need to change some nouns to pronouns.
   The fox met the stork.
   The fox invited the stork for dinner.
   The fox promised to make a special dinner.
   The stork accepted the invitation.
   The stork went to the fox's house.
   The fox put the soup in a saucer.
   The stork could not eat.
   The fox ate all the soup.
   The stork left.

3. Think of a folk story from your country.
   a) Tell it to your partner. Write down the main things that happen in the story.
   b) Look at how *The Fox and the Stork* begins. Think about how folk stories begin and end when you are telling them in your own language.
   c) Write down some typical beginnings and endings in your language.
   d) Translate them word for word into English. Would you say it this way in English?
   e) Now write the story, remember to use time phrases and words like *but, because, so, and*.

THE LONDON LANGUAGE AND LITERACY UNIT

Friends, Families and Folk Tales

12 Banging on the Floor

¹ One of my favourite neighbours is a middle aged lady. She is English and like most of the English she has a pale complexion. She is very tall and flabby, her face is round with a double chin, she has blue eyes, her hair is curly and
⁵ white. Sometimes she dyes it red or blonde.

She is a very nosy person, she knows everything about everyone. She is quite a good natured person, but sometimes she is unpleasant. She does not like children and she is always banging on the floor trying to have a bit of
¹⁰ quiet (she lives upstairs).

She has a sweet tooth, she is crazy about chocolates and cakes. She often comes to my house asking for something. I know that she does not need anything, it is just to be nosy and have a bit of company.

Pina from Spain

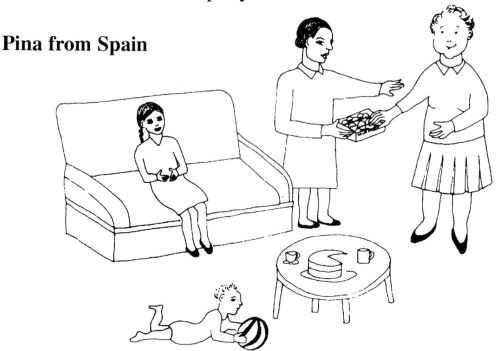

Discussion questions

a) Do you know your neighbours now?
b) Did you know your neighbours where you lived before?
c) Describe one neighbour (now or before).
d) What is a good neighbour?

Banging on the Floor

Reading Exercises

1. Read the story again. Circle true or false.

eg)	My neighbour is young.	True	(False)
a)	My neighbour is English.	True	False
b)	She is small.	True	False
c)	She likes children.	True	False
d)	She likes to eat chocolate and cakes.	True	False
e)	I like my neighbour.	True	False

2. Work with a partner. Read these sentences from the story. Decide whether they are fact or opinion. Fill in the table.

She is English.
She is a very nosy person.
She does not like children.
Sometimes she is unpleasant.
She is always banging on the floor.
She is crazy about chocolates.
She is quite good natured.
She has blue eyes.

	Fact	Opinion
eg)	*She is English*	

THE LONDON LANGUAGE AND LITERACY UNIT

Friends, Families and Folk Tales

Grammar Exercises

1. **Put the words in the right order. Write the sentences on a separate sheet of paper.**

    eg) complexion she a pale has
    She has a pale complexion.

    a) round face her is

    b) and curly hair her white is

    c) dyes sometimes it red she

    d) person a nosy is very she

    e) like she doesn't children

2. **Look at these two sentences from the story:**

    She does not like children   She does not need anything
    Now look at the table:

I you we they	don't (do not)	like children
he she it	doesn't (does not)	like children

    a) **With a partner, make up 5 sentences using don't and 5 sentences using doesn't.**

    b) **Now discuss when you use 'do not' and when you use 'don't'.**

Writing Exercises

1. **This story has 3 paragraphs. Match the label with the right paragraph.**

eg) A: My neighbour's personality — One of my favourite neighbours is a middle aged lady. She is very tall and flabby, her face is round with a double chin.

B: Things my neighbour does — She is a very nosy person, she knows everything about everyone, she is quite a good natured person, but sometimes she is unpleasant.

C: My neighbour's appearance — She has a sweet tooth, she is crazy about chocolates and cakes. She often comes to my house asking for something.

2. **Put in full stops, commas and capitals in the right place.**

eg) she is very tall and flabby her face is round with a double chin
She is very tall and flabby, her face is round with a double chin.

a) she has blue eyes her hair is curly and white sometimes she dyes it red or blonde

b) she is a very nosy person she knows everything about everyone she is quite a good natured person but sometimes she is unpleasant

c) she has a sweet tooth she is crazy about chocolates and cakes she does not like salty food

3. **Write about one of your neighbours, in this country or in your home country. Write about your neighbour's appearance, personality and the things he or she does.**

Friends, Families and Folk Tales

13 A Visit to My Friend

Last week I went to meet my friend. He lives in Peckham. He and his family moved there one month ago. I like him very much. Now he is 40 years old. He is not short, not tall, and is very strong. He is an honest man and a hard worker. He and his wife have 4 children. They are all in school. When he saw me he was very happy, he held me and said:

"Hello, I'm pleased to see you! How are you and your family?"

"Fine, thank you, and you?" I said.

"Fine, fine, thanks! Please come in," he said.

Then he invited me to come into his living room and made Chinese tea for me. His living room was beautiful, everything was tidy. Some pots of flowers in the window were growing large and beautiful. I liked them very much. He talked about different flowers, about their colour and beauty.

"So, you're an expert in growing flowers then," I said.

"No, I am not, but I grew them in Vietnam from time to time," he said.

We talked about living in London and some problems in our lives, but I thought the big problem was language. If we do not speak English we will not get a job; so first we need to improve our reading and speaking skills in English. He agreed with what I said. His wife made food and invited me to have some. After that I said good-bye to him, his wife and everyone.

Thanh from Vietnam

Discussion questions

a) Do you have friends from your own country that you visit?
b) When do you usually visit them? What do you do when you are together?
c) Do you think British people have different customs with their friends?

THE LONDON LANGUAGE AND LITERACY UNIT

A Visit to My Friend

Reading Exercises

1. Read the text again, and fill in the table about Thanh's friend.

name	
where he lives	
age	
marital status	
number of children	
country of origin	
occupation	
skills he has	
skills he needs to improve	

2. Look at the words below.
a) Discuss their meaning with a partner.
b) Look up the words in a dictionary. Write the English definition of these words, and then write the word in your language.

Word	Definition	Translation
a) expect		
b) honest		
c) improve		
d) problem		
e) skill		

THE LONDON LANGUAGE AND LITERACY UNIT

Friends, Families and Folk Tales

Grammar Exercises

1. **Look at the man. Read what he is saying.**

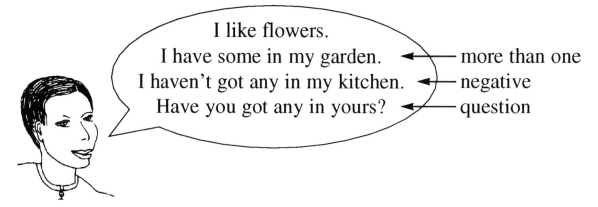

I like flowers.
I have some in my garden. ← more than one
I haven't got any in my kitchen. ← negative
Have you got any in yours? ← question

Work with a partner and use *some* or *any* in these three ways. Here are some ideas you can talk about – books, children, fruit, animals.
Now write four sentences about one of these things.

2. **Look at words in this table:**

I		me	
you		you	
he		him	
she	*saw*	her	*yesterday*
we		it	
they		us	
		them	

a) Underline two examples of *me, you, him* and *them* in the text.
b) Make up five sentences using one word from each column.
eg) *I saw her yesterday.*

Writing Exercises

1. **Read these letters.**

A	B
Flat 3 *12 Bridge St.* *Birmingham B11* *6th October* *Dear Ali,* *Hi! Haven't seen you for ages. Hope you're well.* *How about coming to see my new flat on Saturday? Come for lunch. I'll expect you around 12.00. Give me a ring if there's a problem.* *Look forward to seeing you.* *Cheers!* *Amit*	EAST RIDING SCHOOL The Woodlands, Cheshire Tel. 0121 354 897 12 March 1997 Dear Parent The Governing Body and staff of this school have pleasure in inviting you to its annual Presentation Evening on 26 March 1997. This will be held in the new Sports Hall at 7.00pm. We would be delighted if you would join us for a drink from 6.30pm. Yours sincerely  J. Kelly Headteacher R.S.V.P.

   Work with a partner and discuss what is similar and what is different about them. Consider layout, beginning, ending, ... and anything else.

   Discuss how you would reply.

2. **Write a letter inviting a friend for dinner.**

Friends, Families and Folk Tales

14 Family Life in Morocco

1. A Moroccan family differs considerably from a European family. For example, in Morocco it is very rare to find
5. old people living alone. They usually stay with their relatives, children or grandchildren or other members of the family.

When children grow up, they
10. do not split up from their family. And when they get a job they have to share their earnings with the rest of the family. In any case they would
15. not live on their own if they have to live in the same town. Once married, the girl goes with her husband but usually they live with his family. If
20. they move somewhere else it is not unusual to have another member of the family living with them.

Dinner is always late and it is a
25. very big meal. Very often it will be served on one enormous plate; everyone helps himself either with spoon or fingers, depending on what
30. is being served. If you are invited to a wedding you could find that women do not necessarily eat with men. Most of the parents do not bother to
35. send their children to bed at a certain time. As a result many children can be found wandering around the streets until very late at night.

40. These are just a few things one can say about a Moroccan family.

Mohammed from Morocco

Discussion questions

a) Do you come from a large family?
b) Is family life in Britain different to family life in the country you come from?
c) Are children brought up in a different way in the country you come from?
d) Do you prefer family life in the country you come from or here?

Family Life in Morocco

Reading Exercises

1. **Fill in the gaps. If you need to, look back at the text.**

   A Moroccan family differs considerably from a
   eg) <u>*European family.*</u> For example, in Morocco, it is rare to find
   _____ people living alone. They usually stay with their
   relatives, children or grandchildren or other members of the
   _____.

   When _____ grow up, they do not split up from their
   family. And when they get a _____ they have to share
   their earnings with the rest of the family. In any case they would
   not live _____ _____ _____
   if they have to live in the same town.

2. **Work with a partner and discuss whether the statements are true for Moroccan families, European families or families in your country.**

   Fill in the table. Tick or cross (true or false) for each statement.

		Moroccan Families	English Families	Families in your country
eg)	Once married, young women live with their husband's family.	✔	✘	—
	Young people share their earnings with their families.			
	Dinner is late.			
	Children have a regular bed-time.			
	It is rare to find old people living alone.			
	At weddings, men and women do not eat together.			

THE LONDON LANGUAGE AND LITERACY UNIT

Friends, Families and Folk Tales

Grammar Exercises

1. **a) Read the story and underline these words:**
   Usually, often and always.

   b) Put the words in the right order. Write out the sentences again on a separate sheet.

   eg eat always eight I at – *I always eat at eight.*

   a) relatives they with usually their stay

   b) often she wine drinks

   c) bed to sometimes he early goes

   d) dinner always late is

   e) plate served is meal often one the on

2. **With a partner, discuss these questions.**
a) **Look at the time line. Where would you put *usually* and *often*?**
b) **Can you think of any other words or phrases that show how often you do something? Write them on the line.**

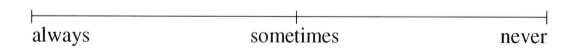

Family Life in Morocco

Writing Exercises

1. **Circle the correct spelling.**

   eg) It is rare to find old   (people) / peeple / pipple   living alone.

   a) When   children / chilblains / shildren   grow up, they stay with their family.

   b) These are just a few   thinks / things / tings   one can say.

   c) Usually they live with his   famaly / famly / family.

   d) Once   marrid / married / meried   the girl goes with her husband.

   e) Most   parents / pearants / partners   do not send their children to bed early.

2. Read the text again with a partner. What are the main points the writer covers?
   Prepare to write about families in your country.
   Make notes of your ideas and put them in order to make a plan.

3. Write about families in the country you come from. Try and use words like *usually, always, often, never*.

THE LONDON LANGUAGE AND LITERACY UNIT

Friends, Families and Folk Tales

15 Escape from Vietnam

¹ My grandfather went from Guangdong in China to Vietnam over a hundred years ago. My father and I were born in Vietnam.

In 1978 I left Vietnam because of the fighting. The ⁵ Vietnamese said all Chinese people had to leave Vietnam. If not, they would die.

So I went with my family and a lot of other people in a small boat. At Bei Hai the boat broke down because it was very old. We waited 40 days for the boat to be mended. We ¹⁰ were not free. We had to stay behind a fence, but one person from each family could go out for two hours every day to buy food. Water was free. After 40 days the boat was mended.

We got more food and water to put on the boat. We went ¹⁵ between Haikow Island and the mainland. It is very dangerous there because the water runs very quickly. Nobody knew the way through, not even the captain. There were whirlpools and strong currents. A lot of people on other boats had died there. It took 23 days to get to Hong ²⁰ Kong.

Tran Phu Canh from Vietnam

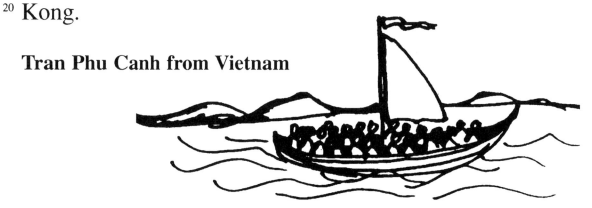

Discussion questions

a) Why did you leave your country? Was it because of war or fighting?

b) What was the journey to England like?

c) What could you bring with you?

d) What did you have to leave behind?

68   THE LONDON LANGUAGE AND LITERACY UNIT

Escape from Vietnam

Reading Exercises

1. Put the sentences in the right order.

a) After 40 days the boat was mended.
b) It took 23 days to get to Hong Kong.
c) In 1978 I left Vietnam.
d) We went between Haikow Island and the mainland.
e) At Bei Hai the boat broke down.
f) We waited for the boat to be mended.

2. Find the word or phrase in the text which has the same meaning as the following:

eg) ship   *boat*

a) went away from   _____

b) stopped working   _____

c) repaired   _____

d) fast moving water   _____

e) water turning in circles _____

THE LONDON LANGUAGE AND LITERACY UNIT

Friends, Families and Folk Tales

Grammar Exercises

1. Fill in the table with the missing verbs:

	Present Simple	**Past Simple**
eg)	wait	*waited*
		left
	break	
		had
	get	
	run	
		knew
	die	

2. Read the story again, and fill the gaps using one of the verbs in the box below.

eg) The boat journey <u>could</u> kill you.

a) They _____ buy food.

b) They _____ stay inside the fence.

c) All Chinese people _____ leave Vietnam.

d) They _____ go out for 2 hours.

e) The boat broke down so it _____ be mended.

had to	could

Escape from Vietnam

Writing Exercises

1. Read the story again. Work with a partner, and discuss:

a) How many paragraphs are there?

b) What is each paragraph about?

c) Write a sentence summarising each paragraph.

   1) _____

   2) _____

   3) _____

   4) _____

2. Find *would* and *could* in the text.
Think of 2 more words with the pattern *ould*, and write a sentence using each word.

   a) _____

   b) _____

Do all the words sound the same?

3. Write about an important or interesting journey you have made.

Friends, Families and Folk Tales

16 My Husband's Ex-Wife

1 I don't like my husband's ex-wife. She is a trouble maker. She always uses the child against him to get the things that she wants.

On the occasions that I have met her, I have found her
5 personality to be weak.

I never know when she tells the truth. She is young and immature. I think she has not been successful as a mother.

I hope that she will improve with age.

Silvana from Brazil

Discussion questions

a) Can you think of a person that you really dislike?
b) Why do you feel this way about him or her?
c) Describe this person's personality.

My Husband's Ex-Wife

Reading Exercises

1. **Read the story and write short answers.**

   a) Does the author like her husband's ex-wife?

   b) Is the ex-wife young or old?

   c) Does the ex-wife have children?

   d) What is the ex-wife's personality like?

   e) Is the ex-wife a successful mother?

2. **Find the following words in the text and circle them.**

like	met	found	think
is	uses	hope	tells

3. **Match the 2 halves of the words and then write the whole word.**

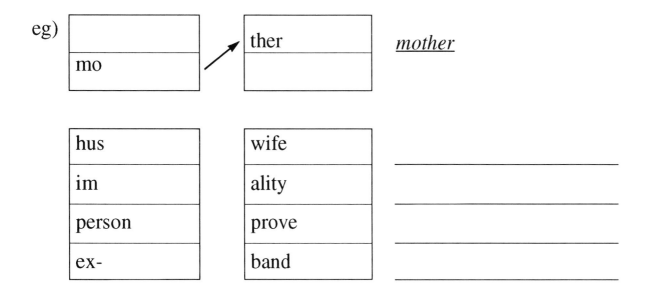

THE LONDON LANGUAGE AND LITERACY UNIT   73

Friends, Families and Folk Tales

Grammar Exercises

1. **Read the text again, then read these phrases.**

I *have met* her	she *has met* her
I *have found* her	she *has found* her

I *have not met* her	*Have* you *met* her?
She *has not met* her	*Has* he *met* her?

   Fill in the gaps.

   a) I _____ lived in Britain for 10 years.

   b) She has _____ finished her coffee. Wait for her.

   c) _____ you seen Penny today?

   d) He _____ _____ been to India. _____ you?

   e) I _____ worn glasses since I was a child.

2. **Work with a partner. Read these words.**
   These are adverbs showing how often you do something.

   |———————+————————+————————+————————|
   always   often   Sometimes   rarely   never

   Discuss where the adverb goes in English compared with your language. Put one of these words into each of the sentences.

   a) I eat breakfast.   d) I walk in the park.
   b) I smoke.   e) I sing in the bath.
   c) I go to bed early.

My Husband's Ex-Wife

Writing Exercises

1. **Choose the correct spelling.**

   eg) She's young and   imature
                                    inmature
                                    (immature) ← circled

   a) She has not been   sucesfull / successfull / successful

   b) On the   ocassions / ocasions / occasions   I have met her

   c) When she   tels / tells / tel   the truth

2. **Write about someone you do not like.**

   a) **Choose from these sentences to begin:**

   " I am going to describe _____ "

   " I do not like _____ "

   " I would like to tell you about _____ "

   " There is a person I do not like very much whose name is

   _____ "

   b) **Describe the person's appearance and personality. Describe your relationship with this person and explain why you do not like him or her.**

   c) **Think about a way of ending the description.**

THE LONDON LANGUAGE AND LITERACY UNIT

Friends, Families and Folk Tales

17 The Cooking Pot

There was an old man called Nasreddin. He was a very funny man. One day he asked his neighbour if he could borrow a big cooking pot.

After a day had gone by Nasreddin gave his neighbour two cooking pots; one was slightly smaller than the other. The neighbour asked,

"Why have you given me two cooking pots back?"

Nasreddin replied to his neighbour:

"The large cooking pot I borrowed from you had a baby."

The neighbour was very pleased.

The next day Nasreddin went back to his neighbour and again he asked if he could borrow his cooking pot. The neighbour gave it to him.

After days went by, Nasreddin did not return his neighbour's cooking pot. He asked Nasreddin,

"Why have you not returned my pot?"

Nasreddin replied,

"I am afraid your cooking pot has died!"

The neighbour asked,

"How can a cooking pot die?"

Nasreddin replied,

"Well, you believed that your cooking pot had a baby so why don't you believe that your cooking pot has died?"

Figen from Cyprus

Discussion questions

a) Have you heard any stories about Nasreddin?

b) Who is he? What kind of person is he?

c) Can you tell one of the stories?

d) Do you have a lot of stories about one person (or animal) in your country? Who is he or she? What kind of person is he or she?

The Cooking Pot

Reading Exercises

1. **Read the story again. Then put the sentences in the box in the right place in the story. Do not look at the text.**

   One day Nasreddin asked his neighbour if he could borrow a big cooking pot.

   After a day had gone by Nasreddin gave his neighbour two cooking pots, one was slightly smaller than the other. The neighbour asked,

   eg) "<u>*Why have you given me two cooking pots back*</u>?"
   Nasreddin replied to his neighbour

   a) " _____ "
   The neighbour was very pleased.

   The next day Nasreddin went back to his neighbour and again he asked if he could borrow his cooking pot. The neighbour gave it to him. After days went by Nasreddin did not return his neighbour's cooking pot. He asked Nasreddin,

   b) " _____ "
   Nasreddin replied

   c) " _____ "
   The neighbour asked

   d) " _____ "
   Nazreddin replied

   e) " _____ "

   > 1) The large cooking pot I borrowed from you had a baby.
   > 2) Well you believed that your cooking pot had a baby so why don't you believe that your cooking pot has died?
   > 3) Why have you given me two cooking pots back?
   > 4) I am afraid your cooking pot has died.
   > 5) Why have you not returned my pot?
   > 6) How can a cooking pot die?

   THE LONDON LANGUAGE AND LITERACY UNIT

Friends, Families and Folk Tales

Grammar Exercises

1. Look at these sentences:

   > [How] can a cooking pot die?
   > [Why] have you not returned my cooking pot?

   [How] and [Why] are used to ask questions.

   Work with a partner. Think of other words you can use to ask questions. Now use some of these words to complete the following questions:

   eg) a) *Why* have you given me 2 cooking pots?

   b) _____ is my cooking pot?

   c) _____ will you give it back?

   d) _____ can a cooking pot die?

2. Look at these sentences:
   Why have you given me 2 cooking pots?
   Why have you not returned my pot?
   This is the present perfect tense. With a partner, make questions using this tense. Make positive and negative questions.

   eg) Why (come) to England?
   Why *have you come* to England?

   a) Where (leave) book?
   b) Why not (come) to see me?
   c) Where (be) in England?
   d) Where not (be) in England?

   eg) Why not (do) homework?
   Why *have you not done your* homework?

   **Can you think of any more?
   Do you have a similar tense in your language?**

The Cooking Pot

Writing Exercises

1. **Read the sentences in the box. Nasreddin and his friend are speaking. They are using direct speech.**

   > The neighbour asked,
   > "Why have you given me two cooking pots back?"
   >
   > Nasreddin replied to his neighbour,
   > "The large cooking pot I borrowed from you had a baby."

   | Open and close speech marks when writing the exact words the speaker uses. | Begin a new line when someone starts speaking. | Use a full stop or other punctuation (!?,) before the closing speech marks. |

2. **Re-write the following two conversations, using correct punctuation. If necessary write on a separate sheet.**

   a) I can't come over this weekend said Amina because Emma is ill oh I'm so sorry said Helen I hope she's better soon

   eg) "I can't come over this weekend," said Amina,

   b) Could you give Amina a message asked Nasreddin yes of course Daniel answered what is it I'm going to be late but can she wait for me he said.

3. **Write about a misunderstanding you have had with someone, or write about an argument.**

THE LONDON LANGUAGE AND LITERACY UNIT

Friends, Families and Folk Tales

18 Education in China

In China, children go to school at 6 or 7 years old. I started school when I was 7. In Chinese schools, there are very strict rules. I remember when I attended classes, we had to put our hands behind our back, straighten our back and sit without talking to each other.

When the teacher asked a question we first had to raise our hands and when the teacher called someone, he or she had to stand up to answer the question. If pupils were late for school, they had to shout "BAOGAO" (meaning "I'm here") outside the door. If the teacher agreed, they could go into the classroom. There were over 40 pupils in each class.

Every year we had two terms and two holidays, one in summer and one in winter, each about a month long. We went to school at 7.30 am and did some practice by ourselves. At 8.00 am the first class started and school went on until 4.00 pm.

There are 6 years of primary school. In the first and second year children learn reading and writing, mathematics, abacus, music and sport. In the third year they start to learn history, politics and nature. There are 2 exams each year, one in July, the other in December. If students pass their exam in July, they can continue in a higher class.

After primary school comes 3 years in secondary school followed by 3 years of high school. There are more subjects than in primary school but the rules are not so strict. The exam system is the same.

I really loved learning but I was often afraid of the teachers.

Jing Hong from China

Discussion questions

a) What are schools like in the country where you went to school?

b) Are teachers strict?

c) Is the system of education in that country similar or different to Britain?

d) Is education in that country better than here?

THE LONDON LANGUAGE AND LITERACY UNIT

Education in China

Reading Exercises

1. Read the text and fill in the missing words.

eg) In China children go to school at <u>6</u> or <u>7</u> years old.

a) There were over _____ pupils in each class.

b) Every year we had _____ terms and two holidays one in _____ and one in winter.

c) At _____ am the first class started.

d) School finished at _____ pm.

e) There are _____ years of primary school.

f) If students pass their exam in _____, they can continue in a higher class.

2. Circle the correct answer.

eg) In China teachers in primary school are (very strict) / not strict.

a) The classes are not large. / large.

b) In China children work by themselves before class starts. / with a teacher all day.

c) Primary school is as long as high school. / longer than high school.

d) The school day is quite long. / short.

Friends, Families and Folk Tales

Grammar Exercises

1.

Now	Past
there is an exam in July	**there was** a strict teacher
is there an exam in July?	**was there** a strict teacher?
there are 6 years of primary school	**there were** 40 pupils
are there 6 years in primary school?	**were there** 40 pupils?

Fill in the gaps using *is are was were.*

a) In class today there _____ many students.

b) Yesterday there _____ a terrible storm.

c) In my house there _____ 2 bedrooms.

d) There _____ a post office near here.

e) _____ there any apples in the fridge?

f) _____ there lots of people in the High Street last Saturday?

2. a) Read lines 31 to 42 of Education in China again.
   b) Change the verbs and put them in the past tense.

There _____ 6 years of primary school. In the first and second year children _____ reading and writing, mathematics, abacus, music and sport. In the third year they _____ to learn history, politics and nature. There _____ 2 exams each year, one in July, the other in December. If students _____ their exam in July, they _____ could continue in a higher class.

Education in China

Writing Exercises

1. a) Read the passage and make notes about term dates, school times, subjects, behaviour and exams.
   b) From your notes, write sentences about education in China.

2. You are writing to ask for information about English classes at a local college. Fill in the gaps using some of the words and phrases given below:

```
                                        36, Priory ¹_____
                                              Bradford
                                              W.Yorks

15th ²_____ 1997

Dear ³_____

I am writing to ⁴_____ about English classes in
your College) I am ⁵_____ evening classes.

I am a ⁶_____ resident.

I ⁷_____ to know how much they ⁸_____, the
⁹_____ dates and ¹⁰_____ of classes.

I ¹¹_____ to hearing from you.

¹² _____

Jing Hong (Mrs)
```

April
cost
enquire
find
hope
interested in
know
look forward
pay
permanent
Road
Sir/Madam
term
time
want
would like
yours faithfully
yours sincerely

3. Write about your school days or education in another country.

THE LONDON LANGUAGE AND LITERACY UNIT

Friends, Families and Folk Tales

19 Pakistani Customs

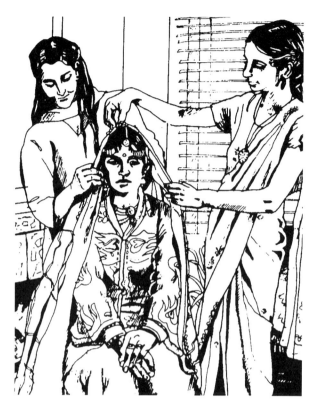

1 I am from Pakistan. We have different culture and customs from this country. I like our customs very much, we have a lot of fun. We celebrate Eid Ul Fitr, Eid
5 Ul Adha, marriages, birthdays, Kunda parties etc. For example, the bride has to sit in the house ten days before her marriage. She cannot go out. She wears a yellow dress. All the young women and
10 girls sit around her. They beat a drum and sing marriage songs. They wear red, blue, pink, yellow and different coloured clothes, and the elders sew the bride's clothes when they give the dowry.

15 One day before the wedding the bridegroom's relatives bring china, fruit, sweets, jewellery and clothes. They bring twenty-one stitched and unstitched sets of clothes. And the girl's parents also
20 send suits, shoes, sweets and fruit to the bridegroom's house. In this way we have fun. We take some photos on the wedding day; when the boy comes, the bride's sisters hide the bridegroom's shoes and
25 they ask for money. If the boy gives them a good amount of money then they return the shoes. When the groom is ready to go home, the bride's sisters do not let her go unless the groom gives them money, and
30 the sisters of the bride give a glass of juice to the groom and take the money.

For Eid, we cook sweets. In the morning we get up early and have a bath and wear different coloured new clothes.
35 The men go to the mosque and say their prayers. When they return home the children ask for some money, which is called "Eidi" from their parents and from their relatives. They go to their relatives'
40 house. All the businesses in Pakistan are closed that day. The youngsters go to see films. We have lots of fun on these days.

Sakina from Pakistan

Discussion questions

a) What are the main celebrations in the country you have come from?
b) What do you do on these special days?
c) What happens on a wedding day in the country you have come from?

Pakistani Customs

Reading Exercises

1. Read the text and find:
a) the names of 3 festivals
b) 3 things the groom's relatives bring on the wedding day
c) 3 things people do on Eid.

2. Read the sentences and choose the most appropriate word or phrase to fill in the gap. Circle the letter with the best answer.

eg) In Pakistan Eid is
   a) a day of sadness.
   b) a day when children get up early and have a bath before school.
   (c) a religious holiday.

i) The day before the wedding
   a) relatives take photos.
   b) the bride receives many gifts.
   c) the bride and groom sew their wedding clothes.

ii) On her wedding day
   a) the bride wears red, blue, yellow and pink.
   b) she sits in her dress for 10 days.
   c) the bride is accompanied by other women who sing and play music.

iii) On his wedding day
   a) children play jokes on the groom.
   b) children hide the bride's shoes.
   c) the groom pays money and goes home with sweets and fruit.

iv) Wedding customs in Pakistan
   a) are similar to those of English wedding customs.
   b) are the same as those of India.
   c) differ considerably from English wedding customs.

THE LONDON LANGUAGE AND LITERACY UNIT

Friends, Families and Folk Tales

Grammar Exercises

1. **Re-order the sentences to make a logical paragraph.**
   We have lots of fun on these days.
   The men go to the Mosque and say their prayers.
   All the businesses in Pakistan are closed that day.
   We celebrate Eid.
   When they return home, the children ask for some money, which is called 'Eidi'.
   In the morning we get up early and have a bath and wear different coloured new clothes.
   The youngsters go to see films.

2. **Read these sentences. Look at the order of the subject, object and verb in the active. Compare the order with the passive. With a partner, discuss the changes. What happens to the verb in the passive sentence? What happens to the subject?**

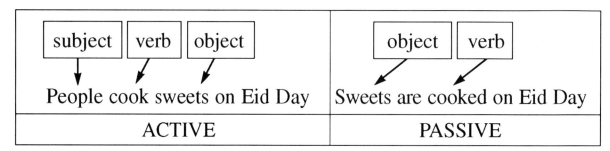

ACTIVE	PASSIVE
People cook sweets on Eid Day	Sweets are cooked on Eid Day

   Change these sentences from the active to the passive.

   eg) Men say prayers in the Mosque.
   Prayers are said in the Mosque.

   a) People bring china, fruit, sweets and jewellery.
   b) Women wear red and yellow clothes.
   c) People take photos on the wedding day.
   d) They return the shoes.

Writing Exercises

1. **Read the text with a partner. Discuss the tense it is written in. Why do you think the writer uses this tense?
Complete the flow diagram using your own words:**

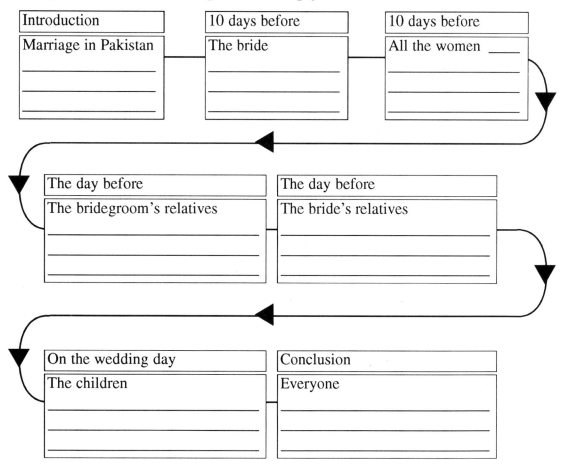

2. **Write about marriage customs you know about.
First complete the plan.**

   a) Write short notes.
   b) Put your ideas in order.
   c) How will you begin and end it?
   d) What tense will you use?

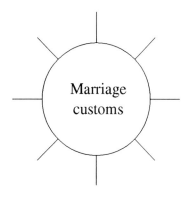

Friends, Families and Folk Tales

20 Future Plans

¹ Today, the teacher gave us homework: write about your future. Do you have future plans? To be honest, I never thought about my future. Here is a woman, 36 years of age who does not speak English well. What can she do?

⁵ What I need now is to learn more English. For me, English is not easy to learn. My problems are these: grammar, English tenses and how to join up sentences. Of course, there are many more problems beside. I believe that people who have a good educational background learn English ¹⁰ faster and catch up quickly. I did not have a good education. I left school when I was 13 years old.

So in the future, I will carry on learning English. Hopefully, one day I will be able to speak English well because my husband and I, and my 2 children will live in England for ¹⁵ good. For this reason it is important to understand the language.

Kit from Hong Kong

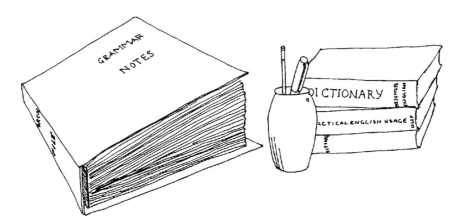

Discussion questions
a) Why are you attending English classes at the moment?
b) What aspects of English do you need to improve?
c) What would you like to do next year?
d) Do you know where to go for information about other courses or training, or for careers advice?

Future Plans

Reading Exercises

1. Tick true or false.

	True	False
eg) The writer's future is well planned.	☐	✔
a) She can learn English fast.	☐	☐
b) She has difficulty with using the past, present and future in English.	☐	☐
c) She is middle-aged.	☐	☐
d) She is not married.	☐	☐
e) She went to university in Hong Kong.	☐	☐
f) She hopes to go back to her country to stay.	☐	☐

2. Match the words from the text with the correct meanings.

eg) carry on ⟶ continue

a) to be honest   for ever

b) for good   reach the same level

c) catch up   to tell you the truth

THE LONDON LANGUAGE AND LITERACY UNIT

Friends, Families and Folk Tales

Grammar Exercises

1. **Fill in the table with the missing verb:**

simple past	present simple	future simple
		will carry on
	live	
		will be able
gave		
	does not	

2. **Look at these sentences:**
   I will carry **on** learn**ing**.
   I am interested **in** apply**ing** for the job.
   I'm fed up **with** cook**ing**.

a) **What is common to the 3 sentences?**
   Work out the rule with a partner.

b) **Fill in the gap with the right form of the word.**
eg) My daughter is good at *singing.* (sing)

   (i) Turn off the gas before _____ (leave) the house.

   (ii) I have had enough of _____ (clean).

   (iii) I look forward to _____ (see) you.

   (iv) I am interested in _____ (become) a teacher.

Future Plans

Writing Exercises

1. **Look at the writer's plan for this piece.**

Introduction:	teacher gave us homework future plans personal information
Main part:	need to learn English problems in English importance of educational background my educational background
Conclusion:	my future plans why they are important

   Prepare to write about either your future plans or your English class. Write a plan. You can write the plan in your own language.

Introduction:	
Main part:	
Conclusion:	

2. **Now write about your future plans.**

THE LONDON LANGUAGE AND LITERACY UNIT

Friends, Families and Folk Tales

21 The Man and The Monkey

¹ Long, long ago there was only one man in the world. One day the man went to the forest to cut wood for his fire.

⁵ When he got to the forest he took off his hat, and hung it on the branch of a tree and started to cut the wood. He cut enough wood to make a big bundle, put ¹⁰ the bundle on his back and walked home.

He was nearly home when suddenly he remembered his hat. So he turned round and ¹⁵ went back to the forest.

A monkey had been sitting in the tree watching the man. The monkey saw the hat and liked it. When the man left the ²⁰ forest, the little monkey jumped down from the tree, picked up the hat and put it on his head.

The man wanted his hat. When ²⁵ he got back to the forest he looked everywhere for it but he could not find it. It was getting dark when, looking up into the branches of the tree he ³⁰ suddenly saw the monkey watching him with the hat on its head.

How was the man to get back his hat? He could not catch the ³⁵ monkey. He thought for a long time. All the time he thought the monkey was watching him. Then the man pulled some hair from the top of his head, held ⁴⁰ it up in the air and threw it away. The monkey watched. Then the monkey pulled the hat from his head, held it up in the air and threw it away.

⁴⁵ At last the hat fell onto the ground. The man quickly picked it up, put it on his head and walked home.

Lan from Vietnam.

	Discussion questions	
a)	When you were a child, who told you stories?	c) Do you have stories about animals in your language?
b)	Do you tell stories to anyone now?	d) Can you remember one? Which animal is it about?

Reading Exercises

1. **There are two stories, The Cooking Pot (page 76) and The Man and The Monkey. They have been mixed together and the order has been jumbled up.**
   Work with a partner. First, separate the stories, then put them in the right order.

   The next day, Nasreddin again borrowed a cooking pot from his neighbour.

   When he was nearly home he remembered his hat. So, he returned to the forest.

   When the man got back to the forest he saw the monkey watching him with his hat on its head. How was the man to get back his hat?

   Long, long ago there was only one man in the world.

   The neighbour replied
   "How can a cooking pot die?"

   The man picked it up quickly and walked home.

   Once upon a time, there was an old man called Nasreddin.

   One day the man went to the forest to cut wood. He took off his hat and hung it on the branch of a tree. He cut a big bundle of wood and walked home.

   Nasreddin said,
   "You believed your cooking pot had a baby, so why don't you believe that your cooking pot is dead?"

   The man pulled some hair from his head and threw it down. The monkey pulled the hat from his head and threw it on the ground.

   Nasreddin gave back his neighbour 2 cooking pots. He said,
   "The large cooking pot I borrowed from you had a baby."

   One day he asked his neighbour if he could borrow a cooking pot.

   A monkey had been watching the man, and when he left, the monkey picked up the hat and put it on.

   Nasreddin did not return the cooking pot. He told his neighbour,
   "Your cooking pot has died."

2. **Read *The Man and The Monkey* again and underline all the words and phrases that show time is passing in the story.**

Friends, Families and Folk Tales

Grammar Exercises

1. Fill in the gaps with *the, a,* or *leave blank*.

Long, long ago, there was only _____ one man in _____ world. One day _____ man went to the forest to cut _____ wood for his fire.

When he got to _____ forest he took off his hat and hung it on _____ branch of _____ tree and started to cut _____ wood. He cut enough _____ wood to make _____ big bundle, put _____ bundle on his back and walked home.

2. Choose the correct preposition. Delete where appropriate.

eg) The man went ~~at~~ **to** ~~out~~ the forest.

a) The man pulled the hat **from / out / on** his head.

b) When he got back **of / at / to** the forest.

c) The man put it **in / on / to** his head.

d) There was only one man **on / of / in** the world.

e) The monkey picked **in / up / to** the hat.

The Man and The Monkey

Writing Exercises

1. Look at the chart. Talk to your partner, and together fill in the missing parts of the story. Write either in the box or on a piece of paper.

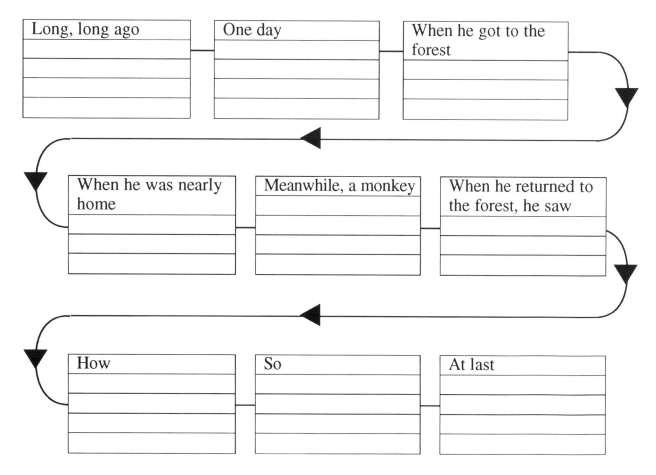

2. Write the story in full. Leave a good margin.

3. In small groups, proof read your stories together, using the code from page 107.

4. Write a story or folk tale that you know.

THE LONDON LANGUAGE AND LITERACY UNIT

Friends, Families and Folk Tales

22 Christmas and New Year in Vietnam

I am Vietnamese. I was born and lived in South Vietnam. Almost all the Vietnamese of South Vietnam joined the Catholic and Buddhist religions. Vietnam came under Chinese, French and American influence.

Annually, in December, the Vietnamese expected the coming of Christmas and of Vietnamese New Year. People sent Christmas and New Year cards to each other and bought new clothes and toys for the children, food and wine for Christmas Day.

On Christmas Eve, people flocked to eat and drink, very merry. In Vietnam, the weather was very warm; on the night before Christmas Day the young people went around the streets in crowds. They blocked the traffic. They wore hats and artificial noses, very funny. They walked in flocks and made a noise. The churches were decorated very nicely outside. A lot of coloured flags and electric lamps were hung. At midnight for the main ceremony, the church bells rang. All of the Catholic people were in the church. After the ceremony they had a party called "reveillon".

The Vietnamese New Year was very merry because it was for everybody. There were four days off. Every house was decorated very nicely. Children and people wore new clothes, new shoes. They visited their friends' houses in crowds to greet each other. The traditional foods and cakes were made. In every family, there were the traditional ceremonies. New Year was an opportunity for relations to meet together.

Nghi from Vietnam

Discussion questions

a) What are the most important festivals in the country you come from?

b) How do you celebrate these special days?

c) What happens in Britain on Guy Fawkes Night?

d) Do you think people in the country you come from have more fun than in Britain?

Christmas and New Year in Vietnam

Reading Exercises

1. **Read the text and answer the questions.**
   a) Which are the most common religions in South Vietnam?
   b) Who was Vietnam colonised by?
   c) What did children hope for at this time?
   d) Was Christmas a quiet celebration?
      Give reasons for your answer.
   e) What were the main features of Vietnamese New Year?

2. **Find the word in the text that means the same as:**

eg) roads   *streets*

a) every year   _____

b) gathered in large numbers   _____

c) jammed   _____

d) false   _____

e) religious service   _____

f) family members   _____

THE LONDON LANGUAGE AND LITERACY UNIT

Friends, Families and Folk Tales

Grammar Exercises

1. **Look at this example of the passive form of the verb from the text:**

   Every house was decorated very nicely

   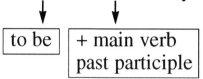

   a) **Find other examples from the story and write them here. Then circle the verb to be and underline the main verb (past participle).**

   i) _____

   ii) _____

   iii) _____

   b) **Why do you think the passive is used in English?**

   c) **How would you say this in your language? Do you have active and passive?**

2. **Put these sentences into the passive.**

   eg) The builders built this house in 1906.
   This house was built in 1906.

   a) The cooks made sweetmeats and fancy cakes.

   _____

   b) The postman delivered the letters late yesterday.

   _____

   c) The earthquake destroyed many buildings.

   _____

Writing Exercises

1. Work in a group.
   Think of as many words as you can to describe Christmas and New Year. Think about Christmas and New Year in Vietnam, Britain or any other country you know.

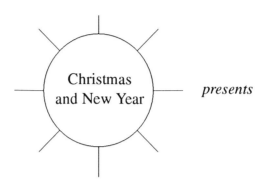

2. Fill in this table using the words you have thought of.

Vietnam	Britain	other countries

3. With a partner, compare Christmas and New Year in Vietnam with Christmas and New Year in Britain or another country.

4. Now work alone, and write your comparison down.

THE LONDON LANGUAGE AND LITERACY UNIT

Friends, Families and Folk Tales

23 I Left My Country with Sadness

I am from Eritrea. I grew up in a small village with my family. It was a very nice place with green grass and big mountains. We had a big farm with animals; cows and goats, sheep and oxen and one horse. We were very fond of it.

Well, when I was about fifteen and a half I went to Massawa (it is by the seaside) to get a job. I started to do a little work and I sent some money to my family. After that I got married and I had two children. So I had a very, very good family and I loved my husband and our children. In the summer for our holiday we used to go to our parents, to that nice village.

Suddenly in 1974, in my country something quite bad started. There was a change of government, and they killed quite a lot of children, men and women. My husband was arrested too. There was no food. There was a lot of sadness for all the people. I went to my village where I grew up. Even there it was quite bad to live, so I decided to leave my country completely, with sadness. My family said to me, "Please don't go away, we'll die all together."

In 1976 I arrived in Sudan. The language was certainly a big difficulty. In 1977 I went to Italy with one son. In Italy finding a house is a big problem so I had to send my son to a boarding college. It was about seventy kilometres from where I lived. I remember how my son and I cried. Every fifteen or twenty days I used to go and see him by train. We always remembered his father I mean my husband, and my little boy. Well, on 8th December 1980 we came to England.

Some people from my country, even some Italians, said to me, "In England life is very difficult and expensive. The language is quite hard to understand, especially in the street, and English people are quite strong and unkind."

Oh dear, what could I do? I was very afraid when I heard this. Anyway, I came to England.

The first problem when we came to England was to find a school for my son. The lady I was working with said, "It's impossible to find a place for your son." She told me to ask in a school but it cost £400 a month. What! I was surprised and quite upset. What could I do?

One day I saw a notice saying "School". Well, I went there. I was afraid. The headmistress of the school said to me "Welcome, are you from Eritrea?" "Yes", I said, "and I don't speak English." She said: "Never mind, I will help you". So slowly she asked me some questions and told me my son had to start on Monday. She told me there was nothing to pay, only £1.70 for meals.

"Thank you very much, see you on Monday," I said. It was quite wonderful because I remembered the words of friends, they told me the English are strict and unkind. It is not true, they are very quiet and gentle and kind.

Well I am very sad to have left my husband, and my son, my home, my nice country, all my family. I brought only one son. But on the other hand I am happy to live in England, because I have my son to live with me. He is not living in a separate place like the college. And I am quite happy to learn English too.

Anon from Eritrea

Discussion questions

a) Do you remember arriving in Britain?
b) What time of the year was it?
c) What things surprised you about this country?
d) Did you have any problems because you did not have the right information?

THE LONDON LANGUAGE AND LITERACY UNIT

I Left My Country with Sadness

Reading Exercises

1. Work with a partner. Read the title – what do you think the story is about? Then, read the first sentence of each paragraph and discuss what you think the rest of the paragraph is about.

2. Now, read the whole story carefully.
   Circle the correct sentence.

eg (i) She grew up in Eritrea.
   ii) She was born in the Sudan.
   iii) She is from Italy.

a) i) Her family lived in the seaside.
   ii) Her family lived in the mountains.
   iii) Her family lived in the city.

b) i) When she was 15 ½ she got a job.
   ii) When she was 15 ½ she got married.
   iii) When she was 15 ½ she changed jobs.

c) i) In 1974 they killed her husband.
   ii) In 1974 they arrested her.
   iii) In 1974 her husband was arrested.

d) i) First she went to Italy and then the Sudan.
   ii) Before she came to England, she went to Italy.
   iii) She came to England, she went to the Sudan.

e) i) She had to pay for the school.
   ii) She had to pay for the dinners.
   iii) She did not have to pay for anything.

Friends, Families and Folk Tales

Grammar Exercises

1. **Compare these sentences**

Direct speech	Indirect speech
The lady I was working with said, "It's impossible to find a place for your son."	The lady I was working with said that it was impossible to find a place for my son.

   Find the differences. How many differences are there? Compare your answers with a partner.

2. **Change the following sentences into indirect speech. Write the sentence on a separate sheet.**

   eg) They said, "In England life is very difficult and expensive."
   <u>They said that in England life was very difficult and expensive.</u>

   b) I said, "I don't speak English".

   c) He said, "I'll see you on Monday".

   d) I said, "I can't come to class tomorrow".

   e) She said, "I will help you."

3. **Look at line 13:** In the summer for our holiday, we used to go to our parents. **Did she do this only once or regularly?**

4. **Another common way of showing that things happened regularly in the past is to use 'would'.**

In the summer, for our holiday we used to go to our parents.	In the summer, for our holiday we would go to our parents.

   Think of 5 things you did regularly when you were a child. Write them down using both *used to...* and *would...*

THE LONDON LANGUAGE AND LITERACY UNIT

I Left My Country with Sadness

Writing Exercises

1. Start to re-tell the story. Make notes using the table as a guide.

when?	where?	what happened?
1954	Eritrea	writer was born
1954 – 1968	small village	writer lived on a farm, with lots of animals
1969		
1969 – 1973		
1974		
1976		
1977		
1977 – 1980		
Dec. 1980		

2. Use your notes to tell the story to a partner.

3. Now write the story in full sentences and paragraphs.

4. Proof-read your partner's story, using the code on page 107.

5. Compare the paragraphing in both your stories.

Friends, Families and Folk Tales

24 Growing and Learning Together

The old home which I looked forward to seeing again was the one in which I had lived when I was born. It was also the place that I spent my happy childhood. Indeed, it was a happy home full of smiles and warmth.

This lovely home was neither well-furnished nor well-decorated. On the contrary, it was a rough stone house. It contained a bedroom, a sitting-room and a kitchen. Since we were poor, the sitting-room was also our bedroom as my brothers, my sister and I slept in there. My parents could not afford to buy or to hire a television set. They gave little pocket money to us. Thus, the only way for us to spend our leisure time was by listening to the radio.

Being energetic, we tried to find out ways to release our energy. My eldest brother, Henry, was a good leader and organiser. Although the games which he organised were free, we got lots of satisfaction.

Sometimes, we fought our civil war in the open space which was in front of my house. We divided into two groups: Henry and Wallace, my youngest brother, were on one side while my elder sister, my younger brother and me were on the other side. We used the cushions to build our shelters, and slippers to be the bombs. We hid behind the shelter and dropped the bombs on our enemy. Then, the war broke out. The group whose shelter was demolished or seriously damaged, was judged to be the defeated group. Usually, Henry and Wallace were the winners because we felt pity for Wallace as he would cry if he knew he was a failure.

Although we were young, we knew how to do business. We collected gravel as the goods. Then, we cut used newspaper into pieces as our bank notes. One of us pretended to be the owner of this small snack bar. The others were the customers. Our transactions were carried out. We trained when we were young, it was not surprising that we were good at mathematics when we grew up.

Our house was situated near the field. So, we normally played in the field and made friends with the farmers. Sometimes we even helped them to water their plants. So, in the harvest season, they sent us some sweet potatoes and maize.

However, we also had our sorrow as the nearby channel system was not well-developed, and flooding often occurred especially after a thunderstorm or heavy rain. We were quite worried about the farmers. Nevertheless, the home was warm and happy.

Later, we moved out and settled in a town. As we grew up, our relationship became less close than before. As time went by, the gap between us became wider, for some of us were married while the others studied abroad. The past happiness and wonderful moments could only be tasted in our memories.

Tze Chui from Hong Kong

Discussion questions

a) What games did you play as a child?
b) Do you know if there are similar games in this country?
c) Do children play with toy weapons in the country where you grew up?
d) Do you think children should play with toy guns?

Reading Exercises

1. Read the title. What do you think this passage is about? Read the first and last lines of each paragraph. What do you think each paragraph will have in it?

2. Now read the whole passage carefully.
   Answer these questions. Read them all before answering.

   a) Say briefly what the author's house was like.

   b) Describe the civil war game the children played.

   c) Which other game did the children play?

   d) How did the children make up for their lack of toys?

3. **Find words in the story which mean the same as those below:**

   eg) a place of safety   *shelter*

   a) small stones

   b) knocked down

   c) people who triumph

   d) to rent

   e) acted out

   f) clients

Friends, Families and Folk Tales

Grammar Exercises

1. **Fill in the blank spaces. Choose from the words given below:**

This old home (1)_____ I looked forward to (2)_____ again was the one (3) _____ which I had lived when I was (4)_____.This lovely home was (5) _____ well-furnished nor well-decorated. On the contrary it (6) _____ a rough stone house. (7) _____ we were poor, the sitting-room was (8) _____ our bedroom. (9) _____ we fought our civil war in the open space which was in (10) _____ of my house.

also
born
front
in
is
neither
nor
opposite
sometimes
since
see
seeing
which
was
were
up

2. **Read these sentences.**

> We fought our civil war in the open space.
> The open space was in front of my house.

> We fought our civil war in the open space **which** was in front of my house.

Using the relative pronoun 'which', make one sentence from these pairs.

a) I saw the tables. You bought the tables.

b) In the library there is a book. The book describes how to make Indian food.

c) There were a lot of houses. The houses were well-built.

d) He borrowed £5. He never returned the £5.

Writing Exercises

1. **Read this correction code table.**

s	spelling
^	missing word
p	punctuation
t	tense
pr.	preposition
v	something is wrong with the verb
( )	not needed
=	capital is needed
s/pl	singular/plural agreement

   Now proof-read the paragraph below which has some mistakes. Correct it using the code.

   although we were young, we new how to do business. We collected gravel as goods then we cuted used newspaper into pieces as our banck note. One of us pretend to be the owner of this small snack bar. We trained when we were young, it wasn't surprising we were good in mathematics when grew up.

2. **Put these words in alphabetical order.**
   a) smiles, shelter, sitting-room, shack, seriously
   b) pieces, pretended, parents, pocket-money
   c) bombs, brothers, bedroom, born, bank, bar
   d) transactions, trained, then, tried, the, television

   Choose one word from each list. Look it up in the dictionary and write the definition underneath.

3. **Write about childrens' games or games you played as a child**

Friends, Families and Folk Tales

25 When Will You Grow Up?

I was born in 1964 in Hong Kong. My father was a worker on a construction site. I was the youngest in the family. I had three brothers and a sister. My eldest brother had been married for four years. He married before he went on to university. My sister had married too. I remember during my childhood, I was very happy. My family gave me everything I wanted.

The first year at secondary school was wonderful and enjoyable. My Form One teacher was a young lady. She was very kind to me and the whole class. She was a really good teacher. She always worried about my work and my health because I was very weak and I was always ill at that time. She made me feel like she was my sister or relation. This year passed quickly and happily.

The following year passed very silently and it seemed nothing had happened. No-one treated me specially and nothing made me upset but I began to change and behaved badly when I was in Form Three. I was very lazy and seldom handed in my homework. I always bunked off. People began to talk about me and my friends because we were always causing trouble. They said we were the problem youth but I did not care. That year I really was in trouble because I failed my exam. My brothers, mother and father always blamed me, but I did not change and continued my life. They always said that I was very clever and could do better than my eldest brother. He had worked very hard and always got higher marks. I did not know why I behaved like this and I hated to talk to them. Maybe they put too much pressure on me and it broke the family. This did not change until I studied in Form Four. My father always said if I could not get good marks, I would be sent to England. This made me confused.

By chance my teacher called me to his room and said, "When will you grow up? Don't behave like that, you are an intelligent person, I know. You can work harder and be better than everyone. You will need to be independent in the future and live on your own one day."

Not long after this, I changed and felt very sorry about the things I had done. My teacher was very surprised but it was too late. Finally, I was sent to England to study. But it seems nothing has changed, people here still say I am a lazy boy and blame me about my behaviour and say my friends are not good.

I am sure I know what I am doing and what I ought to do.

Yin from Hong Kong

Discussion questions

a) What are or were you like as a teenager?
b) As a teenager, do or did you have problems at school or with your family?
c) Are teenage girls different from teenage boys?
d) What is life like for teenagers in Britain today?

Reading Exercises

1. Read the story and then work with a partner to complete the questionnaire. Ask each other questions: eg "Where was he born?" "Hong Kong" Complete in note form.

place and year of birth	
number of brothers and sisters	
father's job	
first year at secondary school	
behaviour during second year at secondary school	
behaviour during third year at secondary school	
family's opinion of his behaviour	

2. Find these words in the text and circle them. Then write a word with the opposite meaning by the side.

independent	*dependent*
wonderful	
enjoyable	
weak	
lazy	
clever	
confused	
happily	
silently	
badly	

Friends, Families and Folk Tales

Grammar Exercises

1. **Read the text. Fill in the correct preposition.**

   eg) My eldest brother had been married *for* 4 years

   a) I was very happy _____ my childhood.

   b) He married _____ he went to university.

   c) Finally, I was sent _____ England to study.

   d) She always worried _____ my health.

   e) Father always blamed me _____ it.

2. **Read these sentences.**

   a) If you get bad marks you will go to London
         [present simple]   [future simple]
   This is a **likely to happen.**

   b) If you got good marks you would stay in Hong Kong
         [simple past]   [conditional]
   This is a **unlikely to happen.**

   c) **Complete these 'if' sentences. Look at the tense and decide if it is likely or unlikely to happen.**

   eg) If I spoke Chinese *I would go to China.* _____ (go/China)

   i) If I won £1,000 _____ (buy/car)

   ii) If it rains tomorrow _____ (stay/home)

   iii) If she rings _____ (go/cinema)

   iv) If she paid my fare _____ (go/China)

Writing Exercises

1. Imagine you are Yin's father and you received this letter from his teacher.

    > Main Road Secondary School
    >
    > 1st January
    >
    > Dear Mrs Ho,
    >
    > I am anxious to discuss Yin's behaviour and attitude with you. I am concerned that he is not working as hard as he should.
    >
    > Could you come in one day next week to talk to me? I am available after 4.00pm.
    >
    > Yours sincerely
    >
    > *Ann Smith*
    > Ann Smith

    Write back to say that you too wish to discuss Yin's work and behaviour. You are able to come next Thursday at 4.30pm.

    > Flat 5, Hong Seng Road
    > Hong Kong
    >
    > Dear _____
    >
    > _____
    > _____
    > _____
    > _____
    > _____
    >
    > Kit Ho (Mrs)

Friends, Families and Folk Tales

26 Somali Tradition

¹ In southern Somalia there is a village called Algooye. The people living there believe that if they do not play the fighting game once a year there will be no rain and no planting.

⁵ The game is called Istunxa. The word means beating each other.

A number of people come together in one area, and they then divide into two groups. Each person has a stick. They first start apart, the groups separated by 50 metres, and they ¹⁰ attack by running at each other, with spiritual voices.

Some people in the battle are injured, and blood drops from the cuts in their skin. That is the aim of the whole seasonal game: if there is no blood there will be no rain.

Ali Ibrahim from Somalia

Discussion questions

a) What do you know about the English traditions of Guy Fawkes Night or May Day? What do people do? Why do they do it?

b) Tell us about a tradition from your country. What do people do? Why do they do it?

Somali Tradition

Reading Exercises

1. **Read the passage, and fill in the table.**

eg)	name of village	*Algooye*
	name of country	
	name of game	
	meaning of name	
	aim of game	
	what happens in the game	

2. **Find the words in the passage that mean the same.**

eg) sowing seeds in the ground   *planting*

   a) hitting, with sticks   _____

   b) come apart   _____

   c) fight   _____

   e) singing and chanting special songs   _____

   f) hurt, wounded   _____

Friends, Families and Folk Tales

Grammar Exercises

1. **Read these sentences:**

   | If there is blood | there will | be rain |
   | If there's blood | there'll | be rain |

   Is the writer sure that this will happen, or does he think it is only a possibility?

   Now, join the two halves to make one sentence.

   eg) If there is snow   we'll go swimming.
   a) If it's hot   you'll move to the next class.
   b) If I feel tired   we'll make a snowman.
   c) If I get paid   I'll stay at home.
   d) If you pass your exams   I'll buy a new coat.

2. **Now read these sentences.**
   i) If there is no blood there will be no rain.
   ii) If there isn't any blood there won't be any rain.

   They both mean the same thing. (i) sounds stronger, so can be more poetic. Show you can use both by writing each sentence again using 'any'.

   eg) If there are no teachers, there will be no classes.
   If there aren't any teachers there won't be any classes.

   a) If there is no money, there will be no books.

   _____

   b) If there are no books, we will learn no English.

   _____

   c) If we learn no English, we will get no jobs.

   _____

114 THE LONDON LANGUAGE AND LITERACY UNIT

Somali Tradition

Writing Exercises

1. Look at the table in Exercise 1 of the Reading Exercises. From these notes, re-tell and write the story in your own words.

2. Take a partner and proof-read your partner's story, using the proof-reading key on page 107.
   Every student has different priorities. Some students need to concentrate on spelling, others on tense or paragraphing.
   What are your priorities when you proof-read your own work? What do you think your partner's should be?

3. Write about a tradition from your own country. Make sure you proof-read it.

Friends, Families and Folk Tales

27 We Want This!

1 Life in a world free from the threat of war.
Ample food for everyone.
Comfortable housing for everyone.

Satisfying employment for all who need it,
5 so they can provide for themselves and their families.

Life that is not marred by sickness and disease.
Enjoyment of security, without danger to one's person
or property from criminals.

A world in which qualities most highly prized include
10 love, kindness, concern for one's fellow man and
truthfulness.

For thousands of years, political rulers have been
promising their people better conditions
with what results?

15 Reflection: man has dominated man to his injury.

Orlando

Discussion questions

a) Imagine you are Secretary General of the United Nations. What bad things in the world would you try and get rid of?

b) Imagine you have 3 wishes for the world. What would you wish for?

We Want This!

Reading Exercises

1. Read the text again. Underline the positive words or phrases. Underline the negative words or phrases with a different coloured pen. Use the dictionary if necessary.
   Now fill in the table.

	positive	negative
eg)	*ample food*	

2. Find the word from the text that means the same as:

   eg) enough   <u>*ample*</u>

   a) illness   _____

   b) jobs   _____

   c) homes   _____

   d) safety   _____

   e) honesty   _____

THE LONDON LANGUAGE AND LITERACY UNIT

Friends, Families and Folk Tales

Grammar Exercises

1. **Fill in the gaps with the correct preposition. Do not look at the original text.**

   Life *in* a world free _____ the threat _____ war.

   Ample food _____ everyone.

   Comfortable housing _____ everyone.

   Satisfying employment _____ all who need it,

   so they can provide _____ themselves and their families.

   Life that is not marred _____ sickness and disease.

   Enjoyment _____ security, without danger _____ one's person or property from criminals.

   A world _____ which the qualities most highly prized include love, kindness, concern _____ one's fellow man and truthfulness.

   Reflection: Man has dominated man _____ his injury.

2. **Fill in the table with the right word.**

	Noun	Adjective	Adverb
eg)	sickness	*sick*	*sickly*
		poor	
			concernedly
		secure	
	possibility		
		kind	
			freely

118 THE LONDON LANGUAGE AND LITERACY UNIT

Writing Exercises

1. **Write a list of the main things that the writer wants.**

   eg) *peace*

2. **Write a short paragraph, summarising the writer's feelings.**

3. **Write between 5 and 10 things that you would like to see in the world, giving reasons. Continue on a separate sheet if necessary.**

Friends, Families and Folk Tales

28 A Woman's Place?

My point of view is that the husband is the most important person in the family, but the wife is the 'queen' at home. Why?

The man must do everything for his wife and children. The husband, when he gets married, promises the Lord to look after his 'compañera' in riches and in poverty, in the good and the bad times. After that, he promises a good future for his family. He brings food, clothes and wages for his wife and children and she looks after him and the children at home, cooking and cleaning the house and helping the children with their study.

I think 'jobs for both' is a mistake. When the wife starts to work it is the beginning of a broken marriage. Why? She looks for new friends, more money, fashionable clothes, and starts to forget the children's care, the husband's care, the home and family. For South American people my opinion is:

"The husband at work and the wife at home."

This saves the marriage, the sons and daughters, the family and the home. Money is not happiness for the family. Money only calms the nerves.

Jorge from Chile

Discussion questions

a) In your country, do men and women have equal rights?

b) Do you think men and women should have different roles in the family?

c) Is British society sexist?

A Woman's Place?

Reading Exercises

1. Read the text with a partner, and work together to complete the table showing whether the statements are facts or the author's opinions.

	Fact	Opinion
eg) The husband is the most important person in the family.		✔
a) When he gets married, the husband promises to look after his wife.		
b) He brings money for his wife and family.		
c) The wife's role is to look after him and the children and cook and clean.		
d) When the wife starts to work outside the home it is the begining of broken marriages.		
e) When the wife works, she looks for new friends and forgets to look after the family properly.		
f) Money does not bring happiness to the family.		

2. Match the 2 halves of these sentences to make 4 whole ones.

   eg) He brings food and wages   cooking, cleaning the house and helping the children.

   a) My point of view is that   is a mistake.

   b) She looks after him and the children   calms the nerves.

   c) I think 'jobs for both'   and the wife stays at home.

   d) The husband goes to work   for his wife at home.

   e) Money only   the wife is queen at home.

THE LONDON LANGUAGE AND LITERACY UNIT

Friends, Families and Folk Tales

Grammar Exercises

1. **Read these sentences. They have similar meanings.**

   a) The husband is the most important person but the wife is the queen at home.

   b) Although the husband is the most important person, the wife is the queen at home.

   c) The husband is the most important person. The wife, however, is the queen at home.

   Re-write these sentences twice, giving all 3 possibilities.

   i) Football is played in Britain, but it is not played in all schools.

   ii) The dog was angry. He did not, however, bite the postman.

   iii) Although it was late, they still went to the party.

   iv) He said he did not want to go, but we persuaded him.

2. **The verb look can be followed by: *after, into, out for, out, at, for, through* and many other prepositions. Fill the gaps with an appropriate preposition from the above. Use a dictionary if necessary.**

   eg) Please look <u>*out for*</u> the bus. I've been waiting for ages.

   a) I've been looking _____ hours and still can't find it.

   b) Look _____! The house is on fire!

   c) She looked right _____ me and ignored me completely.

   d) I shall look _____ it for you and find out what I can.

   e) When I was young, she looked _____ me and took care of me.

Writing Exercises

1. Jorge's wife wants a job. This is a form which she has filled in.

Surname:	*Gomez*
First name:	*Julia*
Address:	*12 Woodside Park, Birmingham B11 5AZ*
Telephone No:	*0121 892 0103*
Age:	*43*
Nationality:	*Chilean*
Occupation:	*Housewife*
Marital Status:	*Married*
No. of children	*four*

Here is a job she has seen advertised

WANTED
St Lawrence School
Western Lane, Erdington.
Dinner Lady required
for friendly Primary School
12.00 – 2.00, Mon – Fri.

Imagine you are Jorge's wife. Write a letter, applying for the job. Give details about yourself.

2. There are four paragraphs in this text. Underline the topic sentence in each paragraph. The topic sentence gives the main idea in that paragraph.

3. Write what you think is the woman's place in a marriage.

Friends, Families and Folk Tales

29 My Grandmother's Life

I thought of writing something about my grandmother's life because it is the most remarkable life in my family.

She came from a fishmonger's family of eleven children, she was the only girl. She started work when she was seven, helping her mother around the house to wash, clean the house, and go to the river to wash the clothes.

When she was twelve she used to go to help her father and brothers to bring in the fish from the trawler in heavy baskets, shoulder deep into the sea. She married at twenty and she had twelve children and she carried on working very hard looking after the children, and the house at the same time. She carried on helping with the fish, and the two trawlers they had at the time. Even when she was pregnant she carried on helping in the sea with the fish.

She breast fed all her children plus two of her neighbour's because they lost their mother.

After my mother married and my grandfather died, she lived with us again, looking after my mother's eight children. She was my mother's housekeeper, doctor and nanny, she looked after everything to do with the house. I never remember her being upset about anything, she was kind and loveable with us, we all loved her very, very much. She used to tell us a lot of true stories about her childhood. She had never had the chance to go to school, something she regretted. She read and wrote a bit only from what she heard from the school next door. She was a good singer as well, she won a competition singing when she was young.

Her cousin came all the way from South America to ask her parents to let her go there to train to be an opera singer, but her mother and father refused because she was supposed to help her mother look after her brothers.

She was a very intelligent person with an incredible memory, also she used to cure sick people with her hands and medicated herbs which she made herself. She always had very good health. She was 95 when she died, and the people who knew her did not want to believe it, they thought she was going to live forever. She was working until her last month. Because she was tired she stopped, but was never in bed. She told my mother and I she was dying, and, yes like that, she passed away. She had all her own teeth when she died. She always used to ask God to let her die without suffering.

Sometimes I never understood why, when I was a child, she used to say all the time, "I am the richest and luckiest woman in the world" and now I know she was right. Health is the most important thing in life.

She died 25 years ago, but for me she lives forever.

Magdalena from Italy

Discussion questions

a) Can you remember your grandmother? What was she like?

b) Was her life very different to yours? How?

c) Describe your relationship with your grandmother.

My Grandmother's Life

Reading Exercises

1. Read the text, fill in the table with the missing events and dates.

	Event	Date
eg)	was born	*1875*
	helped her mother in the house	
		1887
	married	
		1970

2. Find words which have a similar meaning and underline them in the text. Then write them below.

   eg) extraordinary   *remarkable*

   a) a fishing boat   _____

   b) sad or worried   _____

   c) physical well-being   _____

   d) to look back and feel
      sorry about something _____

   e) to heal or make better _____

3. Make a list of all the grandmother's jobs, skills, talents and characteristics, using the table below.

	jobs	characteristics	talents & skills
eg)	*washing*	*hardworking*	

THE LONDON LANGUAGE AND LITERACY UNIT

Friends, Families and Folk Tales

Grammar Exercises

1. **Look at this sentence from the story.**

   She used herds, 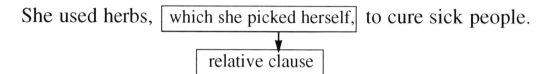 to cure sick people.

   This relative clause is written between 2 commas because the information in the relative clause is not essential to the main idea "She used herbs to cure sick people."

2. **Read these sentences. They all have a main and a relative clause. Some of the relative clauses contain information which is not essential to the main idea, but some contain information which is essential.**

   Find the main and relative clause in each sentence. Underline the relative clause.

   eg) My grandmother's voice, <u>*which was never trained,*</u> was very beautiful.

   a) Thermometers are instruments which measure temperature.

   b) My neighbour's front garden, which has large trees near our fence, has been the source of many disputes.

   c) Coffee, which contains caffeine, is a well known stimulant.

   d) The kinds of diseases which are associated with poverty include cholera and rickets.

3. **Where the information is not essential, write out the main idea as a separate sentence.**

   eg) *My grandmother's voice was very beautiful.*

My Grandmother's Life

Writing Exercises

1. **Read these words and discuss their meaning with a partner.**
   then, next, subsequently, afterwards, simultaneously, finally, eventually, while, previously.

2. **Read paragraphs, 3, 4, 5 and 6 and re-write some of the sentences using these words.**
   eg) <u>She married at 20 and subsequently had 12 children.</u>
   You can rearrange the word order or take out words.

3. **Read the first and last sentence of the story with a partner. Do you think they are a good beginning and ending? Why?**

4. **Read these beginnings and endings and match them to the type of writing they would suit.**

   eg) Once upon a time   a description
   Long ago   a personal experience
   One dark night   a narrative
   When I was a young   a fairy tale
   It all started when   a frightening tale
   I would like to tell you about a folk tale

5. **Write a short description of someone you admire.**
   a) **Do a plan first, showing the main points you will cover.**
   b) **Think about an appropriate beginning and ending, and consider the main tenses you will be using.**
   c) **Proof-read your draft, checking tenses, punctuation and anything else you have frequent problems with (eg use of articles, spelling etc.)**

Friends, Families and Folk Tales

30 The Runaway

It was the 9th May and I was ready to go to the hospital at 8.00 o'clock. For a long time I had had a pain in my right side. I went to my G.P. and told her about it. The doctor said, "In that case, I think I will send you to a specialist. I'll contact the hospital and they'll send you an appointment by post."

After 4 weeks, I received a letter from the hospital. In the letter was the appointment and some advice. I was a midwife in my country and I was not nervous. The day soon came. The night before I had no food and no drink but I did not sleep very well. So, I got up at 5.00 o'clock and prayed and read the Quran. I also put £10 in the charity box in the kitchen. At 7.00 o'clock the friend who was driving me to the hospital rang.

"Are you ready?" she asked me.
"Yes" I said "Come and get me."
After 15 minutes she arrived.
I left my house tidy.

When we arrived at the hospital, I gave my letter to the receptionist and then a nurse came and asked me if I could speak English. I said that I could speak a little. My friend speaks better English than me, but she could not stay with me as she was looking after my little daughter and was not able to leave her alone. We said goodbye then I went inside. They brought me special clothes and asked me to change. One of the nurses helped me to fasten the gown at the back. Then she asked me quite a lot of questions. She was kind but she spoke very fast. I answered some of them and some I did not understand. I waited with some other patients in a special room. I went to the bathroom and was washing my face when I heard a woman's voice calling, "Mrs Ali, Mrs Ali."

I replied and opened the door and went towards her. She seemed in a hurry and spoke fast so I did not understand her. I felt hot. I followed her and found myself in the operating room. I do not think I felt afraid. I climbed onto the bed and lay down. She pressed my arm looking for a vein. She asked me to open and close my hand. I did it twice. She was about to put the needle into my vein when I suddenly sat up and said,"Stop, please." Everybody there turned to look at me, completely surprised. One of them tried to convince me but I refused.

I do not know why it happened but I just knew I could not continue with it. I got dressed and left the hospital.

Salima from Iraq

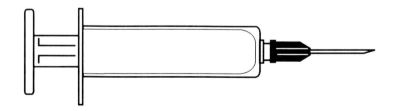

Discussion questions

a) What kind of things frighten you?
b) Are you afraid of the dentist?
c) Are doctors and hospitals different in your country?
d) What are the differences?

The Runaway

Reading Exercises

1. **Work with a partner.**
   Look at the picture and read the title. What do you think the story will be about?
   Now read the first and last sentence of each paragraph and discuss what you think the rest of the paragraph is about.

2. **Read the whole story carefully, and answer the questions.**

   a) Why did Salima's G.P. refer her to a specialist?

   _____

   _____

   b) Was she or wasn't she nervous? Give your reasons.

   _____

   _____

   c) Why do you think she put money in the charity box?

   _____

   _____

   d) Why do you think Salima could not understand the nurses?

   _____

   _____

   e) Why do you think she ran away?

   _____

   _____

Friends, Families and Folk Tales

Grammar Exercises

1. **Find a verb in:**

   eg) the simple past   _received_

   a) the simple present   _____

   b) the simple future   _____

   c) the simple past   _____

   d) the past continuous   _____

   e) the past perfect   _____

2. **a) Look at these examples from the story with a partner:**
   "I went to my G.P. and <u>told her</u> about it....a nurse asked me if I could speak English. I <u>said</u> that I could speak a little...I <u>answered</u> some questions ....I <u>replied</u> ....One of them tried to convince me but I <u>refused</u>."
   b) Discuss their meaning.
   c) Change these sentences from direct to indirect speech, using all the verbs shown above.

   eg) "Get undressed," she said.   <u>She told me to get undressed.</u>

   a) "No, I won't," I said.

   b) "Why not?" she said.

   c) "Because I'm frightened," I said.

   d) " What are you afraid of?" she said.

   e) "I don't know," I said.

The Runaway

Writing Exercises

1. **Change the verbs in the following paragraph from the simple past to the simple present. Write it out again, using the simple present.**

eg) *I reply and open the door ...*

I replied and opened the door and went towards her. She seemed in a hurry and spoke fast so I did not understand her. I felt hot. I followed her and found myself in the operating room. I do not think I felt afraid. I climbed onto the bed and lay down. She pressed my arm looking for a vein. She asked me to open and close my hand. I did it twice. She was about to put the needle into my vein when I suddenly sat up and said,
"Stop, please."
Everybody there turned to look at me, completely surprised. One of them tried to convince me but I refused.
Read it aloud with a partner, and discuss what difference, if any, it makes to the story.

2. **You have an appointment at the hospital next week, but you are unable to attend. This is your appointment card.**

NHS HOSPITAL TRUST	St George's Hospital Blackshaw Road, London SW17 3ST Dental Clinic

You have an appointment to see Mr Chowdhury
in the New Building, Clinic 27
on Monday 8th September 1997.
If you cannot attend, please notify us on 0171 672 5767
or write to the above address.

Write a letter to change your appointment.

The London Language & Literacy Unit

The London Language & Literacy Unit works in the areas of ESOL, basic skills and dyslexia, as well as in language and learning support. We offer consultancy, training, customised and accredited courses and project development in these areas. Our publishing aim is to produce up-to-date, relevant materials at a price affordable by practising tutors. For a full publication list, or for further information about the work of the London Language & Literacy Unit, please contact us at the address printed below.

About the authors/editors

Marina Spiegel was born in Argentina and has taught Modern Languages and ESOL since 1975. She now works at Richmond Adult & Community College and has a particular interest in training and developing support programmes for bilingual adults in mainstream courses. Other publications include co-author of *Chart Your Course in English.*

Helen Sunderland started teaching ESOL in 1977, and has always had a particular interest in teaching literacy skills. She now works at the London Language & Literacy Unit as a teacher-trainer and consultant, where her special interests are teaching bilingual learners and working with dyslexic learners. Other publications she has been involved in producing include *The Teacher's Video; an ESOL Tutor Training Resource, The GNVQ Induction Pack,* and *Dyslexia and the Bilingual Learner.*

London Language & Literacy Unit
Southwark College
Southampton Way
London SE5 7EW.
Tel. 0171 815 1699/0171 639 9512

ISBN: 1 872972 49 7